# Addressing the Elephants in the Room

## Also by Paul J. Thomas

*Bite Size Advice: A Definitive Guide to Political, Economic, Social and Technological Issues*

*Bite Size Advice 2: The Lesson Continues ... A Further Guide to Political, Economic, Social and Technological Issues*

*Bite Size Advice 3: The Concluding Tutorial ... A Final Guide to Political, Economic, Social and Technological Issues*

PAUL J. THOMAS

# Addressing the Elephants in the Room

A Collection of Straight-talking Blog Posts on Contemporary Political, Economic, Social and Technological Issues

InHouse Publishing Pty Ltd
Underwood 4119
Brisbane, Australia

First Edition 2022

Thomas, Paul J.

Addressing the Elephants in the Room: A Collection of Straight-talking Blog Posts on Political, Economic, Social and Technological Issues

ISBN: 978-1-922839-28-2

BUSINESS & ECONOMICS/General
BUSINESS & ECONOMICS/Government & Business
BUSINESS & ECONOMICS/Education



Printed in Australia by InHouse Print & Design.

IN HOUSE PTY LTD PUBLISHING

NATIONAL LIBRARY OF AUSTRALIA

A catalogue record for this book is available from the National Library of Australia

For my grandchildren:

Emma, Jessica, Oscar, Elias, Harrison, Abraham, Nayah, and Emily.

(Just make sure you actually read this one day, please.)

Love, Granddad xx.

This book contains a cross-section of blog posts organised thematically into four chapters. Each chapter contains posts covering a common theme. By arranging the posts into discrete subject areas, the reader can find all the content about a specific topic in one chapter, making browsing by interest easier. Note that the chapters can be read in any order and that each chapter begins with a brief introduction. Please also note that the posts contained in each chapter are not presented in chronological order. Given this, each post ends with a footnote showing the original publishing date to provide a timestamp and historical context.

# Contents

# Acknowledgments

This is the fourth book that I have published, and it's never an easy exercise – the experience is always challenging but rewarding. A lot of work goes on behind the scenes to get the finished product into the hands of the reader, and much of this effort is unrecognised. So, I'd like to thank some of the unsung heroes of this text.

My first and foremost debt is to my wife, Beverley, who is always so supportive of my writing endeavours. She graciously allows me to lock myself away in my man cave – otherwise known as my study – while I pound the keyboard, hammering out another post. She has reviewed every piece of prose that I have written under the *Elephant in the Room* banner, and our writer-editor relationship has gone the distance. Thanks for putting up with me, darling.

Once each post is written, the text is entered into a blog content management system, and this important task is undertaken by Kieran Weston. Kieran is a family friend, talented webmaster, and one of nature's gentlemen. He maintains the website which hosts the *Elephant in the Room* blog. As part of this, he manages the blog content and hits the publish button each fortnight on my latest musings. I salute his unfailing support – on a voluntary basis. Please never abandon me, Kieran!

May I also extend my gratitude to the many individuals whose intellectual capital I have so freely used. All posts reproduced in this book were originally published on my website, and each required me to conduct research. Consequently, I drew on the ideas and opinions of a cross-section of writers. Drawing on this eclectic collection of material resulted in the large bibliography which is included at the end as a resource list for those who wish to explore issues further.

Finally, while my name alone is on the cover of this book, it bears the imprint of many invisible hands. These hands belong to my loyal community of blog readers who click-on each fortnight to view the latest post that I have published in cyberspace. Without them, there would be no blog, and therefore this book would not exist. A heartfelt nod to all of these curious individuals.

# Introduction

We live in an era of never-ending political, economic, social, and technological change. The rapid pace of this change has given rise to a raft of difficult issues which are being inadequately addressed within and between countries, and also between individuals. These "elephants in the room" are real and won't go away just because we pretend that they don't exist. Indeed, avoiding or skirting critical topics for fear of causing awkward situations only makes matters worse.

Due to our tendency to refer obliquely to elephants or discuss them in whispered side-conversations, many of us have become used to living with them, rather than calling out elephants for what they are – tricky but solvable problems. The denial of global realities across several overarching themes – including political unrest, economic inequality, social upheaval, and technological disruption – means that elephants have festered and become deeply entrenched.

Addressing sensitive subjects is, by its very nature, hard. Still, it needs to be done, which is one of the reasons I started my blog, *Elephant in the Room,* in early 2020. While many people look past prickly contemporary issues, I choose not to tiptoe around them, but to give voice to what I often discover reflects the thinking of the silent majority. Openly discussing the unspoken truth helps raise awareness of problems and is the first step to resolving them.

This book showcases 50 of my straight-talking blog posts, divided into four categories – **P**olitical, **E**conomic, **S**ocial, and **T**echnological. Taken together, these four domains represent a **PEST** analysis, a strategic tool that can be used to paint a macro picture of the opportunities and threats confronting an industry sector, a sovereign nation, or the entire world. I cast a wide net in my blog writings and typically examine issues at a global level.

The unifying aim of each blog post is to show how we can make the planet a better place for ourselves and future generations. People have always been key to solving humanity's problems, and this remains true in the third decade of the 21st century. Politicians of all stripes, economists of all ideologies, citizens of all nations, and technologists of all types must work together effectively to confront shared global challenges.

The decisions we make individually and collectively shape our world. We must learn to make better choices in a range of areas, including making more intelligent political judgments, becoming more savvy news consumers, and living more sustainable lives. The sobering reality is that we get the politicians we deserve, the media we deserve, and the environment we deserve. We have no one to blame but ourselves for the deep fault lines that have appeared in our globalised world.

The challenges humanity faces, like countering rampant terrorism, controlling communicable diseases, and protecting human rights, are increasingly transnational in nature and cannot be addressed by any single government. Since no individual nation-state is big enough alone to fix common global problems, we must stop seeing the world through a narrow, self-absorbed national lens.

The Earth is one, but the world is not, as the current governance system – which divides the planet into 195 sovereign nations – creates toxic divisions. Yet we are all part of one global village, and therefore need to act like global citizens. However, our knowledge of supranational issues is often superficial, as many of us lack global competency. Hopefully, this book will help readers think outside themselves and the borders of their country.

*Addressing the Elephants in the Room* shines a light on some of humanity's biggest challenges and, by extension, some personal development issues. The posts are deliberately designed to broaden your horizons as they tangle and weave through disparate but connected topics. By joining the dots, you will gain a helicopter view of where individual disciplines intersect and overlap, thereby enabling you to see more creative solutions to present-day problems.

We live in an interconnected world where our local actions can have global implications. Small acts add up – they initially drive change in a city, then a state, followed by a nation, and ultimately the world. This is how people-power shapes our planet, and we can all play a part by understanding (through education) the cause-and-effect connections between the various roles we undertake in society.

As Nelson Mandela said: "Education is the most powerful weapon which you can use to change the world". Education broadens the mind and helps us see the world afresh, thereby enabling us to make more balanced and insightful judgments. By applying these judgments to societal problems, we can advance the cause of humanity. But education is much more than just bookish knowledge – it must provide the tools to solve real-world problems.

The answers to the big global issues we face – including climate change – cannot be found within traditional single disciplines such as economics, or science, or politics on their own. That's why universities around the world will increasingly be challenged to turn out graduates with broader interdisciplinary degrees. It has long been my contention that dividing universities by academic departments creates barriers to cross-disciplinary learning.

Of course, you don't have to enrol in a formal university degree to keep up with what is happening in the world. As you dip in and out of the posts in this book, you will see that the need to educate yourself continuously – in the dos and don'ts of life – is a subliminal message in many of the posts. Much of the education required is informal learning and includes reading articles, viewing videos, attending conferences, and other self-development activities.

I do all of the above plus maintain a blog to stay abreast of current issues. Most posts require me to conduct research and check facts, and this increases my understanding of an issue. I have an inquiring mind and am always imagining how the world could be a better place. Unsurprisingly, one of my all-time favourite quotes is by Robert Kennedy: "Some men see things as they are and say 'Why?' I dream of things that never were and say 'Why not?'"

In today's world of time constraints and information overload, staying up-to-date can be difficult, which is why *Addressing the Elephants in the Room* is ideal for the time-starved reader. It delivers informed advice in bite size chunks and can be read in order, or you can turn to a page at random. This one volume is a business book, an educational book, and a general knowledge book. Its arguments aim to be intellectually compelling without being academic.

Each post was originally written to be read independently of the rest. Given this fact, some repetition and overlap occur when standalone posts covering the same topic – albeit from different angles – are reproduced together in this publication. Please also note that each post ends with a pithy one-liner, often in the form of an aphorism. Aphorisms are pointed, witty statements which express a general truth and are sometimes paraphrased quotes. My closing one-liners are designed to pack a punch and leave you pondering.

The most common topic covered in this book is COVID-19. On 11 March, 2020, the World Health Organization (WHO) declared the coronavirus a global pandemic. The ensuing health crisis had immense political, economic, social, and technological implications. The posts related to the coronavirus have been assigned to one of the PEST groups to enable readers to see the impact of the outbreak through four different lenses.

It should be noted that the "lens categorisation" is based on my subjective judgment, as the allocation of a given post to a specific PEST classification is not an exact science. The pandemic strikingly illustrated how politics and economics intersect, and how other considerations, such as social issues and technological developments, also overlap. Consequently, a number of the posts classified as "political" could easily have been classified as "economic" and vice versa – and so on.

Politically, the pandemic severely challenged policymakers and put governments across the world under pressure to react quickly and decisively. Some political leaders responded better than others to the extraordinary difficulty of safeguarding the well-being of their citizens. All disasters have political consequences, and the pandemic exposed political villains and heroes. These individuals are identified in the posts included in chapter one.

Economically, the public-health crisis devastated economies, causing the worst downturn since the Great Depression. As outlined in chapter two, the magnitude and speed of the economic contraction were unprecedented, resulting in national governments and central banks spending billions of dollars in direct fiscal and monetary support. Aid packages were designed to prevent business bankruptcies, minimise job losses, and maintain financial stability.

Socially, the Great Lockdown upended people's everyday lives. Not being allowed to see family and friends, undertake travel, or engage in leisure activities impacted the physical and mental health of citizens. Additionally, the virus exacerbated deep-seated social inequalities. The posts in chapter three provide many lessons about human behaviour – and not just during the pandemic. They also highlight how the digital age has changed the way people interact, form judgments, and make decisions.

For the technology sector, the pandemic was an absolute boon. Chapter four reveals how America's Big Five tech titans – Amazon, Apple, Facebook, Google, and Microsoft – benefited richly from supplying the tools that made lockdown life and remote working possible. Beyond Silicon Valley, the big pharmaceutical companies used cutting-edge medical biotechnology to develop COVID-19 vaccines, the sales of which injected billions of dollars into their coffers.

Crises create favourable conditions for learning, and the COVID pandemic is no exception. Indeed, it's another example of our need for lifelong learning. The importance of knowledge and learning has been recognised since ancient times. Aristotle wrote: "The educated differ from the uneducated as much as the living from the dead".

I take this to mean that the educated are mentally alive while the uneducated are mentally dead.

We must be cognitively alive to life's lessons and learn from all of our experiences. For me, the most important lesson arising from the pandemic is the need for governments and citizens to work together to solve national and global issues. To paraphrase the WHO Director-General, Tedros Adhanom Ghebreyesus, we need a whole-of-government, whole-of-society approach to issues, whether defeating a deadly virus or tackling climate change.

Many of the matters discussed in this collection of writings are threats which can be turned into opportunities. While the global panorama may appear pessimistic, humanity is winning more than it is losing, and this very point is made in an uplifting post on page 192. Science and technology will continue to play a key role in making our world a better place. As the last 200 years show, humans are technically capable of solving complex problems.

As I write this introduction, I am 65 years of age. Despite this, I still have much to learn, and this was another motivator in launching my blog, *Elephant in the Room,* after I retired in March 2019 following a 43-year career in the banking and finance industry. The final 14 years of my career were spent as the CEO of a mutual (customer-owned) bank, where I was responsible for strategy and became fascinated by the interplay between a range of PEST issues which had national and international significance.

While at Gateway Bank, I had a desire to write about these strategic issues and was encouraged to start a CEO blog, which I maintained for 11 years. That blog, *Doubting Thomas,* provided me with a creative outlet in which to share my ideas and opinions and, in the process, it positioned Gateway as a thought leader. It also spawned three books with the generic title *Bite Size Advice*.

The *Doubting Thomas* CEO blog taught me that an effective way to become acquainted with a subject is to write about it, and the same holds true for my *Elephant in the Room* blog. Writing improves learning by storing information in our memory, and this aids recall. It has been a joy to share my acquired knowledge with my online

*Elephant in the Room* readers and an even greater joy to share it now with a new audience – those reading this text.

I hope that you discover copious salutary lessons in this book – there is much to learn in its pages.

*Chapter One*

# The Political Landscape

Every day around the world, governments make decisions that affect our day-to-day lives. During the pandemic, policymaking proved to be challenging in the extreme – some governments got it right while others got it wrong. Many of the posts in this opening chapter reveal how different countries responded to the crisis. From social distancing to mask wearing, the focus was on "flattening the curve" of COVID-19 cases. Fighting a common enemy should have united humanity, but it caused divisions within and between nations and left growing political divides.

## How world leaders have responded to the coronavirus crisis

### LEADERSHIP IN A TIME OF CONTAGION

The need for effective political leadership heightens during a national crisis. Citizens expect their governments to rise to the challenge and make wise choices. This puts the political judgments of presidents and prime ministers under the spotlight. The populace expects them to provide concrete solutions to serious threats.

The once-in-a-century COVID-19 pandemic has forced leaders to make diabolical choices, creating a watershed moment in politics. Not since the height of the Cold War have the stakes been higher. Governments are making finely balanced decisions which represent stark trade-offs between life, death, and the economy.

This burden weighs heavily on political leaders and, for many, it represents their ultimate leadership challenge. Decisions need to be made rapidly and, if you get it wrong, the lives and livelihoods of millions of your fellow citizens will be negatively impacted. The COVID-19 mega-crisis has tested the mettle of all world leaders, and some have failed abysmally.

Every drama needs at least one villain, and four political strongmen stand out for special condemnation. The autocratic leaders of Brazil, Belarus, Nicaragua, and Turkmenistan denied the threat that the coronavirus posed to their nations. This resulted in them being dubbed the "Ostrich Alliance" by a Brazilian professor of international relations due to their head-in-the-sand attitude.

As the dreaded COVID-19 ripped across the world, these shameful presidents showed disdain for coronavirus science and failed to take defensive measures against the pandemic. The coronavirus crisis has laid bare their collective incompetence, with their flawed responses unnecessarily killing many of their respective citizens.

Standing above these four ostrich leaders is our archvillain, US President Donald Trump, who has also refused to take the pandemic seriously. He was castigated for his dismissive early response to the health warnings about an imminent threat. Trump's contempt for science is no secret, and his failure to implement a nationwide mitigation strategy has cost his nation dearly.

The US has the ignominious honour of having the world's highest COVID-19 infection rate, with over two million confirmed cases. As of this writing, over 114,000 Americans have died from COVID-19, and the death toll is expected to rise. These tragic figures are the direct result of Trump underestimating the virus's contagion and deadliness.

While no one expected inspired leadership from the president, his disastrous handling of the crisis has put him in a league of his own. His presidency has turned deadly, with many of his citizens dying needlessly due to his breathtaking denial and delay. Trump's irresponsibility is almost criminal, with his erratic behaviour proving that he is clearly out of his depth.

Three other heads of government have not covered themselves in glory in response to the threat. Mexico's President, Andrés Manuel López Obrador, urged Mexicans to "live life as normal". In Indonesia, President Joko Widodo peddled nonsense about "herbal remedies". Meanwhile, the Philippines' President, Rodrigo Duterte, issued orders to kill ("shoot them dead") quarantine violators.

Unsurprisingly, the lack of transparency displayed by China has generated much disquiet. The Chinese government is accused of acting too slowly during the early stages of the outbreak. China was subsequently praised by authorities for implementing unprecedented measures, including quarantining the entire city of Wuhan to slow the spread of the coronavirus.

European leaders do not escape criticism. In the grimmest of league tables, Britain has the second-highest rate of COVID-19 deaths in the world, while Italy comes in fourth. UK Prime Minister Boris Johnson and Italian Prime Minister Giuseppe Conte both botched their initial responses. Johnson gave the virus insufficient attention as he was focussed on Brexit, while Conte underestimated the potential spread of the virus.

It is instructive to note that many of the world's inept leaders are populist politicians. According to two Australian academics, populist leaders – such as Donald Trump in America, Jair Bolsonaro in Brazil, and Joko Widodo in Indonesia – have an incentive to mobilise fake news and information, as:

> … they are not capable of adopting evidence-based deliberation as a strategy. Their ignorance of science reaches a point where truth and lies have no clear boundaries. In catastrophes, the use of such ambiguity to promote a political agenda is magnified. … Populist governments are infamous for "silencing" science. This is because evidence-based policy is not compatible with their approach to public policy.

With regard to Sweden, its unique response to the novel coronavirus has been greeted with mixed reactions. Under the leadership of Prime Minister Stefan Löfven, the Swedish government has taken a hands-off approach to managing the pandemic. Rather than declare a lockdown, Sweden asked its citizens to practice social distancing on a mostly voluntary basis, while keeping schools, restaurants, and most businesses open.

Swedish authorities have not officially declared that herd immunity (when more than 60 per cent of the population has had the virus) is their underlying goal. Even so, many believe that augmenting immunity is part of the government's strategy. With one of the highest COVID-19 mortality rates in the world, Sweden has been accused of playing Russian roulette with citizens' lives.

While the pandemic brought out the worst in some leaders, it provided a stage for many others to shine. This is particularly the case for the Global First Movers Group. This elite club consists of an eclectic group of countries – Australia, New Zealand, Austria, Denmark, Norway, Greece, the Czech Republic, Israel, and Singapore – that adopted a "go hard and go early" strategy to limit the spread of COVID-19.

The club is led by Austria, and all members have done exceptionally well in suppressing the coronavirus outbreak. Austria is one of the standout countries in dealing with the virus. Singapore too won plaudits for its aggressive testing-and-tracing campaign. The efforts of Australia and New Zealand have also been hailed, with both nations recording a case-fatality rate below 1.5 per cent.

Another way to look at the effectiveness of political leadership during the pandemic is through the lens of gender. It is claimed that female leaders around the world rose to the occasion by acting boldly and swiftly in making the unpopular call to shut down life as we knew it. A *Forbes* article – titled "What Do Countries with the Best Coronavirus Responses Have in Common? Women Leaders" – provides a precis of how women have managed the crisis with aplomb. *Forbes* notes:

> Angela Merkel, the Chancellor of Germany, stood up early and calmly told her countrymen that this was a serious bug that would infect up to 70% of the population. ...
>
> Among the first and the fastest responses was from Tsai Ing-wen in Taiwan. ...
>
> Jacinda Ardern in New Zealand was early to lockdown and crystal clear on the maximum level of alert she was putting the country under – and why. ...
>
> Iceland, under the leadership of Prime Minister Katrín Jakobsdóttir, is offering free coronavirus testing to all its citizens, and will become a key case study in the true spread and fatality rates of COVID-19. ...
>
> Sanna Marin became the world's youngest head of state when she was elected last December in Finland. It took a millennial leader to spearhead using social media influencers as key agents in battling the coronavirus crisis. ...
>
> Norway's Prime Minister, Erna Solberg, had the innovative idea of using television to talk directly to her country's children. ...

Around 10 per cent of countries are led by women, who preside over just four per cent of the global population. While the performance of countries with a female head of state is a very small category, it can be safely suggested that their performance has been quite positive.

In the words of *The Guardian*, "Plenty of countries with male leaders have also done well. But few with female leaders have done badly".

It is axiomatic that not all heads of state have passed the COVID-19 crisis-management test. The pandemic has exposed feeble leadership among world leaders, with the US paying the highest price for its gross negligence. A combination of slow starts and mixed messages has seen many leaders erode trust and unleash unrest.

**No wonder the coronavirus leadership test has come back negative for some.**

POSTING DATE | 14 JUNE 2020

## How the pandemic has undermined democracies

### EMERGENCY POWERS ABUSED

The novel coronavirus is the biggest news story in a lifetime. For months, it has dominated the international media and become the most talked-about topic on the planet. Front-page and top-of-the-broadcast news stories have focussed on the public-health and economic consequences of the outbreak.

What has slipped under the public radar, however, is the danger that COVID-19 poses to democracy. Inadequate attention has been given to the political risks associated with the virus, even though ominous warning signs are everywhere. Authoritarian leaders are using the crisis to undermine democracy.

Around the world, citizens accepted previously unthinkable restrictions on their basic freedoms in order to avert countless deaths. The loss of civil liberties – such as no public gatherings – were meant to be temporary. Yet, in some nations, life has not returned to normal.

Unscrupulous leaders, like Hungarian Prime Minister Viktor Orbán, have exploited the virus to impose measures that they have long sought. Orbán has used the health crisis as a pretext to push through legislation which enables him to rule by decree indefinitely, effectively removing any oversight of his government.

In Russia, the assaults on democratic institutions have been even cruder. Foul play is believed to be behind the suspicious deaths of two doctors and the serious injury of another doctor. All three doctors mysteriously fell out of hospital windows. Each had criticised the country's handling of the crisis and the lack of personal protective equipment.

Predictably, US President Donald Trump has also politicised the pandemic. Among other things, he attempted to quash dissent by limiting press access to public health officials critical of his response. Trump also threatened to override the authority of governors to impose stay-at-home orders.

Trump's disdain for independent institutions and for the separation of powers is shared by Brazil's far-right leader, Jair Bolsonaro. He has been following the same playbook as Trump, albeit in a more thuggish way. Bolsonaro called for a shutdown of the Supreme Court and Congress, which are investigating him.

Like Trump, Bolsonaro displays utter contempt for his country's system of checks and balances. Bolsonaro admires Trump, and Trump, in turn, is a staunch ally of Bolsonaro. The nonchalance of both men in the face of a global pandemic is part of their shared political disposition.

Both leaders view the coronavirus threat with skepticism – Bolsonaro called it a "little flu", and Trump labelled it the "kung flu". Bolsonaro sacked one health minister and provoked another to resign, while Trump continues to squabble with his scientific advisers.

The Indian government, under Prime Minister Narendra Modi, has used the virus to advance its anti-Muslim agenda. Hindu nationalists within the government have agitated against the Muslim minority, scapegoating its members for causing the virus. This has led to physical and verbal warfare being waged against Muslims, pushing further their ostracisation in Indian society.

Iran, a government obsessed with tight control, has used the epidemic to deploy security forces to clear the streets. It has also used disinformation and cover-ups to keep the infection rate low so that – like all authoritarian governments – it can look competent and effective.

Across the world, public-health officials are brushing up against ideologically minded national leaders hell-bent on using COVID-19 as a cover for repressive, discriminatory, or unconstitutional measures. Borzou Daragahi, an international correspondent for *The Independent*, writes:

> Months-long anti-government protests in Iraq, Algeria, and Lebanon that have been a severe thorn in the side of the elites have been suspended. In Turkey, the conservative Islamist-rooted government has ordered bars, nightclubs and libraries to close over coronavirus fears, but is allowing shopping malls, stores and restaurants to remain open.

> ... Leaders facing critical leadership challenges such as Benjamin Netanyahu in Israel and Romania's prime minister Ludovic Orban found their political problems vanishing, at least temporarily.

The Romanian parliament reluctantly gave the embattled premier full powers. Meanwhile, Netanyahu was temporarily spared the indignity of appearing in court on three corruption cases after his hearings were postponed for two months due to coronavirus restrictions on large gatherings.

The pandemic has also highlighted how voting systems cannot handle disruption. As noted in one report:

> Local and national elections around the world are being suspended – the logistics are too overbearing and costly in the midst of a crisis, and social distancing impossible during polling. These delays will undoubtedly erode trust in the system as leaders without a credible mandate bungle their way through an unprecedented crisis.

There is also concern over contact-tracing apps. The governments of Singapore and Israel have used the crisis to track people through their mobile phones. Other countries have also loosened their restrictions on privacy by allowing surveillance apps that in normal times would be outrageous.

Guy Verhofstadt, a former Belgian Prime Minister, believes that the mass adoption of contact-tracing apps is a slippery slope. He writes:

> Before long, Europeans, Americans or others could find themselves living more like the Chinese, with every move monitored, every violation – even of unwritten rules – punished, and a "personal rating" dictating one's access to travel and public services. This may seem far-fetched, but one need only consider the latest developments in Hungary or Poland to see just how vulnerable democratic institutions can be. If we are not careful, the biggest casualty of COVID-19 could be democracy.

It's clear from what is happening across the globe that civil liberties have been severely weakened. Despots everywhere have tightened their grip on power to run roughshod over democracy and human rights. A recent article posted on the University of Melbourne's multimedia platform, *Pursuit*, by Associate Professor Tom Gerald Daly, reported that:

> An unprecedented number of countries have partially suspended their commitments under international human rights treaties and simultaneously established a state of emergency. ... More than 50 countries have postponed elections, often with little certainty as to when and how they will be held. Concerns run high.
>
> In a survey of 142 countries' exposure to 'pandemic backsliding', the Varieties of Democracy Institute, which investigates the concept of democracy as a system of government, found emergency measures posed little threat to democracy in only 47 countries, including Australia. It also found that 82 countries are at high (48) or medium (34) risk, with the pandemic response accelerating or emphasising established trends of democratic decay, including some of the world's largest democracies – the USA, Brazil, India, and Indonesia.

The alarming uptick in authoritarian behaviours by governments around the world is concerning. The global assault on liberal democracy is real, with emergency powers being used to arrest protesters and sidestep democratic norms.

**Let's hope that temporary restrictions don't outlive the crisis.**

POSTING DATE | 9 AUGUST 2020

## Why the world has been disjointed in managing COVID-19

### POLITICS OF FIGHTING A PANDEMIC

Around the world, the coronavirus has put multi-level governance systems under unprecedented pressure. It has exposed the immense challenge of developing a collective and coherent response to a public-health crisis when power is dispersed. The virus is a shared external threat, yet – in many democracies – governments at national and subnational levels have failed to confront the virus as one team, united against a common and formidable enemy.

At the height of the pandemic in Australia and other jurisdictions, political posturing and jousting saw politicians at different territorial tiers work against each other, resulting in fragmented and muddled policy responses. In some cases, critical relationships turned toxic as political leaders – in search of scapegoats for rising deaths and infections within their respective geographic patches – played the blame game, attacking opponents and causing an escalation of tensions.

In an attempt to shut out COVID, many national governments rushed to close their external borders to foreign nationals. In contrast, only a handful of countries, including Australia, sealed their internal borders by ring-fencing entire states. The extraordinary decision to impose state border restrictions barring entry to other Australians was made by state premiers against the wishes of the Prime Minister, Scott Morrison.

When the pandemic took hold in February 2020, the World Health Organization (WHO) advised against the closure of even international borders, warning that restrictions could "have negative social and economic effects on the affected countries". The WHO also declared that "restricting the movement of people and goods during public health emergencies is ineffective in most situations and may divert resources from other interventions".

It's a natural human reaction to pull up the drawbridge when under attack, and countless politicians did this in an effort to halt the spread of the virus. Still, many experts believe that border closures were of little benefit in containing the virus. "I think they're mostly useless, to tell you the truth," said Ira Longini, a professor of biostatistics at the University of Florida who has studied the effects of restrictions.

Controlling a pandemic requires effective and integrated leadership at all levels. Yet, in Australia, securing a nationally consistent approach to key issues, including schooling, lockdowns, border closures, and vaccinations, proved elusive. Federal and state governments expressed divergent viewpoints, leaving citizens confused. States set their own agendas and refused to let the federal government call the shots.

In a crisis, words matter, and politicians across the globe dialled up the rhetoric on the need to protect national (country) and subnational (regional) borders. Australia's political leaders did likewise, with some state premiers resorting to a discourse combining fear and tribalism. Humans regress to tribalism when afraid – it's the biological loophole that politicians of all political persuasions have long used to tap in to tribal instincts.

Political tribalism is about identities, and Aussies not only see themselves as Australians but also as members of a state tribe, and this begets proud declarations such as "I'm a Victorian". At its extreme, tribalism means that the tribe never concedes an inch to other tribes. It's an "us versus them" mentality which saw some state premiers frame messages around the need to "protect Queenslanders" and "isolate Western Australians" from other Aussies.

When announcing his decision to segregate his state from the rest of Australia, the WA Premier, Mark McGowan, stated that: "In effect, we'll be turning Western Australia into an island within an island – our own country". This sort of parochial decision-making should not come as a surprise – all politicians do it. Pandering to the immediate demands and desires of voters is the classic way to get elected/re-elected.

Consequently, Australia's states and territories displayed almost unprecedented independence as they responded to the needs of their populations/tribes. Throughout the pandemic, premiers were not afraid to go it alone if they felt that the PM's national strategy was not in the best interests of their "tribal constituents".

Tribalism is also defined as a "blind loyalty group", and the local-town pitch of some premiers made their citizens fearful and insular. Moreover, the rabble-rousing by premiers fuelled political rivalries between state-based tribes. To quote the opinion editor at *The Guardian* Australia:

> It is astonishing to witness the "border wars" as people have become warriors for their state and developed particularly strong parasocial relationships with their premiers along the east coast of Australia. It has featured in Western Australia, Tasmania and South Australia too but is most venomous in NSW, Queensland and Victoria.

Embarrassingly, the childish bickering between the states was reported in no less than *The New York Times* under the banner headline: "Australia's States Are Feuding Like Siblings. What Else to Do but Laugh?" The January 2021 article went on to say:

> In Western Australia, which has a long history of flirting with secession, Premier Mark McGowan, its top official, had an approval rating of 89 percent a few months ago after going further than any other leader with restrictions and rhetoric suggesting that Australians from other states were diseased threats to stability. He is expected to be re-elected in a landslide in March.

That prediction proved to be correct – McGowan was electorally rewarded for his tough stance on border restrictions, achieving a crushing victory at the ballot box. His promise to continue providing a border security blanket to protect the WA tribe from COVID-19 was extremely popular at a state level but divisive at a federal level. McGowan's decision to retreat behind borders is an example of a harmful "beggar-thy-neighbour" policy.

Beggar-thy-neighbour policies were also evident globally, with many world leaders adopting a "my-country-first" approach to the pandemic. As with subnational governments, this resulted in national governments also pandering to their electorates.

This was most evident in the rush by first-world nations to buy up the majority of the world's supply of vaccines, to the detriment of poorer nations.

The WHO labelled such blatantly inward-focussed behaviour as "vaccine nationalism". In fairness to national leaders, their nationalistic stance was driven by their respective citizenry, who expect their elected officials to look after them first and foremost. As every president and prime minister knows, their party's fortunes depend upon giving the majority of people what they want.

It's axiomatic that politics, like economics, is driven by self-interest – the selfish ambitions of politicians (personal advancement) and the self-centeredness of voters (what's in it for me?). Given this dynamic, it's clear that (a) at a national level, domestic political goals will invariably be placed above those beyond national borders, and (b) at a subnational level, regional goals will invariably be placed ahead of national goals.

The only governance organisation that has had a global focus throughout the pandemic is the WHO. It warned national and subnational governments that a "whole-of-government, whole-of-society" approach was necessary to crush the virus, but its pleas fell on deaf ears. The harsh reality is national and subnational governments will always focus on their respective constituents first and echo back the concerns of their electorates.

I have long maintained that Australia is over-governed, and that we should eliminate the states. I also hold the view that individual countries are ill-equipped to deal with global issues like climate change and pandemics, and that we need to move to a new form of global governance. I am absolutely confident that neither of these changes will happen in my lifetime!

Meantime, I believe that the world would be a better place if we acted like global citizens. To paraphrase John F. Kennedy's famous line:

**"Ask not what the world can do for you, but what you can do for the world."**

POSTING DATE | 21 NOVEMBER 2021

## How to prevent the next pandemic

### COOPERATION IS THE KEY

Leaders have two responsibilities in any crisis – solve the immediate problem and stop it from happening again. Now that the world is slowly getting on top of COVID-19, we must look to the longer term and work out how to avoid a future global health emergency.

The world was caught flat-footed by the coronavirus, and medical experts fear that if we don't learn from our mistakes, the next pandemic will be a matter of *when*, not *if*. No one can guarantee a pandemic-free world, as infectious diseases are a fact of life, but we can do better at minimising the impact on public health.

Stopping future epidemics from morphing into pandemics will require unprecedented globally coordinated action. It is only through international cooperation – and not through nationalist rhetoric and policies – that governments will be able to protect citizens, according to the World Economic Forum. In mid-April, the Forum issued a report which stated:

> The world that emerges from the coronavirus pandemic may be a warring collection of countries that are more closed off and nationalistic than before. But without rapid and effective global cooperation, the world may not exit this crisis safely at all. For now at least, heavy-handed nationalist responses predominate. Alongside curfews, lockdowns, and requisitioning, governments are closing borders and using wartime rhetoric to rally their populations. ... Soon, however, governments will need to restart the global economy. And that will require international cooperation.

Many believe that COVID-19 is a creature of capitalist globalisation and that the only way to prevent further outbreaks is to build walls, restrict travel, and decrease trade – in other words, to de-globalise the world. However, historian and author Professor Yuval Noah Harari maintains that the coronavirus crisis is a human failure caused by our inability to cooperate.

In a *TIME* article on 15 March, 2020, Professor Harari wrote:

> … while short-term quarantine is essential to stop epidemics, long-term isolationism will lead to economic collapse without offering any real protection against infectious diseases. Just the opposite. The real antidote to epidemic is not segregation, but rather cooperation.

Professor Harari notes that epidemics killed millions of people long before the current age of globalisation. He cites the Black Plague, which killed between 75 million and 200 million people even though there was no such thing as intercontinental travel or megacities in the 14th century to fuel the spread of the disease.

Over the centuries, humanity has become better at combating diseases, with both the incidence and impact of epidemics actually going down dramatically. In the words of Professor Harari:

> Despite horrendous outbreaks such as AIDS and Ebola, in the twenty-first century epidemics kill a far smaller proportion of humans than in any previous time since the Stone Age. This is because the best defense humans have against pathogens is not isolation – it is information. Humanity has been winning the war against epidemics because in the arms race between pathogens and doctors, pathogens rely on blind mutations while doctors rely on the scientific analysis of information.

Professor Harari asserts that history teaches us two lessons for the current epidemic. Firstly, you cannot protect yourself by permanently closing your borders. And secondly, real protection comes from the sharing of reliable scientific data and from global solidarity. Professor Harari continues:

> When one country is struck by an epidemic, it should be willing to honestly share information about the outbreak without fear of economic catastrophe – while other countries should be able to trust that information, and should be willing to extend a helping hand rather than ostracize the victim.

When politicians squabble, viruses double, which is why the United Nations Development Program (UNDP) has added its voice to those calling for greater cooperation. In the concluding remarks to a report titled "Humanity needs leadership and solidarity to defeat the coronavirus", the UNDP is clear:

> We must rebuild trust and cooperation, within and among nations, and between people and their governments.

Following the Global Financial Crisis in 2008, there was swift and decisive action by the G20 in leading a coordinated global response. In stark contrast, there has been a lack of effective international action regarding COVID-19.

Predictably, governments have been working to protect their own populations first by closing borders and imposing quarantines and lockdowns. "But in doing so," warns Erik Berglöf, Director of the Institute of Global Affairs at the London School of Economics and Political Science, "they are often failing to see the bigger picture. That critical error of judgment, if not corrected, will come back to haunt us all".

Berglöf explains that containing a pandemic requires strengthening the weakest links – in an individual hospital, a local community, a country, or the world. "That is why it is in everyone's interest urgently to shore up weak health-care systems", he implores.

Commenting on the inward-looking focus of most governments, economics professor Jong-Wha Lee, of Korea University, stated in an opinion piece on 25 March that:

> Unilateral travel bans should be eschewed in favor of cooperative responses, including information-sharing and coordination in the development and delivery of vaccines and treatments. Public-health systems must be protected. Cooperation is in everyone's interest. Yet, at a time of intensifying nationalism, weak political leadership, and rising political and economic tensions between the world's two largest economies, effective international action is proving difficult to come by.

Berglöf believes that the G20 needs to listen and work with the World Health Organization (WHO). He acknowledges the heavy criticism that has been levelled at the WHO but sees this as "misdirected, ill-informed, and counterproductive". He staunchly believes that "the WHO remains the only institution that can provide global health leadership and inspire the trust needed to intervene," and that "we undermine it at our own risk".

As outlined in a recent *POLITICO* article, the coronavirus has brought out the best and worst in world leaders, and not everyone has passed the test of character. "Countries may not always get the leader they deserve, but the coronavirus pandemic has certainly revealed what kind of leader they've gotten," said *POLITICO*.

Ultimately, governments should be fighting the virus, not each other or the WHO. The UN's Secretary-General, António Guterres, described the role of the WHO as "absolutely critical" in overcoming the COVID-19 pandemic. World leaders must work together, otherwise history will not judge them kindly.

**A classic case of united we stand, divided we fall.**

POSTING DATE | 31 MAY 2020

## Search for COVID-19 vaccine brings nationalist element to worldwide crisis

### NATIONS ENGAGE IN DANGEROUS HEALTH ARMS RACE

A global competition is underway to defeat the novel coronavirus. More than 140 vaccines are being tested, according to the World Health Organization. Australian researchers are leading several major clinical trials that might help control the spread of the disease.

But in the battle to be the first to find effective protection against COVID-19, nobody wins unless everyone wins. That's the view of American epidemiologist and CEO of Gavi, the Vaccine Alliance, Dr Seth Berkley. In an opinion piece Dr Berkley wrote for *Fortune Online,* he expressed concern that the search for a vaccine has morphed into a geopolitical battle.

> ... Regardless of which vaccines succeed, if we don't take a more global and multilateral approach, one involving unprecedented collaboration, where countries work together with global health agencies toward COVID-19 vaccines and where the rewards are shared, then ultimately we all stand to lose. Because with infectious disease, no one is safe until everyone is safe.

Dr Berkley is not alone in flagging that a lack of international cooperation is driving nations to race against each other and not the real enemy – the virus. Writing in *The New York Times,* a team of senior correspondents observed:

> China, Europe and the United States have all set off at a sprint to become the first to produce a vaccine. But while there is cooperation on many levels – including among companies that are ordinarily fierce competitors – hanging over the effort is the shadow of a nationalistic approach that could give the winner the chance to favor its own population and potentially gain the upper hand in dealing with the economic and geostrategic fallout from the crisis.

Vaccine nationalism and a "my-country-first" approach to vaccine allocation also trouble Thomas J. Bollyky, Director of the Global

Health Program at the Council on Foreign Relations. He warns that such behaviour creates the potential for a deadly zero-sum game which will have profound and far-reaching consequences.

> Without global coordination, countries may bid against one another, driving up the price of vaccines and related materials. Supplies of proven vaccines will be limited initially even in some rich countries, but the greatest suffering will be in low and middle-income countries. Such places will be forced to watch as their wealthier counterparts deplete supplies and will have to wait months (or longer) for their replenishment. In the interim, health-care workers and billions of elderly and other high-risk inhabitants in poorer countries will go unprotected, which will extend the pandemic, increase its death toll, and imperil already fragile health-care systems and economies.

World powers are working at breakneck speed to secure vaccine stocks and score some reputational kudos. But an excess of national pride and one-upmanship are threatening to overwhelm the common good. The jockeying for position and public posturing by nations was the focus of an article in the July 7 edition of *POLITICO Magazine*.

> In China, where a vaccine victory could turn a country that started the virus' spread into the savior of the world, the virologist and major general leading the country's vaccine project has been hailed as a "goddess" on social media. ...
>
> In June ... President Emmanuel Macron announced that [French pharma giant] Sanofi would be dramatically ramping up operations in France to put "Sanofi and France at the heart of excellence in the fight ... to find a vaccine." Invoking the "genius of Louis Pasteur," Marcon [*sic*] hailed France as "a great vaccine country." ...
>
> Meanwhile, across the English Channel, Britain is celebrating the news that its own Oxford scientists are "sprinting fastest" to develop a vaccine, in the words of an April 27 *New York Times* article - though the news site *Irish*

> *Central* took pains to point out that the lead scientist is Irish, not English. ...
>
> And then there's Trump, who stood in the Rose Garden in May and stated definitively that "America is blessed to have the most brilliant, talented doctors and researchers anywhere in the world. And now we're combining all of these amazing strengths for the most aggressive vaccine project in history. There's never been a vaccine project anywhere in history like this."

Of course, governments aren't chasing the vaccine trophy just for prestige and scientific accolades. Beyond the hubris, it's about getting first dibs on any breakthrough drug for the benefit of their own people. Many world leaders are driven by nationalist impulses and the demands of their anxious populations to get a jump start on eliminating the virus and bringing their economies back to life.

While it's still uncertain which countries will get the first inoculations, what is clear is that there will not be enough vaccine for quite some time, even with the unprecedented efforts to manufacture billions of doses. A report in *The Washington Post* noted:

> ... the nationalistic priorities of individual nations could thwart the strategic imperative to tamp down hot spots wherever they are on the planet – including poor countries that cannot afford the vaccine. The United States in particular could be left in the cold if vaccines developed here as part of a go-it-alone approach turn out to be less effective than those produced in China or Europe. The scenario public health experts fear most is a worldwide fight in which manufacturers sell only to the highest bidders, rich countries try to buy up the supplies, and nations where manufacturers are located hoard vaccines for their own citizens.

While richer nations look set to win the battle to find a COVID-19 vaccine, they will lose the war against the spread of the virus if poorer nations remain unprotected. Just immunising a few populations against a universal threat won't be sufficient for global trade and travel to resume. Yet there remains a high risk that the most vulnerable will not get the lifesaving interventions that they need.

African nations were pushed to the back of the queue in gaining access to an antiretroviral therapy (ART) for HIV, and they may well suffer the same injustice regarding COVID-19 vaccine delivery. To help prevent history from repeating itself, the United Nations has declared it a "moral imperative" that everyone has access to a "people's vaccine".

A press release issued by UNAIDS in May cited an open letter signed by "140 world leaders, experts, and elders". The letter demands that all vaccines, treatments, and tests be patent free, mass produced, distributed fairly, and available to all people, in all countries free of charge. The letter states:

> Now is *not* the time to allow the interests of the wealthiest corporations and governments to be placed before the universal need to save lives, or to leave this massive and moral task to market forces. Access to vaccines and treatments as global public goods are in the interests of all humanity. We cannot afford for monopolies, crude competition and near-sighted nationalism to stand in the way.

Like climate change, pandemics are transnational issues that no country can solve alone. Both highlight the need for closer international cooperation and coordinated global action. Yet most nations have acted independently from each other during the pandemic rather than in unison. The world needs to heed the words of Pulitzer Prize-winning science writer, Laurie Garrett:

**"Without equity, pandemic battles will fail."**

POSTING DATE | 23 AUGUST 2020

## Who should be first in line for COVID-19 vaccines?

### INOCULATION QUEUES FORM

The pandemic has forced governments to answer many tough questions, and the virus is currently posing another: Who should be at the front of immunisation lines when vaccines against COVID-19 become available? This vexing decision has come into sharp relief as policymakers grapple with how best to allocate doses for scarce vaccines.

Even if in the coming months some vaccines are declared safe and effective, there will not be enough for everyone who wants a shot right away. While many individuals and groups will argue that they should be at the top of the distribution list, determining who should be given priority access to limited supplies is challenging politicians and epidemiologists.

Bio-ethicists have weighed in on the debate as the mass vaccination of almost eight billion people won't happen overnight. It is widely believed that a phased-in approach – which must be fair and equitable – will be required. But deciding how to apportion supplies of the first batches of coronavirus vaccines – and who will follow the initial jump-start phase and in what order – is the subject of ongoing debate.

From a health equity perspective, there will undoubtedly be disagreements over vaccine rationing, regardless of what priority ranking is introduced. Prioritisation decisions will be fraught as players (the young, the old, pregnant women, health-care workers, those in frontline jobs, people of colour, individuals with pre-existing conditions, etc.) jockey to be early recipients of the drug. Some will claim that it is a matter of life and death that they receive an early jab, while others will refuse immunisation altogether.

Of course, for nations to distribute vaccines, they must firstly obtain supplies from vaccine manufacturers. Will manufacturers just sell their product to the highest bidders? Or will they take a global perspective and ensure that supplies are rolled out to all nations – even poorer ones? The correct course of action was outlined in a recent article by Bill Gates.

> During a pandemic, vaccines and antivirals can't simply be sold to the highest bidder. They should be available and affordable for people who are at the heart of the outbreak and in greatest need. Not only is such distribution the right thing to do, it's also the right strategy for short-circuiting transmission and preventing future pandemics.

Though no final agreement has been reached on a single, global distribution framework for COVID-19 vaccines, two main proposals have emerged. A number of experts have argued that health-care workers and high-risk populations (the over 65s) should be immunised first. In contrast, the World Health Organization (WHO) has suggested that countries receive doses proportional to their populations.

From an ethical perspective, both of these strategies are "seriously flawed", according to Professor Ezekiel J. Emanuel from the University of Pennsylvania. He states:

> The idea of distributing vaccines by population appears to be an equitable strategy. But the fact is that normally, we distribute things based on how severe there is suffering in a given place, and, in this case, we argue that the primary measure of suffering ought to be the number of premature deaths that a vaccine would prevent.

Professor Emanuel led a group of 19 health ethicists from around the world (including Australia) to develop a three-phase plan – the Fair Priority Model – for vaccine distribution. In their proposal, as noted in a news release by Penn Medicine, Emanuel and his co-authors point to three fundamental values that must be considered when distributing a COVID-19 vaccine among countries:

> Benefiting people and limiting harm, prioritizing the disadvantaged, and giving equal moral concern for all individuals. The Fair Priority Model addresses these values by focusing on mitigating three types of harms caused by COVID-19: death and permanent organ damage, indirect health consequences, such as health care system strain and stress, as well as economic destruction.

Preventing deaths is seen as the most urgent of all three dimensions and is the focus of Phase 1 of the Fair Priority Model. In Phase 2, two metrics that capture overall economic improvement and the extent to which people would be spared from poverty are proposed. Finally, in Phase 3, countries with higher transmission rates are initially prioritised.

With regard to preventing deaths, the Model begins by calculating the number of years of life that will be added in a given country by the delivery of, for example, a million vaccine doses. Peru, which has experienced high COVID-19 mortality rates, and the US, where the virus has killed over 200,000 people, would likely be on the priority list.

"But take New Zealand, giving them a million doses, you're probably not going to save but one or two people literally. So, they would be low on the priority list," says Emanuel. The group of 19 rejects the argument that its policies would reward bad management, such as in the US, which leads the world in the number of virus deaths and cases.

"You shouldn't penalise Americans because Donald Trump can't seem to manage this pandemic," he reasons.

Emanuel and his collaborators also object to the WHO's plan, which begins with three per cent of each country's population receiving vaccines and continues until every country has vaccinated 20 per cent of its citizens. While that plan may be politically tenable, it "mistakenly assumes that equality requires treating differently situated countries identically, rather than equitably responding to their different needs," argues Emanuel.

Health-care workers and others most vulnerable are traditionally first in line for a scarce vaccine. But many are calling for geography to play a greater role this time round and to give COVID-19 vaccine priority to people where the outbreak is hitting hardest. Still, the fear remains that many nations will prioritise their own populations first. The resultant uneven scramble may see countries with the greatest need for vaccines being unable to put in place an early and critical ring of protection around their borders.

Another idea that has been floated is to give priority to "super-spreaders". A trio of US academics believes that after taking care of essential workers, "vaccinations should be given to the biggest transmitters of the virus – mostly the young – and only then to the most vulnerable".

One of the lessons from past pandemics is that vaccinating likely asymptomatic spreaders early can avert multiple infections in others. The academic trio note that very few of the COVID-19 super-spreaders are elderly. Rather, it is younger people who have a much greater propensity to resume social lives at school and in other venues.

While the strategy of vaccinating the young to protect the old is counterintuitive, there is ample evidence to suggest that this is the right approach. According to UK researchers, immunising those around the elderly may help protect them. It is also instructive to note that a vaccine against COVID-19 may not be as effective in older people, who are most at risk of suffering complications and dying from the disease.

Clearly, there is an urgent need for international coordination on COVID-19 vaccines to ensure that effective treatments are widely available and appropriately distributed. With many nations likely to adopt a nationalistic approach, there is a high risk that the most vulnerable will not get the lifesaving interventions that they need.

Deciding who gets first dibs will be a challenging and contentious task. Most nations are expected to adopt a tiered approach to vaccine distribution. Regardless of the allocation plan adopted, it needs to be transparent and perceived as fair by a majority of the general public.

**Of course, fairness – like beauty – is in the eye of the beholder.**

POSTING DATE | 18 OCTOBER 2020

## Why COVID vaccines are being distributed unevenly and unfairly

### MOST NEEDY MISS OUT

Imagine this for a second. You're at the beach and you notice two swimmers in difficulty. Each has encountered a beach hazard caused by the powerful surf. A rogue wave breaking along the shoreline has knocked a man off his feet, and he is trying to regain his balance. At the same time, a rip current has dragged a woman out to sea, and she is fighting a losing battle against the fast-moving tide.

You face a dilemma: The swimmers are 100 metres apart, and you can't rescue both at once. You quickly assess who has the greater need. While the man is disoriented, he has not suffered serious injury to his back or neck – he is unsteady, but standing. The woman, however, is clearly in grave danger of drowning – she is unable to stay afloat due to exhaustion and is slipping under the water.

Since the woman is far more vulnerable to the ravages of the sea, you swim out through the breaking waves and rescue her. Bystanders commend you on saving her from certain death. As the male swimmer was able to stumble out of the water on his own, no lives were lost. Your judgment to use "likelihood of death" as a triage criterion was spot on. The swimmer most exposed to the elements was correctly identified, and a fatality was averted.

Now imagine a different life-and-death scenario. This time, you are the boss of the World Health Organization (WHO). You cast your eyes over the latest statistics on the number of COVID-19 deaths around the world. It's clear that Brazil and Australia are navigating the virus differently. Brazil is in treacherous waters and has been unable to quell the pandemic waves. In contrast, Australia finds itself in calmer seas with little headwinds.

You face a dilemma: You don't have sufficient doses of COVID vaccines to inoculate every citizen of both nations. You carefully assess which population is worse-off. Brazil has been unable to stem the tide of deaths, and thousands more are expected to perish as a result of the pandemic. Australia, on the other hand, has done an outstanding job in containing the virus and has recorded an extremely low mortality rate from COVID-19.

As a leading epidemiologist, you know that vaccines should go first to the places where there is the greatest suffering. The primary measure of suffering is the number of premature deaths that a vaccine can prevent. Since Brazil has far more reported COVID cases and deaths than Australia – in both absolute and per capita terms – it's a no-brainer that Brazil's needs are the greatest. Still, your decision to prioritise Brazil over Australia creates a storm of controversy.

As WHO Director-General, you know that each million doses of the vaccine will likely save the lives of hundreds of Brazilians. You also know that the same million doses given to Australians is probably not going to save more than one or two people. However, vaccines are not being distributed based on need but ability to pay. Countries with advanced economies have bigger cheque books, which has enabled them to push in front of countries with developing economies.

The unfairness of this is laid bare when we circle back to the surf lifesaving example. Australia can be likened to the male swimmer whose situation was not life threatening, whereas Brazil is akin to the female swimmer who was in serious peril. While none of the bystanders on the beach challenged your decision to rescue the swimmer needing the most help, you are being severely criticised as the WHO boss for choosing the nation that needs the most help.

The hypocrisy of this double standard is even more pronounced when you learn further facts about the two swimmers. The male is from Australia and the female is from Brazil. You knew this before you plunged into the surf, as you spoke briefly to the distressed families of both swimmers. However, knowing the nationality of each swimmer did not cause you to favour the Australian over the Brazilian – and quite rightly so!

Race and ethnicity should not be factored into the equation when rescuing swimmers or determining vaccine allocation. All lives matter and no life can be neglected. Yet, when it comes to COVID, we are witnessing the injustice of some humans being treated as less equal than others. The sad reality is that nearly 70 poor countries will only be able to vaccinate one in ten people against COVID-19 this year. The UN has labelled this distribution outcome as "wildly uneven and unfair".

According to a press release issued by Oxfam International, rich countries are failing the vaccine equity test.

> ... Wealthier nations have bought up enough doses to vaccinate their entire populations nearly three times over by the end of 2021 if those currently in clinical trials are all approved for use. Canada tops the chart with enough vaccines to vaccinate each Canadian five times. Updated data shows that rich nations representing just 14 per cent of the world's population have bought up 53 per cent of all the most promising vaccines so far.

Anna Marriott, Oxfam's health policy manager, adds: "No one should be blocked from getting a life-saving vaccine because of the country they live in or the amount of money in their pocket. But unless something changes dramatically, billions of people around the world will not receive a safe and effective vaccine for COVID-19 for years to come".

The world has a moral obligation to help those in greatest need first. Given this, Australia, New Zealand, and other nations which are not in immediate danger of "drowning" from COVID-19, should move towards the back of the vaccination queue. Of course, this won't happen, as rich nations are focussed on national recovery, not global recovery, as they are prioritising country over planet.

The WHO labels this behaviour as "vaccine nationalism" and blames it for the lack of solidarity against a common enemy. WHO Director-General Tedros Adhanom Ghebreyesus has warned that the lopsided distribution of vaccines "harms everyone and protects no one". Further, he believes that inoculating certain populations to the detriment of others is "medically self-defeating".

The rising fever of inequality is fuelled by a chronic failure of national leaders to display true global leadership. The inward focus of most countries places the pursuit of domestic political goals above those beyond their borders. In fairness to national leaders, their decision to take a beggar-thy-neighbour stance is driven by citizens who expect their elected officials to look after them first and foremost. Many citizens want first dibs on COVID vaccine jabs.

Yet, it's in Australia's self-interest (and other rich nations' too) to help ensure that every other country's population is vaccinated. Until the fear of COVID-19 dissipates, trade and travel won't return to normal. And health-wise, nobody is safe until everybody is safe. The strategy of every nation just looking out for itself is a path that most ethicists think is wrong.

The frenzied grab for vaccines is driven by the same selfish impulses that drove the hoarding of toilet paper. Coronavirus drives panic buying due to the fear of missing out and leads to the irrational stockpiling of vaccines, toilet paper, and other essential items. Needless to say, no one wins when everyone adopts an "every-man-for-himself" attitude.

If we truly believe that life is sacred and worthy of our deepest reverence, we (as individuals and nations) would let poorer nations and those worst affected by COVID go first. Certainly, I would not have objected if the Australian government had delayed vaccinations until more needy nations had received their jabs first.

My view, of course, puts me in the minority, as many Australians, as well as the federal opposition and some sections of the media, are critical that our rollout has not moved faster. Even though it shouldn't be this way, Australian Prime Minister Scott Morrison knows that his party's fortunes depend upon giving the majority of Australians what they want – a jab in the arm and quickly!

**Shame on us for letting the world's most vulnerable people "drown" in a sea of COVID.**

POSTING DATE | 14 MARCH 2021

## How COVID-19 illuminated the flaws in Australia's system of government

### DITCH THE MIDDLE MAN – NO MORE STATES

Around the world, millions of people have been medically tested for COVID-19, and we have been tested in other ways as well. National economies, political leadership, and individual resilience have also been tested. Additionally, the pandemic has tested the integration and coordination of Australia's three-tier system of federal, state, and local governments.

While Australia's multi-level law-making structure looks like a neatly layered cake, there are hidden overlaps which cause blurred lines of separation. History shows that whenever there is a crisis or issue in Australia which transcends state borders, the inherent weaknesses of our governance structure are laid bare. The latest example of this is the novel coronavirus outbreak.

During the height of the pandemic, it was not possible to secure a nationally consistent approach to schooling. Federal and state governments expressed differing viewpoints, leaving parents confused. The PM was blindingly clear in wanting kids to continue attending classrooms. However, the states undermined him by encouraging parents to home school their children.

While education is a state government responsibility, helping Australians weather the economic consequences of the pandemic falls largely to the federal government. That's why Australian Prime Minister Scott Morrison asked premiers to keep schools open so that parents could continue to work and "put food on the table".

With no clear chain of command on this issue, simmering tensions between the prime minister and state premiers were exposed. It was impossible for the PM to get the premiers to fall in to line. Rebellious states – led by NSW Premier Gladys Berejiklian and Victorian Premier Daniel Andrews – rushed to introduce remote learning so that parents could keep their kids home.

The conflicting messages from the states and the federal government about whether it was safe to send kids to class were seized upon by the media, which had a field day reporting the jostling for power. NSW, Victoria, and the ACT broke ranks by making unilateral announcements about schooling arrangements which put them at odds with their federal counterparts.

Gladys Berejiklian was also involved in another political football match – the Ruby Princess fiasco. Australians were treated to the unedifying spectacle of political finger-pointing over who was responsible for allowing the ill-fated ship to dock in Sydney and for allowing passengers to disembark unchecked.

Authorities passed the buck, with NSW officials claiming that they were given permission by the Australian Border Force (ABF) to let passengers off the ship. The ABF returned serve by laying the blame at the feet of NSW Health. A Special Commission of Inquiry is underway to establish which authority ultimately gave the green light to passenger disembarkation.

Another area where Australian governments were not on the same page was lockdown rules. The nationwide lockdown announced by the PM was, quite rightly, accompanied by a warning that police would charge citizens who flouted the rules. But the raft of restrictions on activities varied, depending on where you lived.

Individual state and territory governments decided the specifics of the lockdown in their jurisdiction. Each introduced differing measures to restrict movement, and this caused confusion among the populace regarding the dos and don'ts of going outside. For example, Victoria closed golf courses while NSW left them open.

There was a crackdown by police around the nation on "non-essential travel". Drivers were told that they were required to have a "reasonable excuse" for leaving home. It was clear that popping out to buy groceries and medical supplies constituted essential travel. However, other reasonable excuses for taking to the roads varied from state to state.

The legality of driving lessons turned out to be a hot-button issue. In Victoria, a hefty fine of $1,652 was issued to a 17-year-old learner driver as her driving lesson was classified as non-essential travel.

The fine made headlines around Australia and, following public backlash, it was withdrawn.

NSW Police took to Facebook to assure citizens of New South Wales that driving lessons were regarded as a "reasonable excuse" to leave home. Police in Tasmania also stated that driving lessons were permitted. South Australian authorities similarly gave the green light to driving lessons provided that they were supervised by a household member.

We also had to contend with state border closures, which left Australia's federal model in strange territory. While the prime minister closed our national borders to foreign travellers, many premiers took the unprecedented step of shutting their domestic state borders to segregate themselves from the rest of the nation. The Premier of WA, Mark McGowan, summed it up this way: "In effect, we'll be turning Western Australia into an island within an island – our own country".

Of course, Australian states and territories are not independent sovereign nations but part of a single Commonwealth of Australia. This view is supported by George Williams, the dean of law at the University of NSW, who opined that there is a constructional issue in closing a state border.

> We have section 92 of the Australian constitution and it says trade, commerce and intercourse amongst the States shall be absolutely free. The idea is that we are one country, and a person should be entitled to travel around Australia as they wish.

While closing state borders caused ructions, re-opening them has created even more political drama. NSW Premier Gladys Berejiklian claimed that those states keeping their borders closed were "hindering" the nation's economic recovery. WA Premier Mark McGowan hit back, saying that he would not be "bullied" by a state (NSW) which allowed the Ruby Princess disaster to unfold.

The Queensland Premier, Annastacia Palaszczuk, was more diplomatic in her response to NSW, saying that Queensland would be "seeing southerners return to our glorious sunshine state" towards the end of the year.

It is instructive to note that there was never national advice issued by the federal government recommending that states should close their borders.

In many parts of the world, the catch-cry for coronavirus is "we're all in this together". Yet, when it comes to Australia, each state and territory stands somewhat alone. This is the result of parochial decision-making at a state level and the power struggle between different levels of government.

I acknowledge that the political actors involved in this life-and-death drama have worked tirelessly to stop the spread of the pandemic and are to be thanked. While mistakes have been made, my biggest criticism is aimed squarely at the stage upon which Australia's politicians had to perform – a three-tier system of government which pitted authorities against each other.

There has long been debate in Australia about whether to abolish the states. Former PM Bob Hawke is one of many prominent Australians to have called for a federation overhaul. The complex nature of contemporary issues facing Australia – like climate change and now a global pandemic – is beyond the current three-tier structure, as there is no express head of power for "the environment" or "pandemics".

The inconsistencies between the states have long frustrated me. I once worked for an organisation which spent over a decade lobbying government for uniform credit legislation throughout Australia. I watched with anticipation Australian Prime Minister John Howard's efforts to secure uniform gun legislation following the Port Arthur massacre. And I've listened to upwardly mobile Australian executives with children complain about the lack of uniformity in school curricula around the country.

Let's be honest – the only reason we have three levels of government is due to the burden of history. Australia started out as six independent colonies. The joining of these colonies into a federation of six states to form the Commonwealth of Australia was a good idea in 1901. Today, I humbly submit that the federal/state structure of government has passed its use-by date.

The Founding Fathers of our great nation would not have envisaged the buck passing, endless bickering, and unnecessary duplication that have come to characterise federal/state relations. Blaming Canberra first is the default modus operandi for the states, and my sense is that many Australians are sick of politicians playing the blame game. No system of democracy is perfect – but surely, we can do better than what we currently have in place.

**It's time to scrap the states.**

POSTING DATE | 28 JUNE 2020

## Lessons learned from the coronavirus outbreak

### WHAT THE PANDEMIC HAS TAUGHT US

COVID-19 has left an indelible mark on the world. The pandemic has upended our lives and changed our daily routines. Billions of people have been forced into lockdown, unable to visit one another, or go to work, or attend school, or meet with friends in public places. With constraints put on our basic freedoms to reduce the spread of the virus, any sense of normalcy has been lost.

The once-in-a-lifetime health crisis brought with it wide-ranging consequences which have tested our resilience. As with anything in life, experience is the teacher, so it's vital for humanity to come out of the pandemic as better individuals and a more tightly knit community. The fundamental question is: What have we learned along the way?

As we reflect on the lives lost, the suffering experienced, and the disruption inflicted by COVID, there are many takeaways for governments, businesses, and individuals. The fallout from COVID has ricocheted into all areas of life, so there are myriad lessons – some painful (exposing our weaknesses and limitations) and others uplifting (spotlighting our strengths and generosity).

COVID-19 has been a wake-up call and – as society looks to rebound from this seismic event – it's not surprising that scholars, think-tanks, consultants, and other experts are jumping on the coronavirus "lessons for the future" bandwagon. I have read many of these opinion pieces and, in the main, believe that these analyses contain sound advice.

To provide a succinct summary of the various articles would be challenging as each analysis comes from a different perspective. Regardless, the pandemic has revealed many underlying societal issues that we've long known existed. To fix these problems, we should set ourselves the overarching goal of *building a healthier and fairer society which is inclusive and sustainable.*

Achieving this goal will require collaboration between governments and citizens, and this is something that the boss of the World Health Organization (WHO) knows only too well. Shortly after the

COVID-19 outbreak, Tedros Adhanom Ghebreyesus warned the world that a "whole-of-government, whole-of-society" approach was necessary to crush the virus.

Predictably, many ignored his advice even though governments and citizens working together is a prerequisite to solving any global or national issue. This, I believe, is the most important lesson arising from the pandemic. Whether it's defeating a deadly virus or tackling climate change, governments and citizens must listen to experts and work hand in hand.

The pandemic's catchphrase, "we're all in this together", rings hollow as key stakeholders have not been joined at the hip. Around the world, collective action has been undermined by a lack of political trust (confidence in political institutions) and social trust (faith in other citizens). Waging a war against a disease has led to pandemic belligerence.

Ultimately, slowing the spread of the virus relies on people having faith in the policy prescriptions of governments. Citizens have been asked to adhere to a range of directives, including stay-at-home orders and physical-distancing practices. Even so, the call to make personal sacrifices for the collective good has been a bitter pill for many to swallow.

Governments everywhere have imposed emergency measures which limit the rights and freedoms of citizens, and this has led to varying levels of civil disobedience. Mass protests around the world have seen anti-vaxxers, anti-maskers, and conspiracy theorists march shoulder-to-shoulder in defiance of lockdown laws, thereby creating super-spreading events.

The pandemic has exacerbated prevailing political discontent and resulted in citizens being quick to blame their leaders for not containing the virus. In some countries, this criticism is completely justified, but in others, it is not. In fairness to governments, there is no rulebook for understanding how a pandemic will play out. We are all in uncharted waters, learning as we go.

Still, this does not excuse the "go-it-alone" attitude of many national governments which quickly retreated into populist nationalism in response to a global threat. As I opined in a previous post, *Why COVID vaccines are being distributed unevenly and unfairly,* wealthier nations have bought up enough doses to vaccinate their entire populations nearly three times over.

Rich nations remain focussed on national recovery, not global recovery, as they are prioritising country over planet. The WHO has labelled this behaviour as "vaccine nationalism" and blamed it for the lack of solidarity against a common enemy. Dr Ghebreyesus warned that the lopsided distribution of vaccines harms everyone and protects no one as inoculating certain populations to the detriment of others is medically self-defeating.

This fever of inequality is being fuelled by a chronic failure of national leaders to display true global leadership. The inward focus of most countries places the pursuit of domestic political goals above those beyond their borders. In fairness to national leaders, their beggar-thy-neighbour stance is being driven by citizens who expect their elected officials to look after them first and foremost.

So, the "my-country-first" approach to vaccines reflects the sentiments of citizens. Even though it shouldn't be this way, Australian Prime Minister Scott Morrison – like every other democratically elected world leader – knows that his party's fortunes depend on giving the majority of Australians what they want – a jab in the arm and quickly!

Politics is nothing if not a mirror of the society it serves. As a society, we crave quick fixes and instant gratification and expect politicians to solve all of society's ills at the snap of a finger. That's why politicians who pander to the immediate demands and desires of voters (e.g., to be at the front of the vaccination queue) are invariably rewarded by the electorate.

Complex public policy problems typically involve changing the behaviour of groups of citizens or all citizens. With respect to the pandemic, we as citizens need to change our selfish ways. Not enough of us have shown grace under pressure. There has been a lack of camaraderie. Panic has prevailed over common sense. Many have behaved like a marauding swarm of locusts stripping supermarket shelves bare.

Beyond national governments and citizens, a third actor in the COVID-19 saga is subnational governments – states, provinces, and municipalities. In most countries, governments at this sub-level have been at the frontline of managing the COVID crisis. Many have recorded operational blunders which have resulted in them playing whack-a-mole with successive outbreaks.

To cover their mistakes, subnational governments have used a classic tactic – shift the blame onto others. When it comes to rising infection rates, some subnational governments have attempted to pin responsibility on citizens for breaking health directives, while others have tried to scapegoat their national governments for health policy failures. Amid all the rancour, it's clear that making a villain of other actors is counterproductive.

Despite this, the blame game – with its finger-pointing and mutual buck-passing – is a familiar feature of politics in Australia. As I outlined in an earlier post, the pandemic has laid bare the inherent weaknesses of our three-tier governance structure. Australians have been treated to the unedifying spectacle of states being pitted against states, and states slinging barbs at the federal government.

The pandemic has been a learning curve for everyone, and its continuance is stirring unrest. Pandemic fatigue is setting in and is eroding social cohesion. Our interdependence means that we are all in the same boat and need to work together. With that in mind, the territorial turf wars must cease, political leaders must present a bipartisan front, and citizens must comply with health orders.

**United we stand, divided we fall.**

POSTING DATE | 29 AUGUST 2021

## Why the problem with democracy is voters

### POLITICAL IGNORANCE IS NOT BLISS

It never ceases to amaze me how people around the world complain about their governments. Yet citizens of democracies – via the ballot box – determine who holds political power. So, it's largely our fault if we end up with poor political leadership.

Voters have a track record of choosing idiots, authoritarians, and demagogues for elected office. These leaders invariably turn out to be incompetent and dishonest and thrive on emotion-driven discourse. They hoodwink people into supporting them by exploiting voters' credulity and prejudices.

Politics is nothing if not a mirror of the society it serves. As a society, we crave quick fixes and instant gratification and expect politicians to solve all of society's ills at the snap of a finger. That's why politicians who pander to the immediate demands and desires of voters are rewarded by the electorate.

We jump quickly into the arms of political charlatans but fail to embrace sensible and rational candidates with policies that have an eye to the future. Such long-term outcomes are rejected by "here-and-now" voters who are selfishly focussed on "what's in it for me".

Voting (free and fair elections) is the cornerstone of a true democracy. Yet, in many nations around the world, much of the public is disengaged from politics. Citizens are not politically informed, and this is dangerous as voters do not make informed choices at the ballot box.

US President Donald Trump owes his victory to the uninformed. Indeed, he is on the record as proclaiming: "I love the poorly educated". Political ignorance accounts for a large part of Trump's success. His followers swallow virtually any lie he tells – no matter how outrageous.

When voters know little, they choose the politician with the highest emotional appeal. Trump and other populists play on this, which is why millions voted for him against their best interests. Trump appealed to the anger and discontent of middle-America, tapping in to their fears about jobs, race, and immigration.

Leaders like Donald Trump prove that doing or saying unintelligent things is no barrier to being elected. "We have unserious and unfit leaders," according to a columnist for *The Washington Post*, "because voters are unserious and too often reject sensible, fit candidates for office".

That voters are poorly informed and make irrational decisions is no surprise to renowned political scientists Christopher Achen and Larry Bartels. These two academics co-authored the acclaimed book *Democracy for Realists: Why Elections Do Not Produce Responsive Government.*

The authors' core belief is that people cast their votes for no particularly good reason and that incumbents often get rewarded or punished for events beyond their control. They illustrate this point by tracing the electoral impact of a random event: a dramatic series of shark attacks in New Jersey in 1916.

In what has become the most famous example in the book, they note that voters on the New Jersey seashore blamed President Woodrow Wilson for the shark attacks in the summer of 1916. As a result, Woodrow Wilson lost his home state in the presidential election.

The beachfront towns – which relied on tourism – were negatively impacted by the attacks. Even though Wilson was obviously not responsible for the string of shark-related fatalities, he was the incumbent, and people vote against incumbents when things are bad.

This, of course, is illogical. As Achen and Bartels declare: "Punishing the incumbents for events beyond their control makes no more sense than kicking the dog to get back at a difficult boss at work" ... yet "... governments are punished willy-nilly for bad times".

At the polling booth, election-year natural disasters (droughts, floods, etc.) and the performance of the economy in the months prior to the election have a major impact on whether an incumbent or challenger wins an election. If things are going well – whether they're controllable or not – voters will reward the party in power. If not, they'll look for someone else to lead them.

Achen and Bartels assert that most citizens are unable to evaluate sensitive information in order to reach an informed opinion about whether times have been good or bad under the incumbent government.

> Citizens are unlikely to know whether crime has gone up or down, only whether gruesome murders appear in the local news. Their judgments about the seriousness of environmental threats are virtually uncorrelated with those of experts. Even in the domain of the economy, where detailed statistical information is plentiful ... voters may fixate on current conditions to the neglect of the incumbent's full record.

The book lays waste the comforting view that citizens cast votes based on rational choice – the so-called "folk theory of democracy". Voters don't have anything like coherent preferences. Most people pay little attention to politics and vote irrationally and for contradictory reasons.

Similarly, the majority of voters are too shortsighted to choose economic policies that will produce long-term prosperity. This, in my opinion, is most evident in the irrational attitude of many citizens to government debt. The ill-informed are seduced by populist politicians who promise to balance the national budget.

Our harmful misunderstanding of economic policy is also evident when interest rates rise and fall. Interest rates go up when things are overheating and go down when times are tough. It is ironic, therefore, that nit-picking oppositions are critical when interest rates rise (a sign of a strong economy), and glory-seeking governments take the credit when interest rates fall (a sign of a weak economy).

Most economic truths are counterintuitive. Even so, an ignorant public cannot help but endorse intuitively appealing policies in any given instance, since it has so little information to go on. In the words of the US-based think-tank, the Cato Institute:

> It is little wonder, then, that incumbent politicians are able to take credit for good economic times – regardless of the success, failure, or irrelevance of their economic policies –

> and that presidents cursed with bad economies usually are booted from office, even if their policies have been sound.

Downright misrepresentations and blatant disregard for facts have always plagued politics, and this holds true in Australia as well. During the 2016 federal election, Australians were falsely told that the Liberal Party was going to privatise Medicare and that the Labor Party's carbon price would lead to $100 lamb roasts.

Since few expect politicians to tell the truth, we are not particularly surprised when half-truths and downright lies are exposed. It's often said, however, that politicians lie because voters do not want to hear the truth. The truth often offends, and no one wants to hear things that they find confronting. As noted in the online magazine, *Psychology Today*:

> It is decidedly better for politicians to tell people what makes them feel comfortable. Why should politicians be the purveyors of bad news (and decrease the likelihood of getting people's votes) when they can tell fairy tales with happy endings (which, of course, everyone wants) and come out the victor.

Education is the key to a more literate electorate. We teach our kids "hard" subjects like maths and science, so there's no reason why we can't add politics and economics to the curriculum. The next generation of voters – unlike many of those who are about to cast a vote in the US presidential election – must be able to discern if political candidates are pulling the wool over their eyes and just marketing political and economic snake oil.

**No wonder it's said that the best argument against democracy is a five-minute conversation with the average voter.**

POSTING DATE | 1 NOVEMBER 2020

## Will globalisation create a world without borders?

### NATION-STATES UNDER SIEGE

The most famous photograph ever taken of our planet is called *Earthrise*. It was snapped by astronaut Bill Anders on Christmas Eve 1968 as the Apollo 8 spacecraft rounded the dark side of the Moon. The now iconic image shows the world as a singular sphere, suspended in a desert of darkness. *Earthrise* changed how we see our blue-white planet and ushered in a collective awareness of the Earth as a whole, transcending borders and boundaries.

When the Earth is observed from space, you see one beautiful and fragile planet, not 195 sovereign nations. Nation-states are represented on maps by lines of demarcation which enclose and define territories. In reality, the Earth has no borders that divide the planet's terrain. The physical world, of course, is interconnected. We are all part of Mother Earth – an indivisible, living community which is interrelated and interdependent.

All of us share the same natural resources – air, water, soil, minerals, plants, and animals. Our three basic needs – food, clothing, and shelter – largely come from these natural resources, and their production is common to all cultures. Yet, we live in a world of "national tribes" who see themselves as different and disconnected from one another. But these tribes experience common issues that extend beyond artificial borders.

The challenges humanity faces – like climate change, global pandemics, natural catastrophes, international crime, and rampant terrorism – are increasingly transnational in nature, which is why they cannot be addressed by any single government. As individual nation-states are too small to fix shared global problems, coordinated and collaborative action among governments, non-government organisations, and international organisations is increasingly required.

Nation-states have also seen their power diminished by decades of global commerce. Capitalism has spread to the remotest parts of the world, with transnational flows of goods, data, and money. Borders no longer fulfil their historic roles as barriers to the movement of people, commodities, and capital. Even so, the prediction that nation-states – as autonomous, independent entities – will collapse under the combined onslaught of monetary unions, global television, and the Internet is hotly contested.

While many scholars have prophesied the decline and eventual demise of the nation-state, others fiercely contend that it does have a future and will not be superseded by a new world order. Three main schools of thought dominate the academic debate on globalisation theory – the hyperglobalist, the sceptical, and the transformational. Drawing on the work of renowned political theorist – the late Professor David Held (et al.) – these perspectives can be described as follows:

- Hyperglobalists argue that the world is heading towards a form of global governance which will increasingly see nation-states relegated to the role of decision-takers and not decision-makers due to the existence of international organisations such as the United Nations and the International Monetary Fund.
- Sceptics strongly resist this view and believe that the intensification of international activities has reinforced and enhanced state powers in many domains and that national governments will continue to shape the nature of world politics with their borders remaining effective.
- Transformationalists narrow the scholarly divide by presenting the middle ground that globalisation is creating new political, economic, and social circumstances which are serving to transform state powers and the context in which states operate.

I'm a proponent of the transformationalist view. While I embrace the belief that nation-states will not vanish in the foreseeable future, I acknowledge that their powers are receding. Globalisation has caused the erosion of the state's authority and made it less important and central. So, I stand with transformationalists in believing that states will continue to dynamically evolve in response to changing socio-economic and technological trends.

These trends have already altered the political landscape, with nation-states coexisting with a patchwork of non-state actors. We are moving towards a more distributed power structure as the world increasingly turns to experts outside of government to guide and shape state decision-making. This transfer of power is evident in the proliferation of international standards over recent years, which most governments have simply incorporated in their national laws.

An example is the work of the International Accounting Standards Board. It sets transnational financial reporting rules which corporations around the world follow, making it a powerful de facto global regulator of accounting standards, even though it is a private-sector body.

Many believe that an even more powerful body is the Basel Committee on Banking Supervision. This committee, which is headquartered at the Bank for International Settlements in Basel, Switzerland, makes decisions which affect every man, woman, and child on the planet. Even so, few know of the existence of this unelected group of central bankers and banking supervisors.

The Basel Committee does not possess any formal supranational authority, and its decisions do not have legal force. Yet its views hold great sway, enabling it to impose stringent rules and standards on the global financial system. *The Economist* magazine described central bankers as "more powerful than politicians, holding the destiny of the global economy in their hands".

Beyond accounting and banking, non-state actors address every conceivable issue and operate in virtually every part of the globe. From buying bananas at the supermarket (the World Trade Organization governs how bananas are traded) to obtaining medicines at the chemist (the World Health Organization issues standards for prescription drugs), international laws impact our daily lives.

Imagine flying overseas to watch a major sporting event. The operation of the plane that transports you is regulated by the International Civil Aviation Organization. On arriving at your destination, you drive to your hotel by following standardised road signs developed by the UN Convention on Road Traffic. Following check-in, you phone home, and this global connectivity is facilitated by a treaty on International Telecommunication Regulations.

You leave your hotel and use your credit card to buy a jumper, and this transaction is governed by technical requirements issued by the Payment Card Industry Security Standards Council. With your jumper to keep you warm, you then watch an international sporting event, where athletes are subject to mandatory drug testing by the World Anti-Doping Agency.

Globalisation has spawned the growth in organisations that regulate and control activity on a global scale. This has made non-state actors a worldwide phenomenon, and there is no turning back the clock. These actors are essential to the smooth working of our globalised world. Nonetheless, nation-states still have an important role to play and will survive, albeit in a different form.

We often forget that nation-states (countries) are late comers to history. The fact is that we didn't always have passports and borders – they are relatively new. Jamie Bartlett, one of the UK's leading thinkers on politics, points this out in an essay he wrote for the digital magazine *Aeon*.

> If you'd been born 1,500 years ago in southern Europe, you'd have been convinced that the Roman empire would last forever. It had, after all, been around for 1,000 years. And yet, following a period of economic and military decline, it fell apart. ... To the people living under the mighty empire, these events must have been unthinkable.
> ...
>
> We are just as deluded that our model of living in 'countries' is inevitable and eternal. Yes, there are dictatorships and democracies, but the whole world is made up of nation-states. ... Try to imagine a world without countries – you can't. Our sense of who we are, our loyalties, our rights and obligations, are bound up in them.

It's true that systems based around national sovereignty struggle to deal with complex companies, sophisticated technologies, and social movements. It's also true that economics and information have grown beyond the authority of national governments. Nonetheless, it is premature to write off nation-states, as they still function under globalisation and will continue to exert significant influence over the daily life of their citizens.

**The rumours of the death of the nation-state have been greatly exaggerated.**

POSTING DATE | 31 JANUARY 2021

## Why nationalism is a threat to globalisation

### COUNTRIES FLEX THEIR MUSCLES

The postponed 2020 Olympic Games – which are now scheduled to kick off in Tokyo in July – will provide an international stage for countries to showcase their elite athletes. Spectators the world over will cheer for their nation's sportsmen and women as they vie for Olympic gold. The fierce but friendly competition will fuel national pride and expose a positive side of nationalism – the celebration of the sporting success of those representing their homeland.

Beyond the Olympic arena, however, chest-thumping nationalistic patriotism has a dark side. It's understandable that every country tries to instil a national consciousness among its own citizens. But when that patriotism morphs into a sense of superiority over other countries, it leads to a combative us-against-them mindset, which is a poisonous ideology. In many parts of the world, patriotism has turned toxic.

Populist politicians have been selling nationalism as patriotism by promoting blind loyalty to one's country to the detriment of global connectivity. Claiming to speak for "the people", populists like Donald Trump have appealed to the anger and discontent of voters, tapping in to their fears about jobs, race, and immigration. In the West, many people feel left behind by technological change, growing inequality, and the global economy.

Events over recent years show that there has been a nationalist backlash to globalisation. The UK's decision to leave the European Union, Donald Trump's win in the 2016 US presidential election, and the growing momentum of right-wing parties in France, Austria, and Germany all attest to this. In an increasing number of countries, the radical right – a group of extremist parties united by their hatred of immigrants – has surged in popularity.

These populist parties and their followers have been variously described as racist, xenophobic, anti-Islamic, and anti-refugee. Parties of the far-right focus on tradition – real or imagined – and play on a nostalgia which yearns for simpler times. They want to turn back the clock to when national cultures were not influenced by immigration (and globalisation), and jobs were the preserve of native-born citizens.

This delusional hankering for the "good old days" was epitomised in Donald Trump's campaign slogan to "Make America Great Again". Trump mistakenly believed that this greatness would be achieved by closing borders, curtailing trade, and building a wall to keep out Mexicans. We should not forget that it was this kind of old-fashioned nationalism which helped fuel two world wars.

Following their defeat in World War I, the Germans felt humiliated, and this enabled Hitler to exploit people's feelings of resentment towards the ruling elite. Hitler also promised to make Germany great again. The parallels between how Trump and Hitler came to power are instructive. The rhetoric of both men was dangerously populist in nature. Unsurprisingly, historians have been comparing Trumpism to fascism. One writer recently opined that:

> It hardly takes a genius to see the similarities. Hitler promised to return Germany to her former glory by weeding out the traitorous politicians who had cost her the war. Trump promised to "Make America Great Again" by "draining the swamp". Hitler blamed Germany's problems on the Jews. Trump blamed Mexican "rapists and criminals". Hitler's supporters chanted slogans like "Im Felde Unbesiegt" (Undefeated on the Battlefield), Trump's supporters had theirs too: "Build the wall", "Lock Her Up", and of course, his latest: "Stop the steal".

As part of rebuilding the world after World War II, the Liberal International Order was created. Liberalism is an international (as distinct from national) worldview that opposes isolationism and protectionism. The liberal vision looks for collective solutions to global problems by working cooperatively with the help of international institutions and alliances to make the world a better place. Nationalists, in contrast, want a more homogenous society and tighter controls by governments over territories and borders.

The mantra of nationalist politicians – "country first" – fuels calls to build fences and erect trade barriers. Yet since 1950, the burgeoning growth in international trade has helped make the world a more peaceful place. Free trade raises the cost of war by making nations more economically interdependent. The more people rely on trade with others, the greater the cost to all parties of a conflict.

One of the hallmarks of liberal internationalism is rule-based relations which are enshrined in institutions such as the United Nations. Under nationalism, however, we would see a more contested and fragmented system of economic blocs and regional rivalries. The desire to increase sovereign control invariably results in isolationist policies, particularly with regard to immigration.

In his final address to the UN General Assembly on 20 September, 2016, US President Barack Obama delivered a stinging rebuke to those who would build walls, saying: "A nation ringed by walls would only imprison itself". In the same speech, he defended liberal globalisation, arguing that open markets, capitalism, and democracy should remain the guiding forces of the international order.

> ... I believe that at this moment we all face a choice. We can choose to press forward with a better model of cooperation and integration. Or we can retreat into a world sharply divided, and ultimately in conflict, along age-old lines of nation and tribe and race and religion. I want to suggest to you today that we must go forward, and not backward. I believe that as imperfect as they are, the principles of open markets and accountable governance, of democracy and human rights and international law that we have forged remain the firmest foundation for human progress in this century.

It is paradoxical that the growing calls for a less open world would actually hurt the poor most of all. Since the end of World War II, free trade has lifted millions out of extreme poverty. It is irrefutable that globalisation has been good for the global poor. This point was also made by President Obama.

> The integration of our global economy has made life better for billions of men, women and children. Over the last 25 years, the number of people living in extreme poverty has

> been cut from nearly 40 per cent of humanity to under 10 per cent. That's unprecedented. And it's not an abstraction. It means children have enough to eat; mothers don't die in childbirth.

President Obama went on to say that "our international order has been so successful that we take it as a given that great powers no longer fight world wars; that the end of the Cold War lifted the shadow of nuclear Armageddon; that the battlefields of Europe have been replaced by peaceful union".

Populist politicians are undermining liberal internationalism, and this poses a threat to peace and prosperity. Less international cooperation will lead to increased distrust between nation-states and may even give rise to conflict. Nativism, with its beggar-thy-neighbour policies, is a backward and dangerous step for the world. In the words of the old adage, it really is a case of "united we stand, divided we fall".

The rise of the new radical right reflects a deep social and economic malaise affecting an increasing number of nations. The past decades have ushered in an unprecedented level of socio-economic change, and voters are expressing their dissatisfaction at the ballot box. Only time will tell how long this anger and resentment last. What is clear is that the rhetoric of the far-right has struck a chord with a critical mass of voters.

**The world's political landscape has been transformed by a nationalist movement which has gone global.**

POSTING DATE | 9 MAY 2021

## Understanding the left-right political spectrum

### THE LINES HAVE SHIFTED

We all understand the difference between up and down. We also know the distinction between north and south. But when it comes to left and right in a political sense, many of us are less clear. What does it really mean to be left-wing? How does this vary from those who lean to the right?

The terms "left-wing" and "right-wing" define opposite ends of the political spectrum, yet there is no firm consensus about their meaning. Over time, these labels have become blurred. Former British Prime Minister Tony Blair once argued that the contrast between the two had melted away into meaninglessness.

The genesis of the political categories "left" and "right" dates back to eighteenth-century France and the French Revolution. Members of the National Assembly were seated according to their political orientation. Supporters of the king sat to the right of the assembly president, with supporters of the revolution to his left.

In line with this historic division, contemporary left-wingers are said to be anti-royalists who favour interventionist and regulated market economic policies. Right-wingers, on the other hand, are said to be monarchists who favour laissez-faire, free market economic policies.

While those on the left support higher taxes on the rich and welfare for the poor, the right favours lower taxes on businesses to help them grow. The left believes in an equal society and big government, whereas the right argues that social inequality is unavoidable and that governments should play a limited role in people's lives.

The Australian Labor Party has traditionally been seen as left-wing (socialist) with historic ties to the union movement. The Liberal Party of Australia has customarily been seen as right-wing (capitalist) with a long-standing pro-business posture. Many see this partisan profiling as outdated in describing Australia's modern political landscape.

A case in point is the issue of Australia becoming a republic. Based on traditional ideology, you would expect this cause to be championed by the "anti-royalist" Labor Party. Yet the push for a republic has been spearheaded by a member of the "monarchist" Liberal Party.

Past Prime Minister Malcolm Turnbull is a Liberal blue-blood. (NB: Left-wing parties are typically associated with red, the colour of revolution, while right-wing parties are often associated with conservative blue.) He is a former investment banker who – uncharacteristically for a conservative politician – is also a staunch supporter of the Australian Republican Movement. Turnbull co-founded the movement.

In trying to discard the monarchy (via a referendum in 1999), Turnbull was seen to have taken a left-wing stance, which caused some right-wing hardliners to label him a turncoat. Still, he is not the only Australian politician to be off course in a strict ideological sense. Former Labor Treasurer Paul Keating lurched to the right economically.

Keating's laudable economic reforms included deregulating the financial system, floating the Australian dollar, reducing import tariffs, and introducing compulsory superannuation – sound initiatives that a Labor treasurer was not expected to do. It's said tongue-in-cheek that Keating was Australia's best "Liberal" treasurer and the architect of neo-liberalism in Australia.

Many of Keating's reforms were based on the 1981 Campbell Inquiry Report into Australia's financial system. John Howard instigated the inquiry when he was Liberal treasurer under Prime Minister Malcolm Fraser. But Howard disappointed his traditional business supporters by implementing only one of Campbell's 260 recommendations.

Ironically, it was Keating who introduced many of Campbell's recommendations. He implemented a globalisation agenda which made Australia internationally competitive and opened our economy to the rest of the world. Unsurprisingly, big business embraced Keating – even though the Labor Party and corporate Australia are supposed to be adversaries.

So, how left-wing was Keating as a left-wing politician? In reality, he moved the Labor Party to the right of centre. So, the message is clear: While some may argue that ideological creeds are reflected in the policies of each party, this is often not the case.

If the truth be told, political viewpoints along the left–right scale do not fit neatly into one ideological camp. Within each camp, there are factional groups who believe that some things outweigh others. So, an individual may identify with left-wing ideals on one issue but consider themselves right-wing for everything else.

Those whose political outlook sits somewhere in the middle of the left–right divide are classified as taking a "centrist" stance. And to complicate things further, those who hold extreme political views belong to either the far-left or the far-right.

People on these outermost poles of the political spectrum often see themselves as aggrieved individuals. They are radicals who are deeply estranged from mainstream political mores. Their degree of alienation from contemporary society can be seen in their extreme ideologies.

Both the far-left and the far-right have a victim-like mentality and employ militant strategies. Their political engagement relies upon force, violation of civil liberties, and disdain for democratic ideals and practices. They normalise violence in their attacks on governments, globalisation, and social elites.

The far-left includes Islamic terrorists, while the far-right boasts white supremacists and neo-Nazis among its ranks. These extremist hate groups engage in violent acts and display many parallels. As they have overlapping tactics and stances, some academics contend that it is misleading to classify the far-left and far-right as opposite poles.

It is suggested that a more realistic classification is provided by the Horseshoe theory. This theory asserts that the political spectrum is not a straight line with opposing ends. Rather, it is a horseshoe, with its farthest outliers bending in toward each other and sharing a number of similar beliefs.

To illustrate, supporters of the extreme right and extreme left are more likely to believe in conspiracy theories even when they are contradicted by mainstream science or factual evidence.

These theories include the belief that coronavirus vaccines are harmful, climate change is a hoax, and the US government planned the 9/11 terrorist attacks.

One area where the far-left and far-right markedly differ is in their interpretation of the past. As noted in the US online newsletter, *The Perspective,* these interpretations dictate their political stances and calls to action.

> The far-right expresses nostalgia for the past and actively works to preserve their history, regardless of what that might mean in today's context. ... Conversely, the far-left ... associates the past with its ills – slavery, sexism, and other injustices. History and its institutions are not to be preserved and cherished, but rather, an embarking point from which to begin reform.

History is in the eye of the beholder and so too is populism. There is no agreed definition of populism – it means different things to different people. In political science, populism is seen as an approach that frames politics as a battle between two opposing groups. In their book, *Populism: A Very Short Introduction,* Cas Mudde and Cristóbal Rovira Kaltwasser label these antagonistic groups as the "pure people" (ordinary masses) and the "corrupt elite".

Populism is not sustained by a single political ideology. Rather, it describes a style and approach to politics. Populism can be deployed in the service of almost any ideology – left or right, moderate or extreme. Populists can come from all parts of the political spectrum, and they have popped up all over the world.

Think Marine Le Pen in France, Viktor Orbán in Hungary, Rodrigo Duterte in the Philippines, Indian Prime Minister Narendra Modi, and, of course, Donald Trump in the US. All of these populist leaders climbed to prominence by dividing people into good or bad. Populism defines our current political age. In the words of one US journalist:

> Once in power, populist leaders represent "a threat to liberal democracy" ... [such as] Trump calling the press the "enemy of the people," criticizing judges, resisting

> congressional oversight, claiming that elections are "rigged," flouting laws, and claiming that a "deep state" of bureaucratic actors is out to get him to deny the will of the people he represents. It happens with other populist leaders all over the world.

It's axiomatic that thinking in terms of a left–right spectrum is outdated. While these binary labels may be convenient shorthand descriptors, they are too generic. People hold a range of opinions on social and economic issues, and these do not fit neatly in the traditional left–right continuum.

Also, citizens care about the matters that affect them and not the political ideology that supposedly underpins a given issue. Further, humans can hold seemingly contradictory beliefs. All of this makes the political spectrum largely meaningless, but we continue to use it due to laziness. As outlined in the online magazine *Quillette:*

> Putting people into one of two ideological boxes is far easier than understanding their unique point of view. Reducing politics to a simple contest between right and left is far easier than reasoning through hundreds of issues. Humans generally prefer simplicity to truth and would rather sign up for a "side" than do the hard work of thinking.

**Whether you swing left, lean right, or aim dead centre, it's incumbent on all of us to stay politically informed.**

POSTING DATE | 6 JUNE 2021

## Two wishes for a peaceful world

### CREATE HAPPINESS AND HARMONY

We've all heard the various jokes about a person who stumbles upon a magic lamp, rubs it, and out pops a genie. Thrilled to be freed after many years, the newly liberated genie grants the person three wishes. People commonly wish for things that satisfy their selfish desire for money, power, or fame. But a higher salary, a loftier title, or a posher postcode do not of themselves make us happier.

As a young boy, I often thought about what I would ask for if I were offered three wishes. Believe it or not, I always came to the same conclusion: I wanted just one wish – world peace. As an adult, I understand that achieving world peace actually requires two wishes. Please let me explain.

World peace (outer peace) is impossible without people being at peace with themselves (inner peace) – one follows the other. So, any attempt to achieve world peace must begin with the individual, as it is the conflict in the individual mind that manifests as war. This interdependency is beautifully encapsulated in "The Peace Poem", which many credit to the ancient Chinese philosopher, Lao-Tse:

If there is to be peace in the world,
There must be peace in the nations.

If there is to be peace in the nations,
There must be peace in the cities.

If there is to be peace in the cities,
There must be peace between neighbours.

If there is to be peace between neighbours,
There must be peace in the home.

If there is to be peace in the home,
There must be peace in the heart.

We all have a part to play in world peace. Through our words and deeds, each of us should demonstrate kindness and forgiveness. One way to facilitate such behaviour is for all of us to adopt the Golden Rule, the moral precept that asks us to treat others as we would like others to treat ourselves. Thus, my first wish would be for *the universal adoption of the Golden Rule.*

Building sustainable peace requires positive reciprocity: I show you kindness and you do the same for me in return, multiplied a billion times over throughout humanity. Changing the behaviour of individuals alone, however, does not guarantee world peace. We must also change how international relations are conducted. Thus, my second wish would be for *the adoption of a renewed form of global governance.*

In theory, these two wishes would see a world full of people with inner peace living under one integrated global governance structure, with no wars between individual nations. The end result would be world peace – people and nations united and working in collaboration to build trust at all levels of society. Trust is the foundation of all human relations, and it begins one person at a time.

The challenges humanity faces – like climate change, global pandemics, natural catastrophes, international crime, and rampant terrorism – are increasingly transnational in nature, which is why they cannot be addressed by any single government. No individual nation-state is big enough alone to fix shared global problems. As outlined in an essay by the Dalai Lama:

> In ancient times problems were mostly family-size, and they were naturally tackled at the family level, but the situation has changed. Today we are so interdependent, so closely interconnected with each other, that without a sense of universal responsibility, a feeling of universal brotherhood and sisterhood, and an understanding and belief that we really are part of one big human family, we cannot hope to overcome the dangers to our very existence – let alone bring about peace and happiness.

While peace has been defined in various ways, understanding it simply as the avoidance of violence is narrow in conception, as peace is more than the absence of war. Peace is also the presence of fairness and justice. Furthermore, it is an internal state (of mind or of nations) to achieving happiness and harmony.

The independent international peacebuilding organisation, International Alert, believes that "... peacebuilding is done collaboratively, at local, national, regional and international levels. Individuals, communities, civil society organisations, governments, regional bodies and the private sector all play a role in building peace".

The Earth is one, but the world is not, as the current governance system – which divides the planet into 195 sovereign nations – creates toxic political divisions. We are all part of one global village and need an overarching global governance structure to sit above nation-states. (Even though it's an interesting thought, I have to accept that even a genie saying "Abracadabra" will not make nations disappear!)

In the absence of a single authoritative institution or world government, global governance is designed to bring together diverse actors to coordinate collective action at the level of the planet. To quote the Global Challenges Foundation:

> The goal of global governance, roughly defined, is to provide global public goods, particularly peace and security, justice and mediation systems for conflict, functioning markets and unified standards for trade and industry. ... The leading institution in charge of global governance today is the United Nations. It was founded in 1945, in the wake of the Second World War, as a way to prevent future conflicts on that scale. The UN does not directly bring together the people of the world, but sovereign nation-states.

According to leading human-rights advocate Suzanne Nossel, the world still needs the UN, which is why she believes that building a new global governance framework from scratch is a fool's errand. In an instructive article she penned for the US foreign policy magazine, *Foreign Affairs*, she imagined a system of global governance that would require all nations to follow rules requiring them to refrain from the use of force, foster peaceful conflict resolution, uphold the rule of law, and enshrine respect for human rights.

Ms Nossel believes that nations truly working in cooperation would be able to "… avert crises and foster cooperation on issues including climate change, pandemics, and migration. Great powers would wield influence but be held in check by one another and a rotating cast of middle powers from every region".

She acknowledges that creating such a system afresh in the 2020s would be impossible, as major countries would never agree on objectives or values, much less concede to being legally bound by them. Ms Nossel acknowledges that:

> The United Nations remains the closest thing to a system of global governance that the world has ever known and may ever achieve. And yet, as the COVID-19 pandemic makes painfully clear, the system can be paralyzed, distracted, and dysfunctional just when it is needed most.
>
> … A strengthened system of global governance, if it is to be, will involve overlapping forums, institutions, and coalitions that collectively shoulder the world's challenges. The UN has a central role to play within such a system. Any effort to reinvent global governance should focus on reinvigorating the body invented to serve as its linchpin.
>
> … Reinventing the UN will require member states to renew their original vows to the ideals of international cooperation. … Ultimately, reviving the UN will require subordinating narrow national interests to the task of protecting the world's best hope for solving grave global threats.

You don't have to convince me that global problems need global responses. My sense, though, is that things will get worse before they get better, as petty nationalism always seems to get in the way of global cooperation. Yet, in an era of climate change, pandemics, and Russian revanchism, we need to reconsider what national security really means.

Sadly, worldwide peace and international solidarity will only happen when distant threats to humanity's existence become an imminent peril to all of us. Until then, the sovereign nation-state will remain the main political actor calling the shots. Nonetheless, as I opined in a previous post, the power of the nation-state is slowly waning.

Meantime, let's not forget John Lennon's wish for world peace, as conveyed in the lyrics to his moving anthem, *Imagine*:

**"I hope someday you'll join us, and the world will live as one."**

POSTING DATE | 13 MARCH 2022

## Why we should send politicians to space

### COSMIC PERSPECTIVE FOR A BETTER WORLD

When astronauts return from space, many of them report that their outlook on life on Earth has been transformed forever. They experience a sort of spiritual awakening which leads them to ponder how we could all live better on our beautiful planet as one human fraternity.

A number of astronauts have suggested that world leaders should also orbit the Earth to feel the same overwhelming sense of oneness when taking in the whole planet in a single glimpse. This image produces a life-changing sense of awe for astronauts and should similarly cause politicians to see the world anew.

National borders are artificial divisions and therefore invisible when you are orbiting the Earth. Anyone gazing down at Earth from space sees a single entity, not 195 sovereign nations. This holistic view brings about a cognitive shift in awareness among astronauts – the so-called "Overview Effect".

This psychological switch causes some astronauts to develop a global consciousness which alters their worldview. Seeing Earth from the vantage point of space is a profound experience that can inspire an overwhelming desire to protect our planet – from ourselves!

Tiny planet Earth is where we worship our gods, fight our wars, and destroy our environment. The fragility of our planet and the pettiness of territorial lines become blindingly clear when seen against the dark expanse of the universe.

Of course, very few of us will get to look back at Earth from a spaceship. Even so, a Dutch company is trying to replicate that experience for school children with an education program called SpaceBuzz. With the aid of some whiz-bang technology, the company wants to "send" 100 million kids a year to space using immersive 4D virtual reality.

Putting children in the footsteps of astronauts will hopefully enable them to feel the Overview Effect for themselves and see the bigger picture. SpaceBuzz is designed to give children a deeper sense of connection with the wondrous living system we call Earth and every living thing inhabiting it.

SpaceBuzz will help the next generation of adults become more Earth conscious by living sustainable and eco-friendly lifestyles. But how do we assist the current crop of adults to be kinder to the planet and each other? One way is to provide them with role models to emulate.

Unfortunately, those who should be examples to all of us – politicians – often fall short of the mark. Politicians the world over tend to focus on local issues to the detriment of global challenges. Global problems, though, can only be solved through shared, collective leadership.

The current day peddlers of populism appeal to the prejudices of voters by tapping in to prevailing anti-immigration and anti-trade sentiments. Yet the populist framing of problems invariably leads to the wrong policy responses, such as the desire to build walls and erect trade barriers.

That's why all world leaders should experience a simulated SpaceBuzz virtual flight so that they – like astronauts – can look down at the Earth and its 7.8 billion human inhabitants and embrace a new reality. All humans need to see themselves as connected with one another and with the planet as a whole.

From space, nationalism, patriotism, and tribal behaviour have no meaning – you see just one planet, and it's the only home we have. On witnessing Earth from space, astronaut Edgar Mitchell proclaimed that it makes you:

> ... develop an instant global consciousness, a people orientation, an intense dissatisfaction with the state of the world, and a compulsion to do something about it. From out there on the moon, international politics look so petty. You want to grab a politician by the scruff of the neck and drag him a quarter of a million miles out and say, 'Look at that, you son of a bitch.'

Former NASA astronaut, Ron Garan, poetically described how the spectacle of Earth suspended in space was an epiphany in slow motion.

> From space, the planet is a constantly changing masterpiece and the sheer beauty is absolutely breathtaking. It looks like a shining jewel and you realise that it's home to everyone who ever lived and everyone who ever will be. But another thing that hit me was a sobering contradiction between the beauty of our planet and the unfortunate realities of life on our planet. It filled me with a sense of injustice. It infuriated me.

On Earth, politicians are accused of not seeing the forest for the trees. From space, the reverse applies – they will see the forest but not the trees. As Einstein explained, the nature of reality depends on the position of the observer. Our frame of reference is flipped when viewing Earth from outside its atmosphere, and this gives rise to an altered state of consciousness.

Hopefully, the sensations triggered by the sight of our planet from space would be sufficiently moving to cause world leaders to transcend borders in their decision-making. Narrow-minded national government agendas must give way to collective action to tackle shared global challenges, such as the need to eradicate extreme poverty, improve health outcomes, create a sustainable planet, and foster world peace.

We have the capability to solve all the problems facing humanity, including world peace. In space, American astronauts and Russian cosmonauts work side-by-side on the International Space Station (ISS), even though we cannot secure peace on Earth. This is ironic as the ISS emerged from the Cold War rivalry of the Space Race between the Soviet Union and the US.

On Earth, nations continue to butt heads. However, on the ISS, 15 countries work collaboratively in an orbiting laboratory for the good of all humankind. The ISS represents the largest peacetime cooperative effort humans have ever conceived and implemented. It is as much a political achievement as a technological one.

The ISS is a shining example of a common goal bringing a divided world together. It has become a beacon of peace for warring nations and proves that we can accomplish remarkable things together.

The ISS has also demonstrated that the politics of nationalism must give way to a "one planet" ideology if we are to achieve greater social cohesion.

Regrettably, moving from 195 independent nation-states to one planetary civilisation is not on humanity's radar, so it certainly won't happen in my lifetime nor my children's. Still, in the words of legendary astronomer and science writer, Carl Sagan: "You spend even a little time contemplating the Earth from orbit and the most deeply ingrained nationalisms begin to erode". Space can heal what divides us.

Even though we need a cosmic perspective, most world leaders are either not ready or are incapable of making that paradigm shift in thinking. In fairness, viewing the world through a global lens has not pervaded the hearts and minds of most citizens either. So, for now, we will continue our journey through the universe aboard Spaceship Earth as a divided crew.

**We are all astronauts – we just don't know it.**

POSTING DATE | 27 MARCH 2022

## Why politicians are not qualified to run a country

### SPECIFIC TRAINING NEEDED

In every sector of society, qualifications play a critical role in determining the minimum level of knowledge and skills required for a given profession or occupation. Qualifications define what a person needs to know – and be able to do – to carry out a certain activity, but no such entry requirements apply to the group of people who are elected to run a country.

Around the world, politicians need no formal training before entering parliament. Those running for public office are elected by citizens, many of whom rate charm and charisma over ability and competence. Most voters in modern democracies do not make informed decisions about the capability of candidates or the efficacy of their policies.

Plato, the father of Greek philosophy, was one of the earliest to see democracy as a problem. He, like later critics, argued that democracy meant rule by the ignorant, or worse, rule by the charlatans who hoodwink the people. It would be much safer, Plato thought, to entrust power to carefully educated wise guardians who would decide upon matters on behalf of citizens.

Fast forward to the present, and John Hewson, the former Liberal opposition leader, believes that Australia's contemporary parliamentarians aren't qualified to run the country. Writing in *The Sydney Morning Herald*, Dr Hewson lamented that politics is dominated by career politicians who concentrate on winning points rather than delivering good policy and good government. He states:

> Unfortunately, the skill sets and experience required of a career politician essentially make them incompetent to govern effectively. Their career path is often from university, community or union politics, through local government/party engagement, perhaps serving as a ministerial staffer, to pre-selection, then election, and so on.

We would not let an unqualified teacher educate our children nor allow a physician without a medical degree to perform surgery on us. Yet, we place no job prerequisites on those seeking to become members of parliament (MPs). In Australia and elsewhere, it is not mandatory for MPs to take part in initial or ongoing education and training programs specific to their role.

While I'm not advocating minimum education standards for aspiring politicians, there is a case for introducing compulsory Continuing Professional Development (CPD) for all parliamentarians once elected to office. This happens in other professions (and many occupations) to ensure continued proficiency and capability in one's chosen field.

As lawmakers, politicians – either directly through regulation or indirectly via industry bodies – compel professionals like doctors, lawyers, engineers, and accountants to undertake CPD as a condition of their ongoing professional registration. Politicians the world over, however, are not subject to defined education and training standards for accreditation, thereby creating a double standard.

Like all CPD programs, the learning activities for politicians should include a combination of structured activities (such as training courses, online modules, and seminars) and unstructured activities (such as reading documents, articles, and publications). Any formal or informal learning activity which improves or broadens an MP's knowledge or expertise can be included in the CPD toolbox.

MPs are involved in decisions that have far-reaching consequences for the populace at large and deal with an almost unlimited range of subjects. As noted in the journal, *Parliamentary Affairs*, "those elected to public office are expected to possess indefinable qualities to accomplish an indescribable job".

I am the first to acknowledge that developing CPD programs for politicians is a huge undertaking. Nonetheless, it should be done, and the two subjects that I would place at the apex of CPD curricula are *debunking economic fallacies* and *understanding game theory*. Please let me explain each in turn.

One of the primary activities of modern governments is to determine economic policies. In every country, the government takes steps to help the economy achieve growth, full employment, and price stability. Given this, it's vital that elected representatives be economically literate, even though many politicians display an astounding ignorance of economics.

Over recent years, for example, populist politicians have driven an anti-globalisation agenda by promoting protectionist and isolationist policies. Specifically, the peddlers of populism have challenged the undeniable economic benefits of free trade (which has lifted millions out of poverty) and immigration (which has increased the size of economies).

Economic ineptitude was also on display following the Global Financial Crisis (GFC). Politicians in many nations (including the UK and Greece) adopted fiscal austerity measures which proved catastrophic. Thankfully, politicians in Australia and America implemented fiscal stimulus policies which gave their economies a much needed boost.

One of the reasons that governments adopted fiscal austerity measures post-GFC was to keep a lid on government debt loads in the mistaken belief that government debt is bad. This old chestnut is arguably the single biggest economic myth of all and is called *the household fallacy.*

Politicians fuel this fallacy by constantly drawing false parallels between household budgets and government budgets. Our elected leaders love trotting out the familiar line that governments – like households – need to live within their means. Yet every time they espouse this untrue analogy, they engage in unnecessary fearmongering about government debt.

Around the world, ill-informed politicians claim that governments should somehow have a balanced budget year-to-year. Politicians show empathy with the electorate by promising to cut government spending in line with belt tightening by households. Governments that run deficits are erroneously accused of being poor financial managers.

In *Fifty Economic Fallacies Exposed,* Geoffrey Wood, Professor Emeritus of Economics, examines a range of popular economic misconceptions and explains how these mistaken beliefs misinform economic discussion. It should be mandatory for all politicians to read Professor Wood's book.

Let me now turn to the second subject that I would include in CPD curricula – understanding game theory. Game theory is a framework for examining competitive situations where "players" have conflicting interests. It models human actions on the presumption that everyone tries to maximise their potential gain against everyone around them.

At its core, game theory – which is a special branch of mathematics – is used to study decision-making in complex situations. It examines how our choices affect others, and how the choices others make affect us (so-called "games"). The "games" involve two or more opposing parties pursuing actions in their own best interest, resulting in an outcome for each that is worse than if they had cooperated.

Game theory is applied in a number of fields, and a classic example can be found in the arms race between two superpowers. Both countries are clearly better off when they cooperate and avoid an arms race. Yet the dominant strategy is for each to arm itself heavily. If a new weapon is invented that is more destructive than any in existence, acquisition of this weapon is seen as enhancing the security of one's country. But if both act accordingly, everyone's security is jeopardised rather than improved.

Game theory was used most notably during the Cold War. Both the United States and the Soviet Union quickly saw its value for forming war strategies. A balance was struck in which neither nation could gain advantage through nuclear attack as the reprisals would be too devastating. This became known as the doctrine of Mutually Assured Destruction (MAD).

MAD is founded on the notion that a nuclear attack by one superpower would be met with an overwhelming nuclear counterattack such that both the attacker and the defender would be annihilated. Given this lose-lose outcome, it is said that only a madman would engage in such a self-defeating strategy.

By this logic, Vladimir Putin has been labelled a madman, given his recent announcement that his nuclear forces are on "high-combat" alert. He is playing the madman card, threatening the use of nuclear weapons to get what he wants out of his war with Ukraine. With 6,000-plus nuclear warheads, Putin can end our world as we know it.

While many suspect that Putin is unhinged, I believe that he is a cunning expansionist with dreams/delusions of restoring Mother Russia to her former greatness. He is a megalomaniac who is obsessed with increasing his power and will do almost anything to get his way. The dilemma the West faces is how to deal with Russia without risking nuclear war. As the UN Secretary-General, António Guterres, recently warned: "The prospect of nuclear conflict, once unthinkable, is now back within the realm of possibility".

Putin's actions in brandishing the nuclear option are reckless. If Putin and every other politician on the planet truly understood game theory, they would not threaten the use of nuclear warfare. Nuclear weapons are an intolerable threat to humanity. Instructing politicians in the nuances of game theory would teach them that a nuclear war cannot be won and therefore must never be fought.

At the risk of sounding defeatist, I accept that studying game theory will not be made compulsory for world leaders, let alone rank-and-file politicians. Equally, I'm sure that politicians will not be forced to study economic fallacies. This is disappointing as both of these educational initiatives would make the world a significantly better place.

**One can only dream!**

POSTING DATE | 10 APRIL 2022

*Chapter Two*

# The Economic Landscape

Economics is a social science. Broadly, it's the study of human nature as it applies to money. It focusses on the behaviour and interactions of households, businesses, and governments and their attitudes to saving, investing, and spending. The fiscal and monetary choices made by these economic agents during the pandemic is reflected in some of the topics covered in this chapter. Around the world, COVID-19 brought economic activity to a standstill. Containment measures, including mobility restrictions, froze the wheels of commerce and plunged many national economies into recession.

## How will the world pay for COVID-19 stimulus packages?

### DEFICIT SPENDING ON A GIGANTIC SCALE

The economic damage caused by the coronavirus is mounting across the globe. In a frantic scramble to cushion economies, governments launched massive stimulus programs. These unprecedented fiscal and monetary interventions come with a staggering price tag. Sovereign debt is set to soar, with governments around the world embarking on one of the greatest peacetime borrowing binges in history.

Most governments run annual deficits as they spend more than they collect. Few have spare surplus funds sitting around that can be redirected to support struggling households and businesses. So, countries are piling on more debt to fund emergency spending to help citizens cope with the economic ravages of the pandemic. Many people understandably worry whether the world can afford this avalanche of new borrowing.

The good news is that debt is incredibly cheap at the moment. Prior to the pandemic, the world was awash with savings, which pushed interest rates very low. As global interest rates are now even lower, it has never been cheaper for governments to borrow. Governments are collectively borrowing trillions of dollars to enable them to spend trillions of dollars in a synchronised shock-and-awe response to the pandemic.

A classic way for nations to "print" emergency money is to borrow it by selling government bonds. This increases national public debt and is how governments have historically dealt with economic shocks such as recessions, financial dislocations, and wars. During such crises, investors prefer the safety of government bonds in lieu of putting their money into the stock market, corporate bonds, or real estate.

In Australia, the federal government is expected to fork out in excess of $150 billion to keep the economy afloat during the pandemic-induced downturn. The first federal response cost $17 billion, the second round cost an additional $66 billion, and the third cash splash rang the bell at $70 billion. All up, Australia's coronavirus stimulus packages are equivalent to nearly 10 per cent of the size of our economy.

As explained by ABC business reporter Gareth Hutchens:

> Essentially, the Government will pay for the stimulus package by creating the money and racking it up as debt. Officially, it will raise the money via the Australian Office of Financial Management (AOFM), which borrows money on behalf of the Government by selling Australian Government bonds.

Institutional investors (e.g., local and overseas banks, superfunds, and foreign countries) will be buyers of the bonds. However, as noted by Gareth Hutchens:

> The ultimate buyer of the Government bonds could be the Reserve Bank, because at the moment, the RBA is stepping into the market regularly to purchase as many Australian Government bonds as necessary to keep the interest rate, the "yield", on three-year Government bonds around 0.25 per cent.

The yield on Australian government bonds is the interest rate we pay on our nation's debt. Given that the current rate of inflation in Australia is around 1.8 per cent and is expected to decline further, we are effectively borrowing for free. This is good news for Australia, yet many Aussies are fearful of our level of sovereign debt.

A recently released paper, by think-tank the Australia Institute, "The Budget Surplus Objective: An example of how economics is broken" highlights the folly of this fear of government debt. Citing the report, economics writer Greg Jericho states:

> ... given Australia's nominal GDP is expected to grow at around 4.5%, if government borrowing pays lower than that (as is currently the case) debt levels will fall over time. This is because the economy is growing much faster than is the interest on the debt. ... It means to quote Larry Summers, the former chief economist of the World Bank, that "public investment is essentially costless – the classic free lunch".

One of Australia's foremost economic commentators, Chris Richardson, from Deloitte Access Economics, has gone public to ameliorate fears that the government has saddled our children with massive debt. According to Richardson, the budgetary impact of the fight against the coronavirus will have a much smaller impact on Australia than many expect.

Notwithstanding the "jaw-dropping" size of Australia's stimulus package, Richardson stressed that we have not sentenced younger Australians to a lifetime of higher taxes and sub-standard services.

> Although the dollars are unprecedented, what's even more unprecedented are the interest rates we'll be paying on this new debt. Never in the two thousand years of recorded history of interest rates has it been cheaper for governments to borrow. Never. And markets aren't fazed in the slightest: they reacted to the latest package by dropping the rate on 10-year Commonwealth borrowing substantially further.

Richardson went on to say:

> Australia's economy will grow again on the other side of this [COVID-19] war. So, here's a simple suggestion: Let's just let our debts from this new war simply become a smaller share of our growing economy over time. That's what we did with the war-time debts of the past. And it's probably the smart play this time too. Self-imposed flagellation rarely makes sense. The same policies that were sensible ahead of this crisis will remain just as sensible after it too.

As counterintuitive as it sounds, government deficits can be very helpful to an economy. Nobel Prize–winning economist Joseph Stiglitz has long argued that deficit spending can be a major stimulus to economic growth and can actually lower long-term government debt. When economic growth is restored and unemployment falls, tax revenues increase, which eventually lessens the need for a government to borrow.

Another world-renowned economist and Nobel Laureate, Paul Krugman, has often observed that government finances are not like personal finances. While consumers on a spending spree ultimately have to pay the piper, a government's borrowing strategy directly affects economic growth, and this delivers social benefits.

All of this means that increased national debt from COVID-19 is not our enemy – it will not leave a deep scar on our economy nor will it result in a day of reckoning. This will be hard for many Aussies to accept, as they have been conditioned to believe that debt is bad and that any political leader who does not pledge to lower Australia's national debt is not worthy of their vote.

Even though Australia has long had one of the world's lowest debt-to-GDP ratios, we Aussies display an irrational and emotive attitude to government debt. Hopefully, the pandemic will challenge some long-standing economic theories, including the idea that responsible government means having no national debt.

The notion that governments can sustain levels of debt far greater than previously thought is the centrepiece of an economic model called Modern Monetary Theory (MMT). It proposes that governments can spend freely, as they can always create more money to pay off debts in their own currency. Orthodox economists see MMT as a fringe economic movement, with some labelling it as "voodoo economics". But it is worth exploring, which I do in my next blog post.

**For now, please do not be spooked by the debt bogeyman.**

POSTING DATE | 12 JULY 2020

## Where is the pandemic stimulus money coming from?

### CREATING MONEY OUT OF NOTHING

Governments around the world are spending up a storm. They have loosened their purse strings and are shovelling truckloads of cash into their respective economies. Collectively, it represents the biggest relief package in history – in excess of US$10 trillion globally. For most nations, every penny of their mind-boggling spendathon is borrowed.

In doing "whatever it takes" to combat the COVID-19 pandemic, governments have shown that they can sustain levels of debt far greater than previously thought. Consequently, the coronavirus has challenged orthodox economics in just a few weeks. The belief in balanced budgets has been thrown out the window. Public debt is no longer seen as a drag on economies but a critical lifeline.

Proponents of an unconventional economic framework – Modern Monetary Theory (MMT) – welcome the ramp-up in government spending. MMT posits that countries which issue their own currencies can't go bankrupt as they can never run out of money in the way businesses and households can. That's because governments with their own sovereign currency are able to "print" (or more precisely "create" with a few keystrokes) as much money as they need to pay creditors.

Not surprisingly, traditional economic thinking warns that such spending is fiscally irresponsible as the debt balloons and inflation skyrockets. Critics of MMT cite Hungary in the 1940s, Brazil in the '80s, and Mexico in the '90s as examples where easy money policies (governments creating piles of cash) led not just to inflation but hyperinflation.

Still, this has not deterred MMT advocates, who argue that increased government spending will not generate inflation as long as there is unused economic capacity or unemployed labour. It is only when an economy hits physical or natural constraints on its productivity that inflation happens, because that is when supply fails to meet demand, jacking up prices.

This is what occurred in Zimbabwe in the late 1990s and mid-2000s. The economy collapsed, but not because Robert Mugabe printed ever-more Zimbabwean dollars. Rather, the economy nosedived when farming production plummeted by 60 per cent as Mugabe forced experienced white farmers off their land and gave it to inexperienced soldiers to farm.

The resultant decline in output caused a shortage of goods. At the same time, demand rose as Zimbabweans had more paper money. The combination of more money chasing fewer goods – the classic definition of inflation – caused a supersonic rise in prices. Wallets were replaced with wheelbarrows as hyperinflation peaked in the African nation in November 2008 at an estimated 89.7 sextillion per cent – an eye-watering number with 21 zeros after it.

Of course, Robert Mugabe's gross economic mismanagement of Zimbabwe cannot be compared to Shinzo Abe's savvy stewardship of the Japanese economy. A basketful of groceries in Japan in 2020 does not cost a bucketful of money, as it did in Zimbabwe in 2008. That's because Japan's expansionary monetary policy has not been inflationary – spending has not exceeded the economy's capacity to produce.

Despite having the highest public debt in the developed world, Japan has not experienced runaway inflation (in fact, it has been battling deflation for two decades!) and remains an economic powerhouse. Supporters of MMT cite Japan's success as proof that their unorthodox ideas work. But critics – including world-renowned economist and Nobel Laureate Paul Krugman – strongly disagree.

Both sides of this debate were outlined in a 2019 article published in *The New York Times* – "Modern Monetary Theory's Reluctant Poster Child: Japan". Notwithstanding Japan's hesitance to be labelled an MMT practitioner, proponents of the theory insist that Japan has been a testing ground. As explained in the article:

> The country [Japan] is their [MMT's] equivalent of Charles Darwin's Galápagos Islands: a natural experiment that reveals a fundamental truth about the way the world

really works. Since the country's boom ended in the early 1990s, Japan has borrowed deeply. Currently, its debt level is approaching 250 percent of its annual economic output. Critics say it is an economic basket case. Despite all that, Japanese inflation and lending rates remain low. In fact, some bond rates are negative, meaning Japan can profit when it borrows money. Its standard of living remains competitive with those of the United States and other developed countries.

Bill Mitchell is a professor of economics at the University of Newcastle in Australia and one of the founders of Modern Monetary Theory. He has been closely studying Japan since the 1990s. "It is my laboratory," he explains, calling the country "a really good demonstration of why mainstream macroeconomics is wrong". He argues that Japan has established "the principles of MMT and the consequences of different fiscal and monetary policy initiatives".

Japan has blurred the lines that traditionally divide fiscal and monetary policy. Other nations, including Australia, are currently doing likewise with their pandemic stimulus packages. Historically, governments have raised money to fund spending by issuing bonds, which are bought by a range of investors. Even so, some nations are now self-funding their stimulus packages by issuing and then buying their own bonds, thereby creating money out of thin air.

This funding mechanism bypasses the need to pay interest to investors on newly issued money and is at the heart of MMT – the fusion of fiscal and monetary policy. MMT links fiscal policy to monetary policy by using the central bank to buy the debt (bonds) issued by its government. If all of that sounds double Dutch, then let me share with you another explanation.

In a recent article in *The Sydney Morning Herald*, "Don't add government debt to your list of things to worry about", economics writer Jessica Irvine quite rightly points out that the Reserve Bank of Australia (our central bank which is responsible for monetary policy) has exhausted its traditional method of stimulating our economy (lowering interest rates). So, the RBA is helping the federal government (which has responsibility for fiscal policy) stimulate the economy by buying Australian government bonds.

In answering the question "Where does the stimulus money come from?", Irvine writes:

> A large part of [it] ... will come from the Reserve Bank. Weird, you might be thinking. Does that mean that one arm of government – albeit a statutory independent agency – is now lending to another arm of government, the executive branch? To whom, in such a situation, do taxpayers ultimately owe the money? Themselves? The answer is: well, yes. ... And if we only owe the money to ourselves, what's to stop us spending as much as we like? Another very good question, and one to keep in mind in the strange debates to come.

Irvine underscores that MMTers would prefer that the government simply print the money, rather than borrow it from the private sector in a money-go-round they decry as "corporate welfare". According to MMT, government issued bonds aren't strictly necessary. Instead of issuing $1 in bonds for every $1 in deficit spending, the Australian government could just create the money directly without issuing bonds.

The belief that governments do not need to issue public debt is supported by Dr Steve Hail, a lecturer in economics at the University of Adelaide and an MMT proponent. He sees no need to match public deficits with debt issuance for a currency-issuing government. Such governments should gain the necessary political approval for additional spending and then be able to do it. "Spending is self-financing," he asserts and "does not have to be funded".

In a recent article Dr Hail wrote for the news and opinion website, *Independent Australia*, he stated:

> ... central governments like those of Australia, New Zealand, the USA, the UK and Japan face no purely financial constraints at all. Never mind a "money tree", they have a money computer. They can create limitless amounts of their currencies when they need to do so. They are not

> dependent on the goodwill of the bond market, or of credit ratings agencies. They are monetary sovereign currency issuers.

It's clear that MMT is a controversial idea that has detractors and admirers worldwide. The coronavirus pandemic has moved MMT from the fringes of economic debate to centre stage. It is receiving unprecedented attention now that policymakers are (knowingly or unknowingly) implementing some of its basic tenets. This is MMT's moment in the sun, and only time will tell if it works as advertised.

For the record, I do not believe that government deficits are inherently bad. Nor do I believe that government budgets, like household budgets, should always be in the black. So, my belief is that MMT should not be dismissed out-of-hand, nor should it be approached with a pre-existing economic ideological bias.

**The economics profession, it is jokingly said, is the only field where two people can win a Nobel Prize for saying the exact opposite thing!**

POSTING DATE | 26 JULY 2020

## How to stop the pandemic and restart the economy

### SAVING LIVES AND RESTORING LIVELIHOODS

Around the world, the hustle and bustle of daily life has come to a screeching halt. Cities have become ghost towns, and virtually every aspect of society has changed. Social distancing is the new catchphrase, with elbow bumps replacing handshakes.

As governments double down on containing the fast-moving pathogen, the question on everyone's lips is the same: When will life return to normal? While no one has a definitive answer, it's clear that we need an exit strategy to lift the forced lockdowns and cease the curtailment of economic activity.

Any exit strategy requires input from both epidemiologists and economists as targeting coronavirus and reopening businesses are intertwined. We need to bring the contagion to heel and resuscitate national economies, but the public-health response must come first – the well-being of citizens is paramount.

From a health perspective, the global imperative is to flatten the contamination curve. Every country is keen to join the few nations that have controlled the epidemic and are focusing on preventing a resurgence. Singapore is being held up as a model for achieving rapid control of the virus.

Arguably, the most important factor in the city-state's fight against COVID-19 is that it had a pandemic response plan in place before the virus hit. This was developed in 2003 following the SARS outbreak and enabled Singapore to act pre-emptively and early.

Singapore did not impose drastic lockdown measures – schools, universities, workplaces, bars, and restaurants remained open. Rather, the government introduced rigorous detection and strict quarantine of those found to be infected. It also moved early to ban incoming flights from the Chinese city of Wuhan, where the virus originated.

"Singapore has done everything right," said a former World Health Organization (WHO) infectious diseases expert. In contrast to Singapore, many other nations have had slow and fumbled responses and lost the ability to replicate Singapore's rapid containment success. These nations must continue with their forced lockdown measures to break the COVID-19 transmission chain.

This begs the difficult question: When is it safe to relax these restrictions? Experts warn that easing shutdowns too early will inevitably result in the virus rearing its ugly head again. A second-wave resurgence of infections might see the number of confirmed cases soar.

Governments and their health advisers are grappling with how to reduce social-distancing measures and ease lockdowns without reigniting the virus and going back to square one. "We do have a big problem in what the exit strategy is and how we get out of this," said Mark Woolhouse, Professor of Infectious Disease Epidemiology at the University of Edinburgh.

A Canadian health expert, Assistant Professor Jason Kindrachuk at Manitoba University, cannot see daily life returning to normal until there is a vaccine, and his view is supported by other experts. However, a vaccine is at least 12 to 18 months away, which is why Professor Woolhouse told the BBC that "waiting for a vaccine should not be honoured with the name 'strategy', that is not a strategy".

A vaccine for COVID-19 will need to be administered to about 60 per cent of the global population to achieve "herd immunity". This occurs when enough people have developed an immunity to the outbreak, and vaccination is seen as the best way to safely develop herd immunity.

The policy of the WHO is to keep things clamped down until drugs and a vaccine are available. COVID-19 is too widespread and contagious to fade out on its own, so science will have to deliver immunotherapies. The pandemic has a firm grip on the world, and there is no reset button that can make it disappear.

In the meantime, national governments are becoming increasingly concerned about the economic impact of keeping widespread restrictions in place. Economists fear that the worldwide economic downturn could be deep and lengthy. Commercial activity cannot return to normal while there are constraints on human interaction.

Authorities are caught between the urgent need to reboot economic activity and the ongoing need to contain the virus. With large swathes of the population unemployed and many businesses teetering on the brink of failure, rebuilding broken industries is a key economic goal of all governments.

China did not wait for a vaccine to be developed before it sent workers back to factory floors and construction sites. The majority of China's workforce have returned to their jobs, and manufacturing activity is beginning to ramp up. Malls and restaurants have re-opened to crowds.

The world is now watching to see if China can keep COVID-19 at bay. To date, China's high-stakes experiment seems to be working – it appears to have successfully dampened the rate of new infections. But work life is very different in China's post-virus economy. Fearing a resurgence in cases, the government – as reported in an (American) ABC News article – is taking a gradual approach:

> Beijing's city government is requiring that the number of people in each office be limited to no more than 50% of usual staffing levels. Protective face masks are required, and office workers must be seated at least 1 meter (3.3 feet) apart. Workers are not supposed to face each other when eating.

Similar measures have been implemented across China. As explained in *WIRED* magazine:

> ... [Office] workers enter in shifts staggered to minimize potential exposure. Infrared cameras and security staff check temperatures as they arrive, and their workspaces are decontaminated three times per day. Workers must wear masks at all times and are required to complete a daily health questionnaire. No more than six people are allowed in elevators; tape on the floor shows where to stand. Face-to-face meetings are discouraged, and people eat alone in the cafeteria using a cardboard "face shield," to minimize risk when a face mask is removed.

Lifting lockdowns and getting people back to work is clearly a mammoth task and there is no one sure fire way for it to be done.

India is talking about a "staggered" re-emergence of the population. Other nations will undoubtedly have different road maps. Only time will tell which strategy proves to be the most effective.

**Putting the COVID-19 genie back in the bottle will challenge every nation.**

POSTING DATE | 19 APRIL 2020

## How COVID-19 exposed inequality among workers

### UNDERVALUED CORONAVIRUS HEROES

While nations were under lockdown during the depth of the pandemic, millions of people around the world worked remotely from home. At the same time, there was an even bigger cohort of essential workers for whom it was business-as-usual as the coronavirus swept the land.

These unlikely heroes drove the trucks which delivered our goods, stocked the supermarket shelves which provided our groceries, and prepared the takeaway meals which kept us fed. Other essential workers – like farmhands, meatpackers, store cashiers, and warehouse clerks – also helped keep the economy's lights on.

When the pandemic hit, jobs previously labelled "low skill" were reclassified as "essential". As cities enforced quarantines, and shoppers squabbled over the last roll of toilet paper on the supermarket shelf, essential employees were out and about keeping societies functioning. Their efforts largely went unnoticed even though they were everywhere.

Doctors, nurses, and other health professionals bore the brunt of the outbreak and were the most at-risk population. They received an outpouring of gratitude from citizens and governments for their tireless patient care. Non-medical frontline workers, however, were less recognised. Still, this other layer of critical workers continued to show up on-the-job to help maintain a semblance of normality for others.

The pandemic has shone a light on the stark workplace divide between people who can work from home and those who can't. Lower-paid workers – like factory employees, security guards, and supermarket staff – don't have the option of working remotely. In contrast, highly compensated workers – like managers and other professionals – are able to shelter at home.

Alison Pennington, a senior economist at the Australia Institute's Centre for Future Work, told ABC News that it was easy to see how the pandemic work regime could compound inequality in Australia.

> We estimate people who can work from home are earning around 24 per cent more than those who can't. They're also more likely to have paid sick leave benefits – while essential workers, who are turning out every day, are more likely to work for lower pay, but also less likely to have sick leave.

Pennington said those differences were creating greater inequality, not only in incomes but also in health outcomes, as essential workers faced the higher risk of infection without the income safety net of sick leave. She stated:

> ... coming through this regime, what we're going to find is that the pandemic is going to require a universal entitlement to sick leave if we're going to be able to work through the virus and keep everyone safe.

The Centre for Future Work estimates that only around 15 per cent of Australian workers currently have the option of working remotely full-time. That figure is expected to double as companies quickly adapt to allow more of their employees to stay away from the office. By way of comparison, about a quarter of US workers can easily do their jobs from home.

COVID-19 has revealed how deeply our fates are tied together. It's not a case of us and them – all workers are in this together. Amid stay-at-home orders, office workers ditched their daily commute, while essential workers continued to drive our buses, clean our workplaces, collect our rubbish, cook our food, and staff our nursing homes.

Essential workers are just that – essential. They keep communities running, so staying home isn't an option for them. Risking their well-being for the greater good, their sacrifice is a moral calling for all of us. The pandemic added another layer of burden and responsibility to their jobs as they braved the frontlines against an invisible enemy. We owe them our heartfelt thanks.

Thank you to supermarket employees. Often working at minimum wages, they had to deal with epidemic levels of abuse from irate customers. Retail workers are our neighbours and fellow citizens and maybe even the children of your friends. They put themselves in harm's way to ensure we had access to essential goods – they deserve our highest praise.

Thank you to delivery drivers. While many of us were safely hunkered down at home in isolation, we asked others to drop parcels to our front door. Fulfilling our online orders required the coordinated efforts of workers in warehouses, sorting hubs, and courier companies. They provided an indispensable lifeline to the outside world. We are in their debt and salute their wonderful service.

Thank you to transit workers. Buses and trains underpin urban life, and during the pandemic they performed the critical task of shuttling workers to and from their jobs. This put transit workers in daily physical contact with members of the public in the confines of a bus or train, making social distancing difficult. Three cheers to these quiet achievers for keeping our cities running.

In the war against the novel coronavirus, these and myriad other essential workers were the life support for communities. Yet their work is chronically underpaid and undervalued by society. The explanation for this can be found in economics – or more precisely, the law of supply and demand.

The harsh reality is that lower paid "essential" jobs require few educational credentials. Moreover, the skills necessary to be, say, a cleaner are easy to pick up as they are non-technical. This means that the pool of eligible workers is large, making it easy for employers to hire and fire.

Around the world, many essential workers just get by, living from pay to pay. Yet, during the pandemic, these "low wage workers," according to Health Policy Watch, continued "to risk exposure to the deadly virus while celebrities and CEOs retreat[ed] to private mansions and islands for self-isolation". This brought the gap between "haves" and "have-nots" into stark relief.

In an opinion piece in *The New York Times* on 24 April, 2020, Gene Sperling, a former economic adviser to Presidents Bill Clinton and Barack Obama, asked: "Will our overdue recognition of the contributions of so many workers lead to only temporary applause and pats on the back, or will it move us toward a true social compact ensuring economic dignity for all?"

Drawing inspiration from legendary human-rights activist Dr Martin Luther King, Mr Sperling wrote:

> Fifty-two years ago, when the Rev. Dr. Martin Luther King Jr. famously asserted the dignity of all work, he seemed to foresee this moment when it would become so clear that the labor of everyone – farmworkers, grocers, delivery drivers, caregivers, nursing assistants – was essential to all of our health and well-being.
>
> "One day," Dr. King told sanitation workers on strike in Memphis in 1968, "our society will come to respect the sanitation worker if it is to survive, for the person who picks up our garbage, in the final analysis, is as significant as the physician, for if he doesn't do his job, diseases are rampant."

**In the words of Dr King: "All labor has dignity".**

POSTING DATE | 6 SEPTEMBER 2020

## How households can create a new model of sustainable capitalism

MANIFESTO FOR A BETTER WORLD

Humans are exploiting the Earth in an unsustainable manner. The current model of capitalism is cited as the main culprit, with a burgeoning chorus of scientists challenging the economic mantra of "grow or die". They argue that perpetual growth on a finite planet will lead to environmental calamity.

In the ongoing debate on sustainability, conservationists feel hampered and businesspeople feel vilified. Meanwhile, ecologists and economists disagree about the limits of economic growth and the ecological capacities of the Earth. There is a mounting view that preserving the planet and expanding the economy are mutually exclusive. But is this really the case?

The reality is that environmental and economic issues are interconnected. The planet is part of the economic system, and the economic system, in turn, is part of the planet. In order to grow, the economy feeds on natural resources and emits waste which pollutes the air and threatens the delicate climate on which life relies.

We must reduce the use of fossil fuels by switching to clean energy such as natural gas, nuclear, and renewables (solar and wind). The energy sector matters greatly in our efforts to slow climate change. Electricity generation has long been the world's biggest source of greenhouse gas emissions. The rest comes mainly from transportation, manufacturing, and agriculture.

Around the world, businesses are making changes to their production systems in order to help stop the degradation of the planet. But what role do consumers play? Businesses argue that they merely *supply* the products and services that consumers *demand.* In an age of rampant consumerism, many of us crave the latest "must haves" thereby fuelling an endless cycle of spending.

To understand our insatiable appetite for products and gadgets that are newer and better, you need only look at the hordes of people around the world who queue for days outside an Apple store for the latest iPhone. Consumerism has caused us to confuse a good life with a goods life. The more we have, the more we want, creating a cycle of compulsive buying.

But many of us buy things we don't really need, and this particularly applies to clothing. Open your wardrobe and take stock of all the clothes that you have either never worn or not worn in the past 12 months. It is claimed that most people wear 20 per cent of their clothes 80 per cent of the time. Put another way, we barely wear 80 per cent of what's in our closet.

When it comes to poor practices that contribute to climate change, the fashion industry is cited as one of the worst offenders. Never have consumers been so quick to buy pieces of clothing, yet this apparel runs out of style within weeks. The fashion industry has a vested interest in selling more clothes, so it sets new trends several times a year to keep consumers buying. It's claimed that throwaway garments contribute more to climate change than air and sea travel.

For consumers, sustainability means getting the most out of the products they buy and not throwing them away on a whim. More than 1.7 billion people worldwide now belong to the "consumer class". These people live on diets of highly processed food, own bigger houses and cars, carry higher levels of debt, and have lifestyles devoted to the accumulation of non-essential goods.

Unsurprisingly, many of the environmental issues we see today can be linked to consumption. Disposable cameras, plastic garbage bags, and other cheaply made goods with built-in product obsolescence inflict a devastating toll on the Earth's water supplies, natural resources, and ecosystems. Demand for cheaply manufactured goods fuels our throwaway mentality.

A magazine article titled "Climate Change Is the Symptom, Consumer Culture Is the Disease", notes that "… industries are spouting carbon because customers demand their products: travel, electronics, entertainment, food, all sorts of stuff. So, what if, instead of solely measuring emissions by economic sector, we looked at consumer demand within those sectors?"

Researchers have done just that, and the results tilt the blame away from businesses toward a different villain – ourselves. The article goes on to say:

> C40 Cities, a network of 94 of the world's biggest cities, released a report ... estimating how much consumption habits drive the climate crisis. The results were staggering: In those nearly 100 cities, where a combined 700 million live, the consumption of goods and services "including food, clothing, aviation, electronics, construction and vehicles" is responsible for 10 percent of global greenhouse gases. That's nearly double the emissions from every building in the entire world.

Billions of citizens around the world are looking to governments and businesses to do something about climate change. Yet the real power for change is in our hands. Our collective actions can provide the leadership necessary to combat climate change. We support governments with votes, and businesses with dollars, which means that we can choose who governs and where we spend our money.

If we don't like what a company is doing, we can stop buying their products and services and force them to change. Consumers drive markets, and sustainable consumer choices can change corporate behaviour. But we all need to take a stand and, for many of us, this will require a lifestyle overhaul, particularly with regard to saying "no" to unnecessary and/or environmentally unfriendly household items.

Research reveals that having more and more possessions does not make us happier, which is why some have adopted a minimalist approach to life. There is a growing minimalist movement which advocates that we should get by with less. The basic premise of the movement is to live without unnecessary possessions in order to have more meaningful and thoughtful experiences.

I remain an avid fan of capitalism and believe that it is the greatest vehicle the world has ever known for creating wealth and prosperity. Even so, it is an economic system in need of repair. All of us as individual consumers working together can drive that repair by making better choices in our day-to-day lives regarding the products and services we consume.

**Let's prove that sustainable capitalism is not an oxymoron.**

POSTING DATE | 29 NOVEMBER 2020

## Why it's important to understand economics

### VALUING ECONOMIC LITERACY

Economics touches every part of our lives. We encounter it as workers, parents, citizens, savers, investors, and borrowers. It's at the centre of public debate on everything from education to immigration to the arts. Yet most of us struggle with basic economic concepts such as bond yields, trade deficits, and GDP growth.

Turn on the TV or radio and you'll be bombarded with economic data that screams for your attention. We are surrounded daily by talk of falling interest rates, rising oil prices, ballooning national debt, and seesawing exchange rates. This statistical information helps explain the world in which we live.

Even so, most of us have not read an economics textbook, which is why the discipline remains shrouded in mystery. The technical language and mathematical models of economists are not well understood by the populace. Surveys confirm that most people have a poor grasp of economics.

This deficit in economic understanding hinders us in making informed judgments about the accuracy of economic statements that are made. Many people do not have the economic literacy necessary to critically analyse the economic headlines which dominate the 24/7 news cycle.

One of the primary activities of modern governments is to determine economic policies. The media play a central role in informing the public about these policies and explaining them in clear terms. Together, politicians and the media shape public beliefs and attitudes about economic matters.

Public perceptions about the economy have important political consequences. Governments are largely re-elected or rejected based on economic perceptions. Yet on many economic issues, the gap between public perceptions and economic reality is very wide.

This is not entirely the fault of voters, who are constantly exposed to plausible-sounding economic misconceptions. These fallacies include many beliefs widely disseminated in the media and by politicians. As noted by American economist Thomas Sowell in the preface to his book, *Economic Facts and Fallacies*:

> Some things are believed because they are demonstrably true. But many other things are believed simply because they have been asserted repeatedly – and repetition has been accepted as a substitute for evidence.

Fallacies abound in economics, affecting everything from domestic housing to international trade. Fallacies also have staying power – even in the face of irrefutable evidence against them. Economists could spend an inordinate amount of their time debunking the scores of economic fallacies.

In *Fifty Economic Fallacies Exposed,* Geoffrey Wood, Professor Emeritus of Economics, examines a range of popular economic misconceptions and explains how these mistaken beliefs misinform economic discussion. Among other things, he looks at the supposed dangers of international trade, the alleged ability of governments to control the economy, and the purported benefits to consumers of regulation.

People embrace economic fallacies due to a phenomenon called *the fallacy of composition*. This fallacy infers that what is true for an individual is also true for a whole group. A classic non-economic example is that of a person who stands up at a concert so that he/she can see better. But if everyone stands, the view of many spectators will worsen. So, what is true for one individual in the crowd is not true for the whole stadium.

Thinking about economic issues using the same flawed logic can also lead to incorrect conclusions. For example, our individual experience as a worker is a poor guide to the workings of an economy as a whole. Despite this, those who lose their jobs due to automation typically surmise that technology is a threat to all workers. However, this is an erroneous assumption as new technology does not result in higher overall unemployment.

The misconception that new technology destroys jobs is referred to as *the Luddite fallacy*. In the early 19$^{th}$ century, English textile workers and weavers protested against the changes ushered in by the Industrial Revolution. These "Luddites" smashed mechanised knitting machines as they believed the new labour-saving devices would steal their jobs.

Paradoxically, by the end of the $19^{th}$ century, there were – according to economist and author James Bessen – four times as many factory weavers as there had been in 1830. Automation reduced labour costs for factory owners. This, in turn, enabled the price of garments to be lowered. This, in turn again, increased product demand, leading to the need for more workers.

Automation allows workers to deliver better, faster, and cheaper services, and that's good for growth and therefore good for the economy. What's also undoubtedly good for the economy is immigration – but not according to *the lump of labour fallacy.*

This fallacy is premised on the mistaken belief that the amount of work available in an economy is fixed, so no one can get a job without taking one from someone else. Unsurprisingly, this fallacy is used to prosecute the entrenched myth that migrants steal jobs from native-born workers. It's an understandable supposition, but it's incorrect.

Immigrants who gain work also gain income to spend, creating new jobs. Immigration, therefore, increases the demand for labour and stimulates employment. Commenting on the positive impact that immigrant workers have on the US economy, *The New York Times Magazine* explained that imported workers:

> ... use the wages they earn to rent apartments, eat food, get haircuts, buy cell phones. That means there are more jobs building apartments, selling food, giving haircuts and dispatching the trucks that move those phones. Immigrants increase the size of the overall population, which means they increase the size of the economy. Logically, if immigrants were "stealing" jobs, so would every young person leaving school and entering the job market; countries should become poorer as they get larger. In reality, of course, the opposite happens.

It is axiomatic that the conventional wisdom which says that immigrants take jobs and lower wages is absolutely wrong. In reality, immigrants create jobs and make native workers more prosperous. As world renowned economist and Nobel Laureate Paul Krugman commented "... the [lump of labour] fallacy makes a comeback whenever the economy is sluggish".

One final economic myth – which has been perpetuated for decades – is *the household fallacy*. A government is not a household and therefore does not need to manage its finances like a household. The household fallacy disguises this truth by falsely claiming that what is true for an individual household regarding debt is similarly true for a government.

The household analogy is simple: Governments need to live within their means (like households) by not spending more than they receive or risk going broke. In reality, governments do not always need to have a balanced budget. In fact, they can run prudent annual deficits indefinitely, as many countries do. Britain has maintained a national debt for more than 300 years. Going back to 1776, the US has been in continuous debt except for seven short periods.

Balancing the national budget sounds appealing, and promising to get it back in the black resonates with many voters. Still, policymakers should avoid playing populist politics by trying to imitate family budgets. Fiscal austerity is commendable at a household level but can equate to economic irresponsibility at a sovereign level. As pointed out in a UK media article:

> The familiar logic of the household analogy has become so embedded into public life that spending proposals that would help tackle some of our most pressing challenges – climate change, the housing crisis, unsustainable household debt – can barely make it out of the door. All too often, such proposals are stopped in their tracks by rival politicians and the media asking where the money is going to come from.

It can be seen that economics is replete with fallacies and has a bad reputation for its lack of precision and certainty. As economics is not a natural science – like physics, chemistry, or biology – its propositions are rarely absolutely true or false. Broadly speaking, economics is the study of human behaviour as it relates to money, and we humans are neither rational nor predictable.

It is incumbent on all of us, therefore, to better educate ourselves in the workings of the economy. What currently passes for a conversation among the electorate about economic issues is often amateurish. So, learning about economics often starts by unlearning what you thought you knew.

**We are ignorant of our own ignorance when it comes to economics.**

POSTING DATE | 28 MARCH 2021

## Why the free-market economy is under attack

### DEFENDING CAPITALISM

It's been called the greatest engine of material prosperity in human history. It's lifted people out of poverty, raised living standards, funded research to cure diseases, given us better nutrition, driven mind-blowing innovations, revolutionised the way we live and work, and provided us with access to goods from around the world.

Capitalism has done all these things and more, which is why I believe it's a force for good. Capitalism has made the world a better place by alleviating human suffering. Today, we enjoy lives that are longer, healthier, and better. This is largely because of advances in science, medicine, agriculture, and technology. These advances have been driven by the foundation stone of a capitalist economy – private enterprise.

Central to a global capitalist system is international trade and this, according to the capitalist peace theory, offers a path to world peace. Free trade is built on voluntary interactions of buying and selling, and this encourages nations to live in harmony. Free trade raises the cost of war by making nations more economically interdependent. The more that people rely on trade with others, the greater the cost to all parties of a conflict.

The essence of capitalism is economic freedom. Individuals and businesses are free, within the bounds of the law, to engage in commerce at their will and peril. The father of modern economics, Adam Smith, asserted that economic behaviour is driven by self-interest. The Global Financial Crisis (GFC) painfully revealed that the pursuit of self-interest does not always lead to outcomes that benefit society overall.

So yes, capitalism is not perfect, but that's because human behaviour is not perfect. Economic theory is premised on the assumption that humans make rational choices. However, the GFC showed that we don't always weigh facts objectively when making financial decisions. As to the ill-conceived subprime lending programs, borrowers, bankers, and brokers were united in the delusional belief that house prices never go south.

Another criticism of capitalism is that it leads to inequalities of wealth and income. Again, this is absolutely true, and it's an undeniable fact that the rich are getting richer. But the poor are not poor because the rich are rich – the two conditions are generally unrelated. The rich did not steal their wealth from the poor. While some do inherit their fortune, most people work very hard to make their money – it has little to do with luck.

No two people are exactly the same – and I say that as an identical twin! You have only to look around you to see that we are not equal in height, weight, looks, intelligence, or on a multitude of other dimensions. Everyone has a unique set of abilities which helps them achieve success. As pointed out by one writer:

> Our inherent human inequality should not lead you to despair. On the contrary, imagine how dull life would be if things were otherwise. The fact that I am not equal to LeBron James is a good thing, and so is the fact that LeBron James is not equal to Albert Einstein and that Albert Einstein is not equal to Katharine Hepburn, inequalities are diversity, and *diversity* is the spice of life.

People will never be wholly equal. Yet those who advocate economic equality would view LeBron James's basketball superiority as unfair. They would call for James to be handicapped in some way, perhaps by forcing him to give less skilled opponents credit for some of the baskets he scores. Of course, this would do nothing to improve the performance of his opponents nor provide them with any incentive to lift their game.

That's why taxing the rich more is not the solution to inequality. Around the world, higher-income workers already pay the overwhelming majority of taxes. As the saying goes: "You can't make the poor rich by making the rich poorer". To paraphrase Warren Buffett, we all live far better lives because of Henry Ford, Steve Jobs, Bill Gates, and the founders of Google. These brave entrepreneurs helped expand the global economy, and this assists the poor as much as the rich.

An open-market, capitalist economy is not designed to deliver equal economic status for everyone. People receive varying financial rewards for the jobs they do and the contribution they make to society. While excessive greed benefits no one, trying to make all of us financially equal is a recipe for disaster. Capitalism rewards productive achievement and provides the necessary incentive for entrepreneurs to take risks and innovate, and this benefits society overall.

Even if we somehow managed to redistribute wealth so that every adult in Australia had exactly the same amount of money, it would be fleeting. The smart, the strong, and the devious would quickly acquire the wealth of the slow, the weak, and the gullible. Moreover, people would use their money in different ways. The prudent would save and invest their money while the irresponsible would squander it.

Given our differing attitudes to money, the equal distribution of wealth is clearly an unattainable goal. Even so, I believe that the widening gulf between workers and executives has become excessive. I find it hard to accept that any one individual is worth an annual salary of, say, $10 million. Equally, I don't believe that sports stars and rock'n'roll artists are worth the millions that they are paid.

Still, I accept that in a free-market economy based on supply and demand, captains of industry, the sporting elite, and entertainment celebrities can command multimillion-dollar incomes. As Winston Churchill observed:

> The inherent vice of capitalism is the unequal sharing of blessings; the inherent virtue of socialism is the equal sharing of miseries.

The world has seen a number of socio-economic systems, including slavery, feudalism, socialism, communism, and capitalism. For all of its imperfections, it's my contention that capitalism, like democracy, is better than the alternatives. This is certainly the view of economist Ha-Joon Chang, who is a reader in economics at the University of Cambridge and the author of 15 books.

In his international bestseller, *23 Things They Don't Tell You About Capitalism*, Chang identifies some of the pitfalls of capitalism. In highlighting these shortcomings, Chang is careful to point out that his book is not an anti-capitalist manifesto. "Despite its problems and limitations, I believe that capitalism is still the best economic system that humanity has invented", he underscores.

Notwithstanding his tough assault on capitalism, Chang acknowledges that there's no real alternative to free-market capitalism, describing it as "the worst economic system except for all the others". He says that "being critical of free-market ideology is not the same as being against capitalism". Rather, his aim is to tell "some essential truths about capitalism".

I am the first to acknowledge that capitalism has failed to cover itself in glory over the past couple of decades and that public opinion has turned against it. Capitalism is not without its faults because economics is an imperfect social science. Still, humanity as a whole is doing better than it ever has thanks to capitalism. While we still have problems to solve, they are less severe than at any time in history.

As for those nations suffering severe poverty, they must be helped and encouraged to adopt capitalism. The uneven distribution of wealth in the world is due to the uneven distribution of capitalism. Swedish writer Johan Norberg makes this very point in his book, In *Defense of Global Capitalism*, wherein he states:

> The poor countries that have liberalized their economies have shown impressive results, while those that have not are stuck in deep misery. Therefore, we need more capitalism and globalisation if we want a better world, not less.

Capitalism offers a practical way to nourish the hungry. Handouts are not the solution to poverty in places like Africa. As US President Bill Clinton explained: "No country can work itself out of poverty with aid alone". Training and assistance must be provided to Africa's private sector to help them drive economic growth and make Africa self-sufficient. Capitalism can do this and more.

**Capitalism has changed the world for the better.**

POSTING DATE | 26 SEPTEMBER 2021

## Why GDP is a flawed yardstick of human welfare

### MEASURE WHAT MATTERS

It's a deceptively simple number which captures headlines, makes or breaks governments, and dominates public discourse. Gross domestic product (or GDP) is used to measure the size and health of a nation's economy and the prosperity of its citizens. Each country's economic performance is ranked and judged using this common top-line metric.

GDP measures the economic activities of individuals (personal consumption), businesses (private investment), and governments (public outlays). It also factors in the difference between the value of a nation's exports and imports. GDP became the prime economic indicator during the Second World War to monitor war production and measure a country's economic progress.

Workers and businesses are generally better off when an economy is expanding, as growth drives profits, jobs, and wages. Still, money isn't everything, which is why an increasing number of economists and politicians believe that GDP is a poor gauge of societal well-being. As a macroeconomic index, GDP has limitations, and many are pointing out its deficiencies.

That GDP is not a perfect metric has been known for decades. It's a measure of raw economic activity, not a complete picture of human progress. As Senator Robert Kennedy famously articulated in a 1968 election speech, GDP fails to capture a lot of what actually goes on in life.

> … The gross national product does not allow for the health of our children, the quality of their education or the joy of their play. It does not include the beauty of our poetry or the strength of our marriages, the intelligence of our public debate or the integrity of our public officials. It measures neither our wit nor our courage, neither our wisdom nor our learning, neither our compassion nor our devotion to our country. It measures everything in short, except that which makes life worthwhile.

GDP is the market value of goods and services produced in a year in a nation – its domestic production. GDP is derived by counting up the dollar value of all new goods and services produced, and includes things such as iPhones, cars, taxi rides, haircuts, computers, steel, apples, university education, and cups of coffee.

Most goods and services are produced for sale, so the money spent by individuals, businesses, and governments buying these outputs is used to measure production. GDP only recognises goods and services that pass through official markets. Therefore, production that is not bought or sold does not get counted, as GDP works by measuring market price.

So, volunteer work or domestic work – like caring for an aged relative or knitting a jumper – does not get counted in GDP as it is "unpaid production". Yet most would agree that family caretaking is of enormous value to society and should be included in GDP calculations. (To be clear, if a family hires someone for childcare, that counts in GDP accounting.)

The GDP framework also takes no account of leisure time. Two countries might have equal GDP but one has workers toiling for 12 hours per day while the other only eight hours. Likewise, GDP is not adjusted for pollution costs. If two economies have the same GDP per capita, but one has polluted the air, the well-being of citizens is different, but that's not captured by GDP per capita.

Another metric not included in GDP is the state of the environment. Economic growth is largely fuelled by consumerism, and the rampant rise in household spending is depleting the Earth's natural resources. Scientists warn that perpetual growth on a finite planet is not sustainable and is causing environmental calamities such as climate change.

A further criticism of the embattled GDP is its failure to reflect inequality as it doesn't measure the distribution of growth. Income and wealth disparities in society have grown exponentially, and extreme inequality is evident in many nations. The rich are getting richer, and this skewing of wealth has created universal inequities in accessing education, health care, and finance.

The shallowness of GDP thinking is further evident in the way it counts catastrophes and natural disasters as economic bonuses. When assessing a tragedy such as a bushfire, GDP treats the rebuilding of homes destroyed as a positive economic impact. Yet, it does not capture the negative social consequences on regional tourism, or the trauma suffered by townspeople.

Most glaringly, GDP is unable to account for the full impact of technology on our lives. Most of us could not get through the day without utilising digital media. But as GDP assigns a zero value to goods with a zero price, complimentary services like Google searches, Facebook posts, and app downloads go largely uncounted in official measures of economic activity. Similarly, the vast amount of knowledge that Wikipedia provides free of charge is worth zilch in GDP terms.

It's clear that GDP does not incorporate many of the negative effects of economic growth and misses the main pillars of a progressive society. Certainly, it does not reflect the quality of life or happiness in any given country, which is why there is a concerted effort to find alternatives to measure the wealth and welfare of nations.

A *CBS News* article, quoting *The New York Times* journalist Catherine Rampell, provides a precis of some of the possible replacements for GDP, including:

> ... China's "green GDP", which attempts to adjust for environmental factors; the OECD's "GDP alternatives", which adjust for leisure; the "Index of Sustainable Economic Welfare", which accounts for both pollution costs and the distribution of income; and the "Genuine Progress Indicator", which "adjusts for factors such as income distribution, adds factors such as the value of household and volunteer work, and subtracts factors such as the costs of crime and pollution". Finally, there are more direct measures of well-being such as the Happy Planet Index, Gross National Happiness and National Well-Being Accounts.

Half a century on from Senator Kennedy, the world is still obsessed with increasing GDP at almost any cost. Indeed, our economies have become structurally dependent on growth. Governments pursue economic expansion as a primary goal, with rising GDP providing ever more taxes. From GDP's perspective, bigger is always better – but not according to an article in the *Oxford Business Review* which states:

> GDP is no longer an appropriate goal by which to measure economic and societal success. ... It is paramount that something must replace the goal of infinite GDP growth. After all, growth for the sake of growth is the ideology of a cancer cell.

Growth as a metaphor for prosperity is deeply imbedded in our language – we like to see our children grow and our gardens too. Growth equates to progress, even though too much can be cancerous. At a UN climate-change summit in 2019, Swedish environmental activist Greta Thunberg declared: "We are in the beginning of a mass extinction, and all you can talk about is money and fairy tales of eternal economic growth".

I reject the notion that growth is always synonymous with improved well-being and therefore accept that the current fixation on perpetual economic growth is not sustainable. But that does not mean that I embrace the other extreme – promulgated by the "degrowth movement" – which calls for advanced countries to adopt zero or even negative GDP growth.

As sometimes happens, I find myself in the middle of an important debate – on this occasion between economists and environmentalists. To be clear, I believe that the economy should not be forced to stop growing or even shrink. Nonetheless, it should be required to adopt more environmentally friendly practices and aim for a slower growth rate.

As I outlined in a previous post, which explained the benefits of sustainable capitalism, we all have a vital role to play as consumers because:

> If we don't like what a company is doing, we can stop buying their products and services and force them to change. Consumers drive markets and sustainable

> consumer choices can change corporate behaviour. But we all need to take a stand and, for many of us, this will require a lifestyle overhaul, particularly with regard to saying "no" to unnecessary and/or environmentally unfriendly household items.

While I believe that the world-renowned abbreviation, GDP, remains a valuable tool for economic discussions, it does not tell the real story of human well-being. There is more to life than buying and consuming stuff, which is why economic and other data would be better presented with a dashboard of broader indicators rather than a single GDP number.

**We can have our cake and eat it if we are prepared to change our ways.**

POSTING DATE | 30 JANUARY 2022

## How big corporations make billions from side businesses

### HIDDEN BUSINESS MODELS

In business, things are not always as they seem. Take the ubiquitous McDonald's – it's synonymous with burgers and fries, yet it's actually a real-estate company disguised as a fast-food restaurant. Profits from menu sales at the golden arches are overshadowed by the significant bottom-line contribution the global chain receives in rental income from its franchisees.

While customers have been chomping on Big Macs, the brand has been sinking its teeth into prime land. Globally, 93 per cent of the chain's 38,000 stores are operated by franchisees, but the burger titan owns the land and buildings beneath its franchised locations. This is the real McDonald's secret sauce – leveraging fast food to lease properties to restaurant owners at large markups.

Being able to collect rents as the landlord to its franchisees insulates the McDonald's Corporation from the ups and downs of the business of flipping burgers. When you break down the company's multibillion-dollar earnings, it boils down to real estate. Profit margins on food sales are slim, whereas the return on the company's $38 billion commercial investment portfolio is lucrative.

McDonald's controls one of the biggest property portfolios in the world. From Times Square in New York to Red Square in Moscow, McDonald's owns thousands of iconic pieces of real estate around the globe. Each franchisee pays rent in addition to royalties on food sales, and this enables McDonald's to maintain inexpensive menu prices.

The company's 2020 financial report confirms that rent contributes more to McDonald's profitability than royalties. Out of the $10.7 billion McDonald's collected in fees from restaurants in 2020, $6.9 billion came from rent, and $3.8 billion was generated from royalty payments. Profit from franchise-operated stores stood at $8.5 billion (as it cost McDonald's only $2.2 million to run these outlets), whereas company-owned stores recorded a profit of only $1.15 billion (as they are dearer to run).

Another company that makes billions from a seemingly non-core activity is Amazon. When you peel back the layers at the world's largest online retailer, you discover that Amazon is a major provider of cloud computing services via its subsidiary, Amazon Web Services (AWS). AWS controls around a third of the global cloud market – substantially more than its nearest rival, Microsoft.

Amazon's business is divided into three segments: North America, International, and AWS. AWS is Amazon's largest source of operating profits and is growing at a robust pace. The commercially rewarding cloud-computing arm supplies over 63 per cent of Amazon's profits, making it an extremely important part of the Amazon empire.

AWS provides data storage and processing for companies that don't want the headaches of running their own IT infrastructure. AWS has been very successful in selling its technology services and, as a consequence, has become a cash cow for its parent, Amazon. According to an article in *The New York Times,* AWS is ubiquitous online.

> If you watch Netflix, that's A.W.S. If you have a meeting on Zoom, there's a good chance that's A.W.S., too. If you check Pinterest, that's A.W.S. If you spend any time scrolling through Twitter, well, A.W.S. provides "global cloud infrastructure to deliver Twitter timelines." These examples are just a few of the thousands of A.W.S. customers big and small (including *The New York Times*).

AWS was launched in 2006 with little fanfare as a side business for Amazon and has since morphed into a highly successful enterprise in its own right. Before it was AWS, it was just Amazon's backend technology. Amazon developed expertise in building state-of-the-art technology infrastructure for itself and ultimately decided to rent those services to other businesses.

Today, AWS provides a low-cost infrastructure platform in the cloud, which is highly reliable and scalable and powers hundreds of thousands of businesses in 190 countries around the world. While Amazon has helped revolutionise the way people shop, AWS has disrupted the technology industry by making computing services accessible through the web.

Like McDonald's and Amazon, Google is another behemoth that, at first appearance, deceives many. While it has always portrayed itself as a tech company, its main business line is online advertising. Even so, most people understandably believe that Google is a web search engine which provides free access to searches, Gmail, Google Maps, and other online tools.

Of course, all of these complimentary services must somehow be paid for, and that's where advertising enters the equation. The bulk of Google's multibillion-dollar revenue is generated from its proprietary advertising service, Google Ads. Google makes money by selling ad space with its search results – and it processes a staggering amount of search requests.

Roughly half of the world's population, or 3.8 billion people, use the Internet every day. Most users rely on Google to carry out their daily searches, making Google the most visited website in the world. It is estimated that in 2021, 5.5 billion searches were undertaken per day using Google – this equates to a mind-boggling 63,600 searches every second.

Each search provides an opportunity for Google to display ads and make money. You see those ads each time you search on Google – they are displayed alongside the search results. The ads are paid for by advertisers on a pay-per-click basis. If you do not click on a link, Google does not make any money directly from your search.

Advertisers submit ads to Google which include a list of keywords relating to a product, service, or business. The price for a particular keyword or groups of keywords depends upon the competition among advertisers for that keyword or groups of keywords. Google uses an auction system, so the company which outbids other competitors wins the right to use the relevant word or words.

Google could not attract advertisers without readers – and it needs lots of them. The more readers it attracts, the more interest that is generated from advertisers. Google lures in users, collects their data, and then sells access to eager advertisers across the planet. The more

Google knows about an individual, the better it can target ads, and the more it can charge for ad space.

Demand for Google's services surged in 2021 as the pandemic forced people to spend more time online. This was a financial bonanza for Google and its parent company, Alphabet. By the numbers, Google is an ad company, and it is getting bigger all the time.

The outstanding success of McDonald's, Amazon, and Google is testament to what corporate strategists have long known – businesses should focus on what they do best. Corporations that concentrate on a few core businesses, based on their core competencies, invariably do better than those that try to be all things to all people.

History shows that when most companies diversify into new markets, their profitability is diluted, and acquisitions are subsequently unwound. They quickly discover that they do not have the experience and capabilities needed to expand beyond their core business. So, the challenge is to find "business adjacencies" in adjacent markets.

Adjacency is about identifying new markets that intersect with what a business already does. It is a strategy where a business leverages something they are good at to develop a new product or service in a related market. No technology company exemplifies adjacent innovation better than Amazon. As one technology strategist noted in an online article:

> While Amazon.com was becoming a retail juggernaut, Amazon's technical teams were optimising internal cloud operations and building a world-class technology infrastructure to serve their own retail business. In 2006 Amazon launched Amazon Web Services (AWS) – yet another adjacent business – for cloud-computing services that has evolved into an enormously profitable product on its own.

It's been said that Google's core competency is matchmaking – pairing Internet surfers with advertisers and taking a cut along the way. As the digital world continues to evolve, Google has taken a multi-pronged approach to maintaining its dominance in the search and ad business. Search continues to migrate across mediums, with users increasingly moving from desktop to mobile devices. As outlined in a research report:

> To maintain its foothold and protect its main source of revenue, Alphabet [Google's parent company] is positioning itself to dominate adjacent sectors – such as digital commerce, branded hardware products, and content – and attempting to integrate its services into every aspect of the digital user experience.

McDonald's also utilised an adjacent innovation strategy with the introduction of the McCafé in 1996. This enabled the chain to move beyond burgers into premium coffee – competing directly with Starbucks. McCafé coffee outlets act as an adjacent or related product to the McDonald's main menu. McCafé is based on the company's core competency of standardisation – every coffee has precisely the same taste and texture.

McDonald's, Amazon, and Google prove that masquerading as one thing but doing another can be very profitable. All three have followed the same broad playbook to gain market share and cultivate a world-beating brand. Their hidden business models are profit machines which have made them juggernauts.

**It pays not to be a one-trick pony.**

POSTING DATE | 27 FEBRUARY 2022

## Explaining the bizarre world of non-fungible tokens

### RISE OF DIGITAL OWNERSHIP

Collectors have long been willing to shell out huge sums of money on unique items such as fine art, classic cars, and antique books. Collectables are tangible assets which can be hung on a wall, stored in a garage, or displayed in a cabinet. Historically, the buying and selling of rare and desirable items has occurred at auction houses. However, a new trend is emerging which enables investors to buy intangible digital assets online.

Collectable items have moved into the virtual world using trendy new technology called non-fungible tokens (NFTs). An NFT (also called a crypto-collectable) is a one-of-a-kind asset which can be bought and sold like any piece of property, even though it has no physical form of its own. Almost anything can be minted as an NFT, including digital art, music videos, film clips, video games, luxury goods, and sports collectables such as football cards.

NFTs are changing how musicians and artists can earn a living. NFTs offer a way for "creators" of music and art to monetize their work via the sale of a token and get a slice (in the form of a royalty) of any resale value in the secondary market. Each token is unique, can't be duplicated, and is basically a certificate of authenticity. While other people might have a copy of the artefact that you have purchased as an NFT, they don't own the original item.

Think of Leonardo da Vinci's painting, the *Mona Lisa*. It is the most famous portrait in the world and there are hundreds of thousands of reproductions of this masterpiece – but only one original. The same principle applies to NFTs – you can copy and paste an image, though only the original – digitally signed by the artist – holds value. Buying an NFT is like buying the original *Mona Lisa*, but instead of receiving an oil painting on wood, you get a JPG file.

Some people compare owning a crypto token to buying an autographed print. Each token contains computerised code that verifies it is the only asset with its specific digital identity. The tokens, as asset identifiers, are considered to be non-fungible since their uniqueness makes them irreplaceable and impossible to swap.

As non-fungible tokens cannot be replicated, they are incapable of mutual substitution. An example will help here.

You and a friend are travelling together on a plane and have been issued with boarding passes. If the information on each pass were identical, they would be considered fungible – i.e., capable of being swapped for one another. However, each boarding pass contains unique information, such as passenger name, seat number, and airline membership details. Consequently, they cannot be randomly exchanged with anyone else, thereby making them non-fungible.

In contrast, a fungible asset is something that can be readily interchanged – like money. If I lend you $20, it doesn't matter whether you pay me back with a different $20 banknote from the one that I gave you – any $20 bill will do. Equally, you can repay me with two $10 bills since the total equals $20. Items are considered fungible if exchanging them is meaningless, such as two people swapping $5 notes with each other.

Details of (non-fungible) digital tokens are recorded on an encrypted and publicly accessible ledger called a blockchain. Blockchain is the software architecture that underpins Bitcoin and other cryptocurrencies. Blockchain ledgers are not stored in one place but are distributed over thousands of computers around the world. These replicated ledgers are spread geographically across multiple sites, countries, and institutions.

Blockchains work by using a network of computers to create a shared digital ledger that no one computer can change. All computers must approve a transaction that has taken place before it is recorded in a "chain" of computer code. Every transaction is cryptographically chained to the previous transaction, making blockchains perfect for creating unique digital identifiers which can be easily and securely exchanged – hence the creation of NFTs.

The idea of registering digital assets as NFTs on a blockchain began with CryptoPunks in June 2017. CryptoPunks are a set of unique collectable characters (10,000 to be precise) of randomly generated pixel-based avatars. However, NFTs did not come to prominence until October 2017, with the release of the blockchain-based

CryptoKitties game which enables players to buy and "breed" limited-edition virtual cats.

This past August, the global card-payments processor, Visa, bought a CryptoPunk for nearly $150,000. Visa's CryptoPunk is a pixelated digital image of a woman with a mohawk. Commenting on the purchase, Visa's Head of Fintech, Terry Angelos, said: "We see an emerging new category of commerce that we're calling NFT commerce".

Cuy Sheffield, Head of Crypto at Visa, believes that NFTs will play an important role in the future of retail, social media, entertainment, and commerce. "To help our clients and partners participate, we need a first-hand understanding of the infrastructure requirements for a global brand to purchase, store, and leverage an NFT".

Sheffield remarked that CryptoPunks have become a "cultural icon for the crypto community" and that Visa's CryptoPunk purchase signalled that the company was "jumping in feet first". He added: "This is just the beginning of our work in this space".

According to online financial magazine *Barron's*, Bitcoin was predicted to take middlemen, like Visa, out of commerce entirely by allowing people to transact directly over the Internet, but that has not come to pass. That leaves an opening for incumbent players to maintain their importance. To quote *Barron's*:

> Visa sees an opportunity to be the rails for the new digital economy just as it has been the rails for the current one. It's already connected to consumers and businesses, so people don't need to use a completely new system. Visa's interface with the public can be similar whether they pay through cryptocurrencies or dollars. The company already has helped crypto exchanges issue credit cards and other products.

Other companies to jump on the NFT bandwagon include Pizza Hut (pixelated pizza), Pringles (CryptoCrisp, the chips you can't eat), Nike (Cryptokicks, limited edition sneakers), Vodaphone (augmented reality game), and McDonald's (pixelated Big Mac). These brands have seized on NFTs as a way to engage with their audiences and promote their products. All want a seat at the NFT table because the crypto economy is expected to evolve rapidly.

Recently, the Australian Federal Government, along with the Reserve Bank of Australia, leading companies, and universities set up the Digital Finance Cooperative Research Centre (CRC). The CRC will undertake a decade-long research program examining the digitisation of real-world assets. The projected growth in this market is staggering, with tokenised assets expected to grow from virtually nothing today to $US24 trillion ($A32 trillion) by 2027.

The government believes that the CRC's work could add billions of dollars to Australia's gross domestic product each year. The aim of the project is to unlock new assets and make them efficient to trade. As reported in the *Australian Financial Review*, the CRC's CEO predicts that the creation of digital versions of real-world assets "will have a profound impact on the rate of achievable economic growth and pave the way for new types of investable assets".

As the craze of cryptocurrencies gains momentum, NFTs are emerging as a new investment option. New-age collectors and investors are paying thousands and even millions of dollars to own digital collectables. Even so, is this a bubble waiting to burst? Are NFTs highly speculative bets or do they offer value for money? The bottom line is that the NFT market is too immature to judge its long-term worth as an investment option.

So, it's a case of buyer beware because the NFT market's recent stratospheric rise is no guarantee of future returns. The harsh reality is that while some early investors have achieved insane windfalls, others will fork out inflated amounts for digital assets that may wind up being worthless. Another point to note is that the underlying technology is complicated for a layperson to understand, let alone use on their own.

Right now, NFTs are in the midst of a hype-cycle and trending upwards. Still, there is no assurance that demand for digital assets will continue at current levels. As with any new disruptive technology, there are pros and cons. So, take care to closely examine what could go wrong – the dark side of investing in NFTs is real, particularly as the value of art and other collectables is fundamentally subjective.

**When it comes to NFTs, value lies in the eye of the beholder.**

POSTING DATE | 10 OCTOBER 2021

*Chapter Three*

# The Social Landscape

Social forces are always at work changing our world and the lives of individuals. Societal change is an ongoing process driven by a combination of gradual change and sudden events, and this chapter contains posts covering both types of change. The life-threatening impact of the pandemic caused rapid dislocation, which led to fear and panic among the populace. At the same time, slower-moving trends reached a tipping point and have given rise to a growing number of citizens demonstrating irrational decision-making and embracing conspiracy theories.

## Why the coronavirus outbreak has driven panic buying

### COVID-19 HAS EMPTIED SUPERMARKET SHELVES

Around the world, people have flocked to supermarkets and stripped shelves of household essentials. Panic buying has reached fever pitch, with shoppers piling trolleys high with toilet paper and other items. Supermarkets have imposed limits on customer purchases to quell unnecessary hoarding. In some cases, police intervention has been required to contain the behaviour of stampeding customers.

The coronavirus has caused us to fret, and this has brought out the worst in humanity. Irrational stockpiling has turned people's fear of a shortage into a self-fulfilling prophesy. Pleas by public authorities for calm have fallen on deaf ears. Worry about the scarcity of supplies has driven panic buying, which has bred more panic buying – a classic case of herd mentality. Illogical behaviour has become contagious.

Blindly following the crowd has created public unrest which, in turn, has led to pandemonium due to confronting reporting. Television and social media have whipped people into a frenzy by triggering anxiety and uncertainty. The rolling news coverage with minute-by-minute online updates has stoked public hysteria and induced panic.

Professor Karin Wahl-Jorgensen, a journalism expert from Cardiff University, stated that the coronavirus reporting is a "bigger contagion" than the virus itself. She expressed concern at media coverage which used "sensationalist and frightening language" such as "killer virus" and "deadly disease" and said that she found this "particularly problematic".

One online media outlet, *Euronews*, ran an article which asked the question: Which is the real pandemic – coronavirus or the hysteria that follows? It answered as follows:

> The world is clearly in the grip of not one, but two pandemics, caused by a new coronavirus, the "novel Coronavirus 2019" or nCoV-2019 for short. The first pandemic is the actual infection caused by this virus. The second is the panic, hysteria, threat inflation, associated

> racism and xenophobia that are exploding in the shadow of the viral outbreak. The latter pandemic may claim more lives than the first.

One Australian newspaper, Darwin's *NT News*, made light of the loo roll hysteria. It printed several blank pages for readers to use if they ran out of toilet paper. "We've printed an eight-page special lift-out inside, complete with handy cut lines, for you to use in an emergency," the paper's front page cheekily read.

Consumer psychology experts opined that herd mentality coupled with over-exposure to coverage of the coronavirus is to blame for stores being ransacked of groceries and long-life pantry staples. One such expert, Steven Taylor, is a professor and clinical psychologist at the University of British Columbia and author of *The Psychology of Pandemics.*

Taylor argues that panic buying is fuelled by anxiety and a willingness to go to irrational lengths to quell those fears, such as queueing for hours or buying way more than you need. He says: "If everyone else on the Titanic is running for the lifeboats, you're going to run too, regardless if the ship's sinking or not".

Many shoppers insist that they are only in a frenzy because everyone else is, not because they are scared of the coronavirus. So, fear of missing out is allegedly driving them to join the hordes of other shoppers whose self-preservation instincts have also kicked in. People argue that it is "only normal" to want to look out for themselves and their families. No one, it seems, wants to take responsibility for their own overreactive behaviour.

Outraged customers have vented their fury on social media at the chaotic scenes created by the reaction to the virus. "Just ridiculous" and "insane" and "outrageous" are some of the comments recorded. During the height of the run for toilet rolls, the top trending topic on Twitter in Australia was #toiletpapergate. Clearly, people did give a sh*t that stocks were wiped out!

History shows that a consumer buying frenzy ahead of a potential crisis is not an uncommon phenomenon. For example, it famously occurred in 1962 during the Cuban missile crisis, when nuclear war seemed imminent. Sensible American families stocked their basements with enough canned goods and bottled water to survive an atomic blast.

There's nothing more fearsome than the great unknown, and this describes the coronavirus. Many in the community see it as a dramatic event which requires a dramatic response – such as descending on supermarkets and stripping the shelves bare of toilet rolls, hand sanitisers, and surgical masks. A much better response is something far more mundane – properly washing your hands.

Once a sense of normalcy and balance returns, we must examine our collective behaviour. It's clear that we have to get better as a society in responding to the surprises and shocks of modern living. This requires us to take a more holistic approach by focussing on "we" rather than "me". Our narrow self-interests must give way to the optimum outcome for all parties.

Trying to achieve the best for the collective rather than the individual led to the development of a branch of economics called game theory. This theory describes how the gain of one player is offset by the loss of another player, equalling the sum of zero (a.k.a. a zero-sum game).

The best-known example of game theory is the prisoner's dilemma, where two criminals are enticed by police to betray each other. The prisoner's dilemma – to confess or not to confess – underscores how our choices affect others, and how the choices others make affect us.

The Global Financial Crisis was a modern-day prisoner's dilemma, where the "every-man-for-himself" attitude saw markets crash as everyone tried to get to the exit door first. All the efficiencies of the free market flew out the window as institutions hid their bad loans, causing credit markets to freeze as players did not trust each other.

The notion that someone has to lose for someone else to gain is narrow-minded. We humans must learn to modify our self-defeating behaviour, which is why game theory should be a compulsory element of the core curriculum of educational institutions. We all need to be taught the benefits of cooperation over conflict, and this training should begin in the home.

After all, parents are the world's first and foremost teachers. We can all play a part in making our planet a better place.

**Let's wipe out crap behaviour.**

POSTING DATE | 22 MARCH 2020

## Why the COVID-19 outbreak has led to mass hysteria

### OBSESSIVE COMPULSIVE CORONAVIRUS DISORDER

The reaction to the coronavirus has created catastrophic economic and social disruption. It has spooked investors, causing them to wipe trillions of dollars of value from global financial markets. It has panicked consumers, driving them to clear out supermarket shelves in order to fill household pantries. And it has besieged governments, forcing them to impose travel restrictions, quarantines, and shutdowns.

Volatility is now the new normal as the pandemic brings with it unprecedented changes to daily life. To break the chain of transmission, people are embracing a combination of hygiene measures (e.g., hand sanitising) and social-distancing measures (e.g., remote working). We are all being asked – quite rightly – to change our usual habits to curb the virus and protect the most vulnerable in society.

Many of the disruptions that we are experiencing are not caused by the outbreak itself. Rather, they are the result of people's panicked responses to the coronavirus. Many believe that the media must take some responsibility for fuelling unnecessary alarm. The pathogen is dominating the news cycle, with radio stations and television networks bombarding us with dire forecasts about the pandemic.

Media outlets around the world have been breathlessly reporting virtually every new diagnosis of the coronavirus. However, they rarely tell you that catching the virus is non-life-threatening for most people under 65 years. In a recent press conference, Australian Prime Minister Scott Morrison said that for most people infected with the coronavirus, it "will be a mild illness and it will pass". He acknowledged that the most at-risk members of the community were the aged, which is why authorities moved to lockdown aged-care facilities to protect vulnerable residents.

I commend governments and medical authorities around the world for being concerned and taking the coronavirus seriously. The outbreak has plunged us into the unknown. We know what to expect from the long-observed seasonal flu and have a vaccine to treat it.

But the coronavirus has taken us into uncharted territory – its novelty means that scientists aren't sure yet how it behaves.

Understandably, many find this frightening, and that's all the more reason why reporting of the pandemic must be measured and balanced. The media has an important role to play in letting the public know the dangers without inciting panic. But they have hyped the outbreak with alarmist information such as worst-case scenario death-toll predictions. This has driven fear rather than build an understanding about the illness.

US academic Kalev Leetaru is a senior fellow at George Washington University. He recently published the results of an analysis which sought to identify the degree of responsibility the media holds for "fomenting" coronavirus panic, arising from their "wall-to-wall, end-of-days coverage". His conclusion is that the media has "played a measurable role in driving public attention to the virus and likely worsening behaviors such as panic buying".

Of course, scaremongering by the media is nothing new. In his 2011 book, *Sideshow: Dumbing Down Democracy*, Lindsay Tanner, former Australian federal minister for finance, described how the media manipulates the discussion of issues in ways that entertain rather than inform. He argued that media reporting is blatantly designed to manipulate the public's emotions. Tanner cited a number of examples where the media created unnecessary panic, including the Global Financial Crisis, the Y2K computer bug, and the swine flu epidemic.

The media reporting of these events produced a public response out of proportion to the threat. I vividly recall the exaggerated Y2K reporting. While technology legend Bill Gates saw the millennium bug as "a minor inconvenience", less qualified IT commentators promulgated doomsday scenarios and were aided in their deception by the media, who spun compelling but inaccurate stories.

A gullible public bought in to the outrageous predictions about planes falling from the sky and missiles self-launching. But the bug did not bite, and the New Year passed with nothing more than the expected hangover. Those who foretold of a global computer apocalypse caused unnecessary panic but were never brought to account.

Nothing had changed by the time of the Fukushima power plant disaster in 2011. Yet again, the media wheeled out instant experts who hyperventilated over the very modest amounts of radioactive fallout. Fears about radiation contamination were clearly overblown but made for dramatic headlines which trumpeted the dangers of nuclear energy. The same tactics are being used by the media with regard to the coronavirus.

During an address at a conference in Munich on 15 February, Tedros Adhanom Ghebreyesus, the Director-General of the World Health Organization, said: "… we're not just fighting an epidemic; we're fighting an infodemic. Fake news spreads faster and more easily than this virus, and is just as dangerous". Two weeks later, Dr Ghebreyesus ended a 28 February media briefing with a similar remark: "Our greatest enemy right now is not the virus itself. It's fear, rumours, and stigma".

Another voice worth listening to is that of Clare Wenham, assistant professor of global health policy at the London School of Economics. In an opinion piece that she recently co-authored with two colleagues for online global health-care knowledge provider, *BMJ*, Wenham wrote:

> We conceptualise this as two different outbreaks: one outbreak of a coronavirus, and one of viral fake-news. This sensationalised panic and fear concerning the nCoV2019 outbreak is a consequence of the proliferation of sources of information which exaggerate the severity of this outbreak…

She went on to say:

> … we need to consider the media's role and responsibility in informing and shaping understanding and reaction to this outbreak. Are they aware of the public health impacts of headlines such as "killer virus", "deadly disease" or a "killer coronavirus epidemic"? Alarmist headlines like these incite further fear among populations and

> communities [and] challenge the more measured public health communications from the government or WHO ... The scarier the language and voice, the more this false narrative of coronavirus takes hold.

Every public-health outbreak inevitably involves communication, and panic prevention is an integral part of managing any pandemic. Panic is contagious and destructive and should be avoided at all costs. All new contagious diseases receive extensive media attention, with the media coverage setting the agenda for public debate and concerns.

Media executives know that people are predisposed to fear what they do not understand. Dire warnings by news outlets of a "horrific" and "catastrophic" disease tap into our anxieties and play to our primal fears. Care must be taken, therefore, not to use fear-inducing language but to employ a narrative which tempers fear and provides reassurance.

**Let's work together to stop the virus of fear.**

POSTING DATE | 5 APRIL 2020

## What lessons can we learn from the coronavirus outbreak?

### THE WORLD IS SICK AND IN DISARRAY

Everywhere you look, you see disruption. International markets are in turmoil, with a recession in many nations almost assured. National governments are in crisis mode, implementing unprecedented financial and social measures. And worried citizens are in a state of panic, with fear causing irrational and unhelpful behaviour.

Welcome to the world of COVID-19. What confronts you is not a scene from a disaster movie but the brutal reality of a global health emergency. The coronavirus started as an epidemic in China and quickly morphed into a global pandemic. It has upended life as we know it and has reshaped how we work, learn, shop, travel, and interact.

We are dealing simultaneously with a health crisis and an economic meltdown. Saving lives is killing jobs, as governments make impossible choices between health and wealth. Epidemiologists and economists alike are unable to put hard numbers on the human and financial costs of this rolling calamity. What is clear is that infection rates globally have been rising while the job market has been in free fall.

There is no unanimity of opinion as to how long it will take to curb the spread of the coronavirus, and how the pandemic will end. Predictably, many apocalyptic forecasts have been made about COVID-19. If we ignore the doomsday scenarios, the best case is that we will get it under control in the coming months, and life will largely return to normal. The worst case is that it may keep infecting people for some time, causing outbreaks until there's a vaccine.

In the meantime, the pandemic should act as a wake-up call for humanity. There are serious lessons to be learned for all of us. The ground is shifting beneath our feet, and this will change the social and political landscape. Like the Global Financial Crisis, the coronavirus is an Earth-shattering event which will have far-reaching consequences.

Already, commentators are writing opinion pieces about lessons arising from the pandemic. One such commentator is world-renowned author and historian Professor Yuval Noah Harari. In an article he penned for the London-based international daily newspaper, *Financial Times,* on 20 March titled, "The World After Coronavirus", Harari stated:

> ... the storm will pass, humankind will survive, most of us will still be alive – but we will inhabit a different world. Many short-term emergency measures will become a fixture of life. That is the nature of emergencies. They fast-forward historical processes. Decisions that in normal times could take years of deliberation are passed in a matter of hours. Immature and even dangerous technologies are pressed into service, because the risks of doing nothing are bigger. Entire countries serve as guinea-pigs in large-scale social experiments. What happens when everybody works from home and communicates only at a distance? What happens when entire schools and universities go online? In normal times, governments, businesses and educational boards would never agree to conduct such experiments. But these aren't normal times.

It's said that life is lived forward but evaluated backward. Put another way, in the thick of the moment it's hard to see the forest for the trees, but with the benefit of hindsight things become clearer. Given this, it's too early to draw definitive conclusions about the lasting impact of the COVID-19 saga. While there will undoubtedly be more to come, here are some early lessons.

The first lesson is that the coronavirus will force the return of big government. The pandemic is a stark reminder of the role governments play in our lives and how vital they are in times of crisis. A key duty of any government is to protect the well-being of its citizens, which is why governments have been leading the battle against the coronavirus. Hearing the words "I'm from the government and I'm here to help" is no longer terrifying. The outbreak will strengthen nation states – the need for them has become infectious.

The second lesson concerns the illusion of borders. Global challenges have no national borders, and viruses do not carry passports. No one is geographically immune to a virus as it easily crosses borders. Neither screening nor banning travellers creates an impermeable barrier that absolutely protects a country from importing diseases. Undetected cases slip through – borders cannot be completely sealed and will always be leaky. This is the reality of living in a global village.

The third lesson is that we need to change our self-centred ways. Not enough of us have shown grace under pressure. There has been a lack of camaraderie. Panic has prevailed over common sense. Many have behaved like a marauding swarm of locusts stripping supermarket shelves bare. We needed to be at our selfless best but have been at our selfish worst. The crisis has unmasked who we really are and proved beyond doubt that individual behaviour has a profound impact on society. Many of us have failed the civic-responsibility test.

The fourth lesson concerns the role of the media and the dangers of using fear-inducing language. "Facts, not fear" will stop the virus, said the World Economic Forum. "Words matter", warned the World Health Organization, which urged the media not to use terms like "plague" or "apocalypse" or to describe people with COVID-19 as "spreading the disease". These pleas have fallen on deaf ears. Sensationalist reporting is seen as a "bigger contagion" than the virus itself. The media stands accused of whipping people into a frenzy with irresponsible coverage.

The fifth lesson comes in the form of an almost unspeakable question: Should we sacrifice the economy to save lives? Put another way: Is the cure worse than the disease? Policy-making invariably involves trade-offs, and governments have prioritised mortality risk over economic risk. But containment policies to "flatten the curve" have cost millions of jobs and trillions of dollars, and some see this as too high a price to pay. I believe that governments were correct in not letting the pandemic play out unchecked. However, the policy of "do whatever it takes and whatever it costs" may be challenged as the playbook for future crises.

Undoubtedly, more lessons will reveal themselves as the pandemic unfolds. For example, is it possible to quickly resuscitate an economy following a "controlled hibernation" or is growth stunted for an extended period? Only time will tell the full extent of the damage caused by a microscopic, invisible enemy that has brought us to our knees. But one thing is clear:

**The human species is not invincible.**

POSTING DATE | 3 MAY 2020

## How the coronavirus pandemic will change the world

### READING THE TEA LEAVES

Right now, the degree of uncertainty in the world is immense, which is why thinking about what life will be like after COVID-19 is daunting. Still, that has not stopped futurists from taking out their crystal balls and making predictions about the type of society the pandemic will leave in its wake.

Will we revert to business as usual, or will humanity have a changed worldview? Will the outbreak of an invisible virus redefine globalisation, causing nation-states to seal their borders, or will we better understand that we share a single planet and need each other to survive?

No one, of course, can answer these questions with absolute certainty. However, one way to gain a sense of what might lie ahead is to look at previous crises. Other dark times in history have united people against a grave challenge, and the hope is that this will happen again.

Throughout history, nothing has killed more humans than infectious diseases. Plagues and epidemics have ravaged humanity since the dawn of civilisation. Each global disease outbreak has taught us how to manage its spread as well as providing vital lessons for containing future outbreaks.

Our understanding of the need for social distancing comes from the bubonic plague. King Henry VI of England implemented one of the world's first anti-contagion measures. He banned his subjects from kissing on the cheeks when greeting someone. To this day, Brits favour a firm handshake over a peck.

During this current pandemic, we have gone one step further – handshakes are out and elbow bumps are in. Many argue that handshakes will never return. My hope is that this everyday gesture – which establishes a positive connection between two people – will eventually become commonplace again.

History shows that major upheavals also leave their mark on geopolitics. This happened in the aftermath of World War II when the liberal world order was created. Liberalism is an international (as distinct from national) worldview which opposes isolationism and protectionism.

The liberal vision looks for collective solutions to global problems by working cooperatively with the help of international institutions (such as the WHO) to make the world a better place. Liberalism as a political ideology is linked to globalisation, whereas nationalism is driven by anti-globalist sentiments.

The liberal worldview is not embraced by President Trump and other right-wing politicians. During his election campaign, Trump declared that "Americanism, not globalism, will be our credo". Until a few months ago, it seemed that the resurgence of this nationalist political ideology would define the remainder of the 21st century.

However, the pandemic has forced governments around the world into solidarity and cooperation. It has also demonstrated that a world without deep cross-border engagement is not tenable. The international system will certainly be challenged but will survive, whereas America's go-it-alone policy will be found wanting.

While World War II devastated Europe and Asia, the US emerged in strong economic and military shape, making it the undisputed world leader. Coming out of the COVID-19 pandemic, it is the US which is now being challenged – China wants to become the new hegemon.

China will accelerate its manoeuvring for international leadership, while the US continues to falter (unless Joe Biden wins the November election). COVID-19 has intensified the rivalry between the world's two superpowers, with both nations engaging in mutual recrimination in lieu of collaboration.

In times of great uncertainty, the strong dominate the weak, and China has used the pandemic to cast itself as the global saviour. China has provided many nations, including Australia, with hundreds of thousands of test kits, respirators, and face masks. Ironically, several countries reported faults with the masks, and they were returned.

For over two decades, China has been known as "the world's factory" as it dominates many manufacturing industries, including the production of face masks. If nations do not want to be beholden to China post COVID-19, they must break China's stranglehold on global supply chains.

Depending on one country to provide vital products for industries such as the pharmaceutical sector is a recipe for disaster. About 80 per cent of pharmaceuticals sold in the US are produced in China. This number, according to experts, hides an even greater problem: China is the world's largest and sometimes only global supplier for the active ingredient of some vital medications.

The label "Made in China" will diminish in the coming years. National governments will intervene to force strategic industries to diversify their supply chains to reduce their dependence on any single country. By its very nature, a global economy will always be interconnected and interdependent, but this does not mean that one powerful nation should be able to hold others to ransom – no matter how attractive their price proposition might be.

Another thing that we will encounter when the dust settles on the pandemic is a massive increase in sovereign debt. The world is awash with stimulus packages as nation-states have raced to help people and businesses survive the economic contagion. Collectively, the various fiscal and monetary interventions are estimated to exceed a staggering US$10 trillion, according to the Council on Foreign Relations.

The pandemic is the biggest hit to the global economy since the Great Depression, which is why the world has opened its wallet. But it is citizens who will be forced to pay the bill. The burden of reducing higher net public debt will fall on taxpayers, just as wartime spending did. In many nations, this payback will be via a combination of higher taxes and less government spending.

A final change that we will encounter is the same as that experienced post September 11 – citizens around the world will be required to sacrifice liberties for safety. Just as travellers are now searched before boarding a plane, the price of continued vigilance against new viruses will be some loss of privacy and personal freedoms.

The rise of mass surveillance after 9/11 offers a cautionary tale about the use of technology to keep tabs on people's movements.

During this current crisis, location-tracking apps on mobile phones have been used by China, Singapore, Israel, Hong Kong, Taiwan, and Thailand. These nations have kept a very close eye on people who have been exposed to the virus.

In the fight against COVID-19, civil liberties have been treated as a casualty of war. However, the right to privacy is enshrined in the Universal Declaration of Human Rights. Civil Liberties Australia recently warned that "a health emergency is no excuse for abusing secret powers" and that Australia must not use a crisis "to permanently implant more draconian security measures including excess surveillance".

Please allow me to conclude by underscoring that a number of possible scenarios have been developed by scholars, analysts, columnists, and other commentators to describe what society might look like on the other side of COVID-19. Many are predicting that the pandemic fallout will significantly impact all domains of life and will drive huge shifts in how we live and how governments govern.

I accept that some things will change but reject the assertion of many commentators that the world will be unrecognisable. One assessment which I do embrace is by the influential foreign policy magazine *Foreign Affairs*. In a recent article titled "The Pandemic Will Accelerate History Rather Than Reshape It", the magazine stated that "the world following the pandemic is unlikely to be radically different from the one that preceded it".

Yes, the world feels awfully strange right now, but life on Earth as we know it will return. There will not be an upheaval of everything that we once took for granted; however, lifestyle patterns will experience some changes. My hope is that we will all be part of a more humane society, and that we have all learned at least one lesson:

**You don't know how much you will miss normal life until it's gone.**

POSTING DATE | 17 MAY 2020

## Don't be fooled by self-appointed COVID authorities

### BEWARE OF ARMCHAIR EPIDEMIOLOGISTS

Throughout history, fake experts have suddenly appeared during times of crisis. They emerge from obscurity, stand on their various soapboxes, and proliferate misinformation. Such falsehoods create a climate of fear, which is fuelled by those eager to put in their two cents worth.

Periods of great uncertainty always provide a fertile breeding ground for the spread of mistruths. The current COVID outbreak is no exception and has thrust previously obscure individuals into the pandemic limelight. People claiming to be health experts have popped up everywhere as talking heads in the media.

In response, the World Health Organization (WHO) issued a statement in February warning that humanity is not just fighting a viral pandemic but also an "infodemic". Like the virus, the infodemic has proven to be highly contagious but, unlike the virus, has been transmitted by mainstream and social media.

Public nervousness and the desperate search for cures have made it impossible to completely immunise a gullible public against fabricated stories. In the words of the WHO boss, we are "battling the trolls and conspiracy theorists that push misinformation and undermine the outbreak response".

We should not heed the barrage of half-baked COVID health advice from Twitter, Facebook, or deranged politicians like former President Trump. Yet millions have listened to their quack remedies and pseudo-scientific explanations. While some of these cures seem legitimate, most are patently wrong.

The WHO's mythbusters site pours cold water on a raft of dodgy health tips that allegedly prevent or cure COVID-19. These include eating garlic, drinking bleach, snorting cocaine, rinsing the nose with saline, gargling with salt water, and spraying alcohol or chlorine all over your body.

The Australian Government also has a mythbusting site, and it debunks a number of COVID-19 myths, including that hot temperatures kill the virus, 5G networks spread the virus, drinking water every 15 minutes prevents infection, and hydroxychloroquine is an effective treatment.

Around the world, mass-media coverage of the pandemic has contributed significantly to the COVID-19 infodemic. The mainstream media's penchant for sensationalism has resulted in inaccurate news dissemination, including the reporting of unscientific cures and unverified medicines. As reported in *The Harvard Gazette*:

> At many major news outlets, reporters and editors with no medical or public health training were reassigned to cover the unfolding pandemic and are scrambling to get up to speed with complex scientific terminology, methodologies, and research, and then identify, as well as vet, a roster of credible sources.

The media's failure to correctly identify qualified and trustworthy sources of information about COVID is a case of history repeating itself. From major incidences like terrorist attacks to routine events such as interest rate hikes, the media's modus operandi is to call upon supposed "authorities" to act as instant experts and explain what has happened and why.

But these so-called pundits are often no more than self-proclaimed gurus. Indeed, they typically know little more than the rest of us. Even so, put them in front of a camera, and these publicity seekers can't resist asserting their opinions on subjects in which they have little or no formal training or expertise.

The Y2K computer bug is a classic example. While technology legend Bill Gates saw the millennium bug as a "minor inconvenience", less qualified IT commentators promulgated doomsday scenarios and were aided in their deception by the media, which spun compelling but inaccurate stories.

A naïve public bought in to the outrageous predictions about planes falling from the sky and missiles self-launching. Nonetheless, the bug did not bite, and the New Year passed with nothing more than the expected hangover. Those who foretold of a global computer apocalypse caused unnecessary panic but were never brought to account.

Nothing had changed by the time of the Fukushima power plant disaster in 2011. Yet again, the media wheeled out instant experts who hyperventilated over the very modest amounts of radioactive fallout. While fears about radiation contamination were clearly overblown, they made for dramatic headlines which trumpeted the dangers of nuclear energy.

A report released five years after the disaster by the United Nations Scientific Committee on the Effects of Atomic Radiation (UNSCEAR) found that not one person had died because of the meltdown. Referencing the UNSCEAR Report, a *Forbes* magazine article stated:

> No one will die from Fukushima radiation, there will be no increased cancer rates, the food supply is not contaminated, the ocean nearby is not contaminated, most of the people can move back into their homes, and most of the other nuclear plants in Japan can start up just fine.

Almost three years to the day after Fukushima, the world was gripped by the mysterious disappearance of a Malaysia Airlines Boeing 777. The aircraft vanished without a trace, bringing a gaggle of know-it-alls out of the woodwork. They went into overdrive speculating about what may have happened to the plane.

Many of their theories were not supported by a shred of solid evidence. Nonetheless, their views were given airtime by media outlets. This helped networks maintain rolling coverage of the tragedy and filled the huge gap in reliable information about the plane's fate.

Suggestions from armchair sleuths, aviation experts, and conspiracy theorists were broadcast. Fringe theories flourished and ranged from the sinister (electronic warfare), to the far-fetched (remote island landing), to the insane (abducted by aliens).

Clearly, listening to near-experts is a fool's errand, which is why the media must do a better job of identifying opportunists who simply want 15 minutes of fame. Around the world, television, radio, and print interviews have contributed to new-found notability for charlatans who were not properly vetted prior to being unleashed on an unsuspecting public.

The coronavirus has shown, once again, how easy it is for someone to claim to be a subject-matter expert. And if the "expert" is deemed to be camera-ready, there is always the temptation by the media to forgo a credentials check. Even so, background checking should never be optional, even when working to a tight deadline.

Fact-checking the experience of an "expert" may seem like a tedious extra step to a journalist, a reporter, or a broadcast producer – but it's essential. The media is critical when politicians and CEOs – who also work to tight deadlines – get facts wrong. So, the same standards should apply equally to news outlets.

Please allow me to end with an observation. The media does a great job in holding others to account for their failings and shortcomings and is quick to throw stones. Despite this, the media reacts negatively to feedback about its own performance and is poor at self-examination and reflection.

"Journalists and media professionals automatically take up defensive positions when confronted with criticism," notes Julie Reid, Associate Professor in the Department of Communication Science at the University of South Africa.

In an article published in *The Conversation*, A/Professor Reid acknowledges that, in many countries, political and governmental interference in the editorial independence of news outlets is still prevalent. This causes journalists and media professionals to feel that they are under attack. This, in turn, gives rise to a siege mentality which is reflected in the news media's reluctance to embrace genuine critique or evidence-based scrutiny of its performance. She writes:

> The rantings of a crooked politician who dismisses the news media's reportage as fake news and calls for draconian media regulations to conceal his own corruption is one thing. The critique and criticisms of media analysts, but more especially of ordinary citizens, whose only request

> is that the news media works better for them, is an entirely different matter. And ought to be respected.

I'm an ordinary citizen who merely seeks better accuracy in news reporting. Like all citizens, I have the right to hold the media's feet to the fire over its reporting of the pandemic. On all continents, mainstream media outlets have aided and abetted charlatans in spreading bogus COVID information, and this has circumnavigated the planet in seconds.

Media professionals seeking advice on best practice in responsible journalism during a health crisis would benefit from reading an article by Catriona Bonfiglioli. Ms Bonfiglioli is a senior lecturer in media studies at the University of Technology, Sydney. In a 2020 piece she wrote for *The Journalism Education and Research Association of Australia,* she stated that when journalists report on the coronavirus, it is important that their words:

> ... help people understand best prevention tips, minimise stigmatisation of people with COVID-19, reject fake health news, and resist the allure of "sexy" controversies and contrarians hitching a ride on the news wave by contradicting public health advice or calling for extreme measures.

**Responsible journalism IS possible during times of crisis.**

POSTING DATE | 25 APRIL 2021

## How to make the world a better place

### EDUCATION IS THE KEY

The idea of changing the world can be daunting. With so many problems to tackle, where do you begin? The list of global challenges is long and includes the need to eradicate extreme poverty, improve health outcomes, foster world peace, and build a sustainable planet.

Believe it or not, education can assist in solving these issues and more. Education broadens the mind and helps us see the world afresh, thereby enabling us to make more balanced and insightful judgments. By applying these judgments to societal problems, we can advance the cause of humanity.

You certainly don't need to wave a placard or chain yourself to a tree to make a difference. To quote Nelson Mandela: "Education is the most powerful weapon which you can use to change the world". It provides us with the knowledge to critically examine our response to all life situations.

We all need to take educated action in a range of areas if we are to genuinely improve life on this tiny planet which we call home. This belief accords with the oft-quoted advice of English sociologist and philosopher Herbert Spencer: "The great aim of education is not knowledge, but action".

There is a vast difference between knowing something and acting on it. Understanding alone does not solve problems, which is why awareness must be backed up with specific measures. In the words of Dale Carnegie: "Knowledge isn't power until it is applied".

Periodically, we are exposed to awareness campaigns which are designed to mobilise us to take action on a particular cause or issue. The hope is that once we know that a problem exists (which is the purpose of this post!), we will be motivated to behave in a way that mitigates the issue.

Citizens of all nations are surrounded by problems, many of which are not contained to national borders. Still, it's understandable to see ourselves as inhabitants of a community or a country. Yet, we are also citizens of the world and must learn to broaden our focus to effectively tackle cross-border issues.

All of us need to act like global citizens, as we are all part of one global village. But our knowledge of supranational issues is often superficial, as many of us lack global competency. Even so, we cannot continue to see the world through a narrow, self-absorbed national lens.

The aid and development organisation Oxfam defines a global citizen as "... someone who is aware of and understands the wider world – and their place in it. They take an active role in their community and work with others to make our planet more peaceful, sustainable and fairer".

We live in an interconnected world where our local actions can have global implications. Small acts add up – they initially drive change in a city, then a state, followed by a nation, and ultimately the world. This is how people-power shapes our planet, and it can take many forms.

We can all become agents of positive change by improving our decision-making capabilities. To facilitate this, we must understand the cause-and-effect connections within and between the various roles we undertake in society. Changing our behaviour in the following three critical areas would be a good start.

**1. We need to be better educated as voters to make informed decisions at the ballot box.**

Thomas Jefferson wrote that a well-informed electorate is a prerequisite to democracy. How well-informed and educated were the people who voted for Donald Trump in America? Or those who voted for Jair Bolsonaro in Brazil? Or Rodrigo Duterte in the Philippines, and Viktor Orbán in Hungary?

The harsh reality is that right-wing populist politicians enjoy massive support from uneducated voters. Yet after seeing how unscrupulously and divisively these leaders have behaved, many have come to regret how they cast their vote. Around the world, voters have learned that populists make empty promises.

Populists exploit people's discontent and raise expectations, but cannot deliver solutions. Unrealistic campaign promises are the trademark of populists, and when these pledges are left unfilled, voters feel duped. The electoral gamble of millions of ordinary people has not paid off.

In my post, *Why the problem with democracy is voters,* I stated that:

> Voters have a track record of choosing idiots, authoritarians, and demagogues for elected office. These leaders invariably turn out to be incompetent and dishonest and thrive on emotion-driven discourse. They hoodwink people into supporting them by exploiting voters' credulity and prejudices.

Voting is a choice with consequences. When the electorate gets it wrong, the repercussions can be devastating – not just for an individual nation, but the entire world. Populists shun globalisation and international cooperation, and this poses a threat to world peace and stability. That's why your domestic vote has global implications.

*Educate yourself to make more intelligent political choices.*

**2. We need to be better educated as consumers to make environmentally sustainable purchases.**

Many people understandably jump up and down about humanity's need to take climate change seriously. These same people typically look to governments and businesses to find eco-friendly solutions, when the real power for change is in our collective hands.

We support governments with votes and businesses with dollars, which means that we can choose who governs and where we spend our money. In my post, *How households can create a new model of sustainable capitalism*, I advised that:

> If we don't like what a company is doing, we can stop buying their products and services and force them to change. Consumers drive markets, and sustainable consumer choices can change corporate behaviour. But we all need to take a stand and, for many of us, this will require a lifestyle overhaul, particularly with regard to saying

"no" to unnecessary and/or environmentally unfriendly household items.

It's incumbent on all of us to become responsible consumers. From the clothes we wear to the food we eat and everything in between, our choices matter. We can reduce our ecological footprint by shopping responsibly, buying less, and recycling more. Adopt the mantra: reduce-reuse-recycle.

*Educate yourself to live more sustainably.*

**3. We need to be better educated as media readers, viewers, and listeners to evaluate the credibility of mainstream and citizen journalism.**

We should be able to trust and rely on the news. We look to the media to tell us what is happening in the world as many people don't have the time or skills to sift through vast amounts of information themselves. The media sets the news agenda and political tone, and this informs our decision-making as citizens.

So, the power of the media comes from its ability to influence and shape the perception of the public. In return for this privileged position, people expect journalism to be fair, balanced, and accurate. But like every sector of society, the media has its own prejudices and biases.

In 2018, the Australian edition of *The Guardian* published an article: "Why is populism suddenly all the rage?" The article explained the reasons why "populism is sexy". Instructively, the article identified the role of the media in the rise of populism by acknowledging that:

> Because of dwindling subscription rates, traditional media increasingly focus on topics they expect to sell well, such as scandals and conflict, fuelling the sense of crisis that populists can draw on.

In fairness to the media, I acknowledged in a previous post – *Why media standards have fallen* – the claim made by media outlets that they simply produce (print/broadcast) what consumers want. I further conceded that:

> As a society, we would rather read about the sordid private lives of celebrities than have a serious debate about the

> long-term benefits of public policy. So, just as we get the politicians (and businesses) we deserve, we also get the media we deserve.

Fake news and misinformation are problematic in democratic systems. One way we can combat this is by being aware of the natural human tendency to only seek information that aligns with our personal views. Academics refer to this inbred preference as "confirmation bias", and it impacts the judgments we make.

Online social media platforms – like Facebook, Twitter, and YouTube – run on algorithms which "feed" us information based on our desire to hear only one side of every story – the side which confirms what we already believe. Algorithms capture what we "like", "retweet", and "share" and then send us additional confirmatory content, thereby creating a reinforcing echo chamber.

According to Kristina Lerman, a University of Southern California professor whose research focusses on the structure of modern social networks:

> … echo chambers strengthen polarization and the divisions in our society. It's common to feel uneasy because of the disassociation between the warm blanket of a like-minded social media community and the cold reality of a real-world populated with challenging perspectives.

*Educate yourself to become a savvy news consumer.*

Contributing to the greater good does not require you to develop a vaccine or win a Nobel Prize – you just need to be educated and informed about contemporary issues. Education is the key to better politicians, better companies, better media, and ultimately a better world.

**Education helps us become better versions of ourselves.**

POSTING DATE | 15 AUGUST 2021

## Why we don't recognise our own incompetence

### TOO DUMB TO KNOW IT

Imagine that you are hosting a dinner party for a group of friends. Throughout the meal, one guest is spouting off on a topic that he claims to know well. As those around the table listen to his opinions, it's blindingly clear to everyone that he is grossly ill-informed. Yet, he arrogantly prattles on in the belief that he is the fount of all knowledge.

All humans have blind spots, which is why many of us are oblivious of our own ignorance. We can believe things about our ability that are just not true because – to be blunt – some of us are so dimwitted we don't realise how dense we really are. A good example is Donald Trump, whose confidence and bluster as US president never wavered, despite his woeful grasp of policy matters.

That we are lousy at accurately evaluating ourselves is not a surprise to social psychologists David Dunning and Justin Kruger. Their research shows that people who are capable at a particular task or in a certain topic typically underestimate their ability, while people who are incapable at a particular task or in a certain topic frequently overestimate their ability.

This disconnect is called the Dunning-Kruger effect, and it reveals that while the competent are often plagued with doubt, the incompetent are habitually cocksure of their excellence. Put simply, the Dunning-Kruger effect is the tendency for people to misjudge their abilities, with the skilled putting themselves down and the inept hyping themselves up.

We have long known that fools are blind to their own foolishness. As renowned British naturalist Charles Darwin wrote in 1871 in *The Descent of Man:* "Ignorance more frequently begets confidence than does knowledge: it is those who know little, not those who know much, who so positively assert that this or that problem will never be solved by science".

Another wise man (allegedly Aristotle) said that "the more you know, the more you know you don't know". Smart people are clever enough to know that they don't know everything, so they read and study to fill the gaps in their intelligence. In contrast, asinine people don't read or undertake continuous education because they are clueless to the fact that they have knowledge gaps.

The Dunning-Kruger effect stems from our ignorance of our own ignorance. It is a cognitive bias which causes unskilled individuals to suffer from illusory superiority. One way to avoid falling victim to this phenomenon is to inject a healthy dose of humility into your sense of self-regard. For many people, that is easier said than done.

As English philosopher Bertrand Russell observed: "The whole problem with the world is that fools and fanatics are always so certain of themselves, and wiser people so full of doubts". We have seen both sides of this cognitive pitfall in action during the COVID-19 outbreak.

Highly qualified epidemiologists – and other scientists who have devoted their careers to studying infectious diseases – readily admitted the limits of their knowledge regarding the behaviour of the novel virus. As true experts, they know where their expertise ends. Fortunately, when the pandemic hit, they knew enough to urge the introduction of social-distancing practices and lockdowns.

Still, many people, including political leaders like Trump (USA), Bolsonaro (Brazil), and Modi (India), were dismissive of – and even hostile towards – medical experts and flouted health warnings. Unsurprisingly, coronavirus outbreaks in these countries spiralled out of control due to the incompetence of self-absorbed "Covidiots", as evidenced by their Dunning-Kruger performances.

Around the world, many populist politicians masqueraded as health professionals yet refused to take even basic precautions to keep the public safe. In doing so, they displayed their absolute ignorance of science to the detriment of their citizens. By rejecting COVID-19 countermeasures and downplaying the threat, millions of innocent people died unnecessarily.

Defiant perspectives on COVID have come not just from ignorant people but also lawyers, engineers, accountants, and other professionals. Otherwise astute members of society, including Elon Musk, rejected the assessment of medical experts. Musk – who many consider to be a genius – fell foul of the Dunning-Kruger effect. As pointed out in online magazine *InsideHook*:

> ... Elon Musk is not a medical genius. In this instance, he is no more than yet another unqualified mouthpiece in a growing list of blowhards regarded as armchair epidemiologists.

Similar to the coronavirus pandemic, many citizens and politicians show disdain for the science of climate change in the conceited belief that they know better than the experts. (No wonder disaster movies typically begin with the government ignoring a scientist – a case of art imitating life!) The world is full of climate-change deniers who are blissfully ignorant of their ignorance.

The science has been settled to the highest degree that climate change is primarily due to human activity. Consequently, air and ocean temperatures are rising, arctic ice is melting, ecosystems are shifting, and sea levels are rising. The signs are all around us – the Earth is patently warming, which makes the endless debates questioning the truth of climate science gobsmacking.

While many governments agree with the science, politicians make cosmetic changes and largely adopt a business-as-usual philosophy. Meanwhile, climate activists continue to express their frustration and disbelief, while climate deniers remain dogmatic in their opposition to climate action. Humanity is fiddling while Rome burns.

As psychologist David Forster observed, the Dunning-Kruger effect is:

> ... more noticeable in the denier set because most of them lack scientific or climate science credentials and training and yet they are challenging the collective views of thousands of trained scientists who do have the required training, credentials, knowledge and skills to discuss climate science.

Science-based arguments are rejected by citizens around the world. These same people voted for climate-denying governments in places like America (under Trump) and Brazil. Deniers spend a lot of time on social media eagerly absorbing anything that supports their unscholarly position, even when it's outrageously absurd and completely uncorroborated by evidence.

The political landscape is replete with evidence of the Dunning-Kruger effect. Take Trump's rise to the presidency, which can be largely attributed to ignorance – his popularity was highest among voters without a university degree. As described in a 2016 *POLITICO Magazine* article:

> Their expertise about current affairs is too fractured and full of holes to spot that only 9 percent of Trump's statements are "true" or "mostly" true, according to PolitiFact, whereas 57 percent are "false" or "mostly false" – the remainder being "pants on fire" untruths. Trump himself has memorably declared: "I love the poorly educated."

Over the past decade or so, citizens who elected populist governments have been let down badly. Voters were lied to by politicians like Trump but were not smart enough to know it. In democracies such as Turkey, Hungary, Poland, and the Philippines, citizens unwittingly elected governments which normalised authoritarianism and diminished their democratic rights.

The "right" leaders were not elected as voters lacked the skills to assess the abilities and competencies of others. Votes were cast based on personal feelings or false information, which is why two eminent political scientists believe that the problem with democracy is voters. While many of us rate ourselves highly in political knowledgeability, the harsh reality is that most of us are ignorant as voters.

The Dunning-Kruger effect is real and permeates all aspects of life. It is evident in people's viewpoints on education, vaccination, work, sports, and even investing. In all walks of life, you will find people who think that they are much better and/or knowledgeable than they really are.

Overconfidence is the mother of all psychological biases and has been blamed for the sinking of the Titanic, the explosion of the space shuttle Challenger, the 2008 meltdown of the subprime mortgage market, and the 2010 oil spill in the Gulf of Mexico. Overconfidence accounts for a wide range of poor outcomes – including war.

That a little knowledge can be a dangerous thing has been known by philosophers since Socrates. This perceptive ancient Greek thinker said that "the only true wisdom is knowing you know nothing". As wise as this is, I'll end with the words of Benjamin Franklin, which resonate with me:

**"Being ignorant is not so much a shame, as being unwilling to learn."**

POSTING DATE | 18 JULY 2021

## Are we living in an age of ignorance and stupidity?

### FOOLS ARE EVERYWHERE

Uninformed voters repeatedly elect politicians who are demagogues and incapable of delivering on their promises. Anti-vaxxers fervently oppose immunisation and base their denunciation on fake news and conspiracy theories. Climate-change deniers doggedly undermine scientific experts and cast doubt on well-established findings and conclusions.

The world is fast becoming fact-phobic and is awash in wilful ignorance. A growing number of people are rejecting science and expertise in favour of junk news, with online users an eager audience for gibberish. The line between fact and fiction has shifted and – while questioning is fine – social media echo chambers have turned healthy scepticism into unhealthy paranoia.

The Internet was supposed to spur universal enlightenment; however, it's taking us back to the Dark Ages. We know more but understand less because the social-media algorithms which feed us information are based on our desire to hear only one side of every story. That's the side which confirms what we already believe, and this strengthens the radical polarisations which divide society.

Everything, it seems, is up for debate – even reality itself. During his presidency, Donald Trump made alternative facts a way of life and took the degradation of the truth to new lows. The twice-impeached president peppered his time in office with a barrage of falsehoods and misleading statements and left a legacy of shameless, blatant lies.

Around the world, people viewed Trump's outrageous fabrications with disbelief and disdain – but not his credulous supporters. Over 72 million Americans voted for Trump and swallowed the egregious claims that he made over four tumultuous years. As outlined by Nobel Prize–winning economist Paul Krugman, Trump empowered America's "anti-rational streak".

While Trump is a compulsive liar, his loyalists are compulsive believers, and believers enable liars. Many people have argued that Trump's supporters were insane for embracing his many deceits, with the late Sen. John McCain claiming that Trump "fired up the crazies". Others contend that the effusive admiration for Trump was due to the president's pathological appeal.

This explanation aligns with an arm's length diagnosis of Trump by forensic psychiatrist Bandy Lee. In her book, *Profile of a Nation: Trump's Mind, America's Soul,* Dr Lee helps us understand the Trump presidency from a mental-health perspective.

Dr Lee, who is also president of the World Mental Health Coalition, was interviewed by online magazine *Scientific American* following the release of her book. When asked why people are attracted to Trump, she answered that it was due to two major emotional drives: narcissistic symbiosis and shared psychosis.

> Narcissistic symbiosis refers to the developmental wounds that make the leader-follower relationship magnetically attractive. The leader, hungry for adulation to compensate for an inner lack of self-worth, projects grandiose omnipotence – while the followers, rendered needy by societal stress or developmental injury, yearn for a parental figure. When such wounded individuals are given positions of power, they arouse similar pathology in the population that creates a "lock and key" relationship.

Simply put, the president's mental health affected the mental health of Americans. His narcissism was like a contagion which spread through the population and infected millions of uneducated (some say "stupid") voters. While democracy is supposed to enact the will of the people, many of Trump's followers had no clue what they were doing.

Trump proved that doing or saying unintelligent things is no barrier to political success. That a diabolic charlatan was even elected as the leader of the free world is a damning indictment on the American electorate. Notwithstanding the "shared psychosis" explanation, Trump's mass appeal remains incomprehensible to many, particularly to those of us outside the USA.

It's said that we are living in a post-truth world. The *Oxford Dictionary* defines "post-truth" as "relating to or denoting circumstances in which objective facts are less influential in shaping public opinion than appeals to emotion and personal belief". Post-truth includes forms of public discourse colloquially referred to as "bullshit" and has given rise to the phrase "post-truth politics".

Of course, it's not just in politics that Homo stupiens cannot tell the truth from the untruth. In seemingly all walks of life, the world has become untethered from reality and lost its mind. We are in a battle between logic and emotion – those who think with their head, and those who know with their heart. America, in particular, has descended into Fanstasyland, according to author Kurt Andersen.

Inspired by the unlikely accession of Donald Trump, Andersen published *Fantasyland: How America Went Haywire.* Shortly before the book's release, Andersen penned an article for *The Atlantic* in which he lamented that America had gone "overboard" in "letting the subjective entirely override the objective; thinking and acting as if opinions and feelings are just as true as facts". He went on to say that many Americans inhabit untrue realities as they:

> ... believe that the government and its co-conspirators are hiding all sorts of monstrous and shocking truths from us, concerning assassinations, extraterrestrials, the genesis of AIDS, the 9/11 attacks, the dangers of vaccines, and so much more.

According to Andersen, the great unbalancing and descent into full Fantasyland was the product of two momentous changes – one of which was the onset of the new era of information. Andersen notes that digital technology empowers real-seeming fictions.

> Among the web's 1 billion sites, believers in anything and everything can find thousands of fellow fantasists, with collages of facts and "facts" to support them. Before the internet, crackpots were mostly isolated, and surely had a harder time remaining convinced of their alternate realities. Now their devoutly believed opinions are all over the airwaves and the web, just like actual news. Now all of the fantasies look real.

Many people are know-nothings yet see themselves as know-everythings. This, as I explained in a previous post, is an example of the Dunning-Kruger effect, which reveals the tendency for people to misjudge their abilities. It's a cognitive disconnect which results in the skilled putting themselves down and the inept hyping themselves up.

All humans have blind spots, which is why many of us are oblivious of our own ignorance. We can believe things about our ability and knowledge that are just not true because – to be blunt – some of us are so dimwitted we don't realise how dense we really are. This includes those who argue that the Earth is flat, Elvis is still alive, and the Apollo 11 Moon landing was a hoax.

Humans are naturally drawn to wild conspiracy theories, and these theories are more prevalent in times of crisis. The US elections and COVID-19 both provided fertile ground for alternative takes on reality – with disastrous consequences. Misinformation spurred the insurgent mob which swarmed the US Capitol Building, and insidious false claims have underplayed the severity of the coronavirus pandemic, causing unnecessary deaths.

Far-fetched theories threaten our democracy and safety, yet people latch on to them. Apparently, we are wired to be attuned to plots by the powerful, who we fear are out to exploit us, but we mostly get "false positives" – conspiracies that don't exist. Given this, it's baffling to watch family and friends pass on such theories like they are gospel.

We had a good laugh when Trump suggested injecting bleach to clean out the coronavirus from the lungs, but that doesn't mean it was a joke. What we face is not a laughing matter, as conspiracy theorists are becoming more extreme, more violent, and more globalised. They are trying to disrupt our way of life, which is why their baseless theories have no place in serious conversations.

**We all need a healthy dose of scepticism to make us less susceptible to fake news.**

POSTING DATE | 24 OCTOBER 2021

## How our lives are shaped by the choices we make

### LIFE DOESN'T JUST HAPPEN

Ever since Adam and Eve's original decision to eat fruit from the forbidden tree in the Garden of Eden, humans have made some spectacularly poor choices. History bears witness to these monumental mistakes, including the crew of the Titanic ignoring warnings of icebergs in their path, NASA proceeding with the space shuttle Challenger launch despite known problems with the solid rocket boosters, and engineers filling the Hindenburg with highly flammable hydrogen.

Bad decisions are part of life, though most do not have consequences that weigh as heavily as those just cited. Examples of non-fatal, flawed judgments include the 12 publishers who rejected J.K. Rowling's first *Harry Potter* manuscript, the Decca Records executive who declined to sign the Beatles, and the Yahoo co-founder who turned down a US$44-billion takeover offer from Microsoft.

Hindsight may be 20/20, but risk is an inescapable part of every decision. We never know the outcome of a decision in advance – sometimes our choices turn out to be spot on, while on other occasions our judgments prove to be seriously flawed. In the words of the late French philosopher Albert Camus, "life is the sum of all our choices". History, by extrapolation, equals the accumulated choices of all humankind.

Our lives are defined by the series of choices we make every single day. They play out over a lifetime, and ultimately determine our destiny. Our choices not only change our lives but the lives of others. We are not alone in our choices as we are part of a bigger picture – there is a chain of events associated with every decision we make. Thus, an individual deciding to buy environmentally friendly products can help change the world and make it a better place for everyone.

Some of the life-changing decisions that we make include where to live, how many children to have, and what career to follow. More mundane and routine choices include what to wear and what to watch on Netflix. One of the paradoxes of life is that our bigger decisions are often less calculated than our smaller ones. We can agonise for weeks over what new car to buy but rapidly end a long-term relationship with little thought or deliberation.

Sometimes a snap judgment or instinctive choice is appropriate. Your emotions, though, can easily cloud your judgment, which is why most experts agree that the best decisions are made when there is a balance between logic and emotions. The invisible tug-o-war between the head and the heart is not a bad thing, as you are more likely to carefully weigh the pros and cons of each decision before choosing an alternative.

When your emotions are running high, your logic will be low, which can lead to irrational decisions. To illustrate, anger makes you vulnerable to high-risk, low-payoff choices such as the rash decisions made during a bitter divorce. Happiness, on the other hand, makes you confident and optimistic about the future but can cause you to overestimate your chances of success, such as believing that your winning streak at the casino will continue indefinitely (a.k.a. gambler's fallacy).

Knowing how to make good decisions is one of the most important skills we can possess. Many people look back at some of the terrible decisions they made and ask themselves: "What was I thinking?" We make endless decisions, so we are bound to regret some of them. A Cornell University study estimated that the average adult makes thousands of remotely conscious decisions every day.

Each decision you make is a trade-off as everything you say, do, or pursue has a cost and a benefit. In the language of economists, this trade-off is called an "opportunity cost". The term "opportunity cost" is defined as "the cost of an alternative that must be forgone in order to pursue a certain action". Put simply, it's what a person sacrifices when they choose one option over another. An example will help here.

Let's say that you have $100 in your purse, and you can spend it on a pair of jeans or a meal. You choose to buy the denim jeans, so the opportunity cost is the restaurant meal you cannot afford.

For everything you choose to do, there's something else you won't be able to do. Every day as consumers, we are forced to make such choices due to "scarcity". Scarcity and opportunity cost are two interlinking economic concepts.

Economists view the world through the lens of scarcity. Indeed, without scarcity, the science of economics would not exist. Scarcity arises because, as a society, we have unlimited wants but limited resources. We all know that you can't have everything you want – we have to choose and make trade-offs. Economics examines how individuals, businesses, and governments deal with the limitations imposed by scarcity.

Broadly speaking, economics is the study of human behaviour as it relates to money. When it comes to financial decisions, economists erroneously claim that humans are rational and unemotional decision-makers. Psychologists, on the other hand, correctly contend that economists' models bear little relationship to actual human behaviour. The harsh reality is that humans do not obey the efficient, orderly principles espoused by free-market thinkers.

The Global Financial Crisis (GFC) confirmed that we are far too emotive for rational economic models to accurately predict our conduct. Many people in the US bought houses at grossly inflated prices and expected their value to keep rising. In the process, borrowers saddled themselves with loans that they could not afford, which led to the subprime mortgage meltdown and ultimately the catastrophic GFC.

This "irrational exuberance" was not confined to the housing sector. Borrowers, bankers, and brokers were united in the delusional belief that house prices never go south. Post-GFC, many people turned to behavioural economics to understand what happened. Behavioural economics combines psychology and economics to explain how people really make decisions when they spend, invest, save, and borrow.

Unsurprisingly, few people reach the level of expertise necessary to rightfully claim that they are expert decision-makers. The development of genuine expertise in any field requires years of struggle and sacrifice. Still, you can be a good decision-maker if you choose actions that produce the best outcome for yourself and others. The trick is to make each decision with an open mind and be aware of your unconscious biases.

Cognitive biases distort thinking, influence beliefs, and sway the decisions we make every day, yet most people are unaware of them. Over the course of our lives, we all develop cognitive biases. Just watch the daily news, listen to talkback radio, or scroll through social-media posts to witness biases in action as people argue over politics, climate change, and other hot topics. Everyone, of course, claims that their position is the right one.

Differences of opinion occur because we all have our own perspectives based on our preconceptions, past experiences, and the information we draw on in forming judgments. When it comes to gathering information, many of us are guilty of confirmation bias – readily embracing information and conclusions which align with our views and largely ignoring anything which contradicts our beliefs.

The next time that you make a bad decision, just remember that it could have been worse. Imagine being the individual responsible for allowing the famous Trojan Horse to be brought inside the City of Troy, not realising it was full of Greek soldiers. And how would you have felt standing in Napoleon's shoes after he invaded Russia, suffered a catastrophic defeat, and returned home with just a fraction of his once-grand army?

You can minimise regrettable decisions by learning from your mistakes – history does not have to repeat itself. Humans have a tendency, however, of replicating the same blunders over and over (poor diets, dysfunctional relationships, impulsive buying, etc.), causing us to relive our errors. If you want a different result, you have to do something different – make better decisions!

**We are what we choose to be.**

POSTING DATE | 8 MAY 2022

## Has the world gone mad?

### THINGS DON'T MAKE SENSE

Maybe it's due to the persistent drumbeat of bad news. Or perhaps social media has messed up our brains. It could even be the fault of the pandemic which has pushed some of us over the edge. Whatever the cause, the world seems to have gone a bit bonkers. We have lost our collective minds and our ability to make intelligent judgments.

Humans, of course, have always been notorious for making irrational decisions. Today, however, poor choices have become a mental contagion which has infected normally sane people and fuelled a growing disconnect between fact and fiction. An increasing number of us embrace conspiracy theories, reject scientific consensus, elect populist leaders, and promote wacky cures.

Even the smartest among us have moments when common sense escapes them; but things have got out of hand. During these uncommon times, illogical thinking has come to the fore in the face of uncertainty. Uncertainty causes our brains to overact, and many of us have capitulated to irrational fear. Fear, in turn, influences our risk assessments by overestimating threats.

Fear can become problematic when it's disproportionate to the actual risk faced, such as with COVID-19 vaccines. Despite irrefutable scientific evidence to the contrary, millions have embraced the misleading claims and outright lies about the safety of COVID inoculations. This misinformation has largely been spread on social-media platforms including Facebook, Instagram, and Twitter.

Unquestionably, vaccinations are one of the greatest achievements of modern medicine and have turned many childhood diseases into distant memories. Like all vaccines, COVID shots were proven to be safe and effective through rigorous testing processes. Even so, anti-vaxxers have been unwilling to roll up their sleeves for a jab – because they are fearful.

Vaccine deniers have been spooked by the spurious and unsupported claims about COVID vaccines, including that they contain microchips for government tracking, include metals and other problematic ingredients, alter your DNA and stunt fertility, and have caused widespread death and disease. It's even claimed that the pandemic is a ruse by big pharmaceutical companies to profiteer off a vaccine.

While these conspiracy theories might seem harmless, they demonstrate a detachment from verifiable reality that can cause someone to believe almost anything. To paraphrase a sub-headline in *The New York Times,* the real horror of anti-vaxxers is that their behaviour isn't just a public-health crisis – it's a public-sanity one.

Another group that clings to beliefs which are at odds with conventional scientific thought is climate-change sceptics. These sceptics hold a range of views, from outright denial (it's a hoax) to interpretive denial (it's not a threat). This latter form of denial causes people to reframe climate change as natural and climate action as unwarranted. Thus, they do not contest the facts but interpret them in ways that distort their importance.

Humans instinctively push back against or completely reject facts that are contrary to their beliefs, and this cognitive bias (the backfire effect) impacts how new information is processed. On the other hand, humans look for evidence which supports what they already believe to be true, and this causes them to give credence to data which confirms that their view is right (confirmation bias).

These two cognitive biases work in tandem and help explain why climate deniers (a) ignore the hundreds of studies which show that humans are responsible for climate change and (b) latch on to the one study that they can find which casts doubt on human culpability arising from anthropogenic emissions of greenhouse gases.

Many believe that the catastrophic framing of climate change is self-defeating as it alienates people. I agree that doomsday scenarios don't inspire action among deniers and also accept that merely talking about evidence or data does not change the mind of a sceptic.

So, I was drawn to a story in *The New York Times* which is void of scare tactics. The feature story, "The Science of Climate Change Explained: Facts, Evidence and Proof", is written by a journalist with a PhD in geology. She calmly and pragmatically explains what will happen if we fail to address climate change.

Beyond vaccines and climate change, large swaths of humanity still snub science when it comes to Darwin's theory of evolution. The beginning of the Earth, along with the birth of humans, remains a contentious issue between creationists and evolutionists. These protagonists continue to debate whether life on Earth was created in the blink of an eye, or whether it evolved over millions of years.

Creationists insist that everything in nature was created by a deity who formed all life over a period of six days, as described in the Book of Genesis. Evolutionists reject this assertion by biblical literalists, citing scientific evidence showing that the Earth is about 4.5 billion years old, and that all life evolved from primitive, single-cell organisms.

To any evolutionary biologist, creationism is ludicrous. But to millions of creationists, particularly those in America's Bible Belt, God remains the supernatural "intelligent designer" of the universe. The clashes between creationists and biologists can be explained, as discussed in one blog, through the lens of confirmation bias.

> The latter [biologists] use scientific evidence and experimentation to reveal the process of biological evolution over millions of years. The former [creationists] see the Bible as being true in the literal sense and think the world is only a few thousand years old. Creationists are skilled at mitigating the cognitive dissonance caused by factual evidence that disproves their ideas. Many consider the non-empirical "evidence" for their beliefs (such as spiritual experiences and the existence of scripture) to be of greater value than the empirical evidence for evolution.

Debating creationists is a slippery slope, as they do not adhere to facts or logic. What is scientific fact for evolutionists is irreverent blasphemy for creationists. As creationism argues that faith should take precedence over science, there is little hope for enlightenment – the scientific worldview is unlikely to ever supplant a creationist one. Well may we say, "Let there be light"!

Belief in ideas that have clearly been disproven by science remains widespread around the world. Rejecting scientific consensus has given rise to scientific denialism (dubbed the anti-enlightenment movement), and it has moved from the fringes to the centre of public discourse. An article in the international science journal, *Nature*, put it this way:

> Science deniers – whether on vaccines, evolution or climate – all draw on the same flawed reasoning techniques: cherry-picking evidence, relying on conspiracy theories and fake experts, engaging in illogical reasoning and insisting that science must be perfect.

We view our ancestors as being blinkered by myth and superstition yet see ourselves as reasoned and enlightened. However, for all our advancement as a species, humans still behave irrationally. You just have to witness the global rise of a new political culture based on emotion and fear, in lieu of fact and policy, to know that something is wrong.

Perhaps there is no better example of this political irrationality than the election of Donald Trump, which left millions of people around the world perplexed. His campaign – described in one critique as "a toxic mix of exaggerations, lies, fearmongering, xenophobia and sex scandal" – succeeded in elevating an unsuitable and unpopular nominee to the office of president.

Irrationality has defined much of human life and history and will continue to do so. We make irrational decisions with regular monotony, such as stripping supermarket shelves bare of toilet paper during a pandemic. As I explored in a recent post, *How our lives are shaped by the choices we make,* our reasoning processes are imperfect, and this leads to poor choices.

**To suggest that humans are rational is an irrational idea.**

POSTING DATE | 5 JUNE 2022

## Do as I say, not as I do

### THE HYPOCRITE IN ALL OF US

How many of us practice what we preach? While it's easy doling out gratuitous advice to others, living by the principles and values we espouse is another matter. The hard truth is that many of us display glaring contradictions in our behaviour, adopting one pose in public and another persona in private.

In all domains of life, people put on false fronts. Examples of double standards include pious politicians promoting family values while secretly having an affair to two-faced parents telling their children not to smoke while doing so themselves. Inconsistencies between what we say and do abound, as we often fail to meet our own moral code.

While most humans can be accused of duplicity, higher standards are expected of those who claim the moral high ground. Priests and other religious figures implore us to love our neighbour, yet some have committed unspeakable transgressions against children. Such unvirtuous behaviour is repugnant and has exposed the heinous moral hypocrisy of religious institutions.

Just as churches need to put their own houses in order before damning others, so do we. Everyone is prone to hypocrisy at one point or another in their life. Humans are not cold, logical robots but fallible emotive beings, which is why we suffer from a misalignment between words and deeds, thereby making hypocrisy unavoidable.

High-status people are some of the worst hypocrites in society. These individuals are frequently admired by others and often occupy leadership roles. Yet, as author Peter Schweizer outlined in his 2006 book, *Do As I Say (Not As I Do): Profiles in Liberal Hypocrisy,* famous people are not holier-than-thou and also fall short in living their beliefs.

Schweizer conducted an investigation into the private lives of a handful of prominent US citizens and found a long list of blatant contradictions. To quote the book's promotional copy:

> Michael Moore ... claims to have no stock portfolio, yet he owns shares in Halliburton, Boeing, and Honeywell

> and does his postproduction film work in Canada to avoid paying union wages in the United States. Noam Chomsky opposes the very concept of private property and calls the Pentagon "the worst institution in human history," yet he and his wife have made millions of dollars in contract work for the Department of Defense and own two luxurious homes. Barbra Streisand prides herself as an environmental activist, yet she owns shares in a notorious strip-mining company. Hillary Clinton supports the right of thirteen-year-old girls to have abortions without parental consent, yet she forbade thirteen-year-old Chelsea to pierce her ears and enrolled her in a school that would not distribute condoms to minors.

The business world is similarly guilty of hypocrisy, with companies displaying a lack of coherence between talk and action. Consumer activists have long argued that most business models prioritise profits over people, despite the assertion by firms to the contrary. The classic example is the rag trade, where global clothing brands have been complicit in the exploitation of sweatshop workers.

Sweatshops are as old as the industrial age and were started by heartless businessmen. Still, modern-day consumers must be careful of being too sanctimonious about the plight of garment workers because they (as shoppers) have knowingly bought high-street brands supplied by factories which mistreat their workers.

One of the reasons that high-street clothing has been getting cheaper and cheaper for decades is that sweatshop workers do not receive a living wage. The suffering of these unknown workers on the other side of the world is easy for us as consumers to ignore, particularly as we have become accustomed to reaping the benefits of lower production costs.

Something else that we have become accustomed to is politics in sport, and this was on full display during the Beijing Winter Olympics. The overwhelming message of the opening ceremony was about peace and togetherness. A giant LED snowflake sculpture was used to symbolise all people coming together and living in harmony.

Yet human rights organisations branded the 2022 Olympics as "the genocide games" and accused China of holding a million Uyghurs (a largely Muslim ethnic group) against their will in re-education centres. In response, many nations – including the US, Britain, Canada, and Australia – staged a diplomatic boycott of the games in protest at China's repressive policies toward the Uyghur minority group native to Xinjiang.

Many saw the International Olympic Committee's decision to award China the games as political hypocrisy. Having an alleged human-rights abuser as host was called out as clashing with one of the fundamental principles contained in the Olympic Charter – a commitment to "the preservation of human dignity".

Another international body which recently came in for criticism is the United Nations entity that supports and coordinates action on climate change. For nearly three decades, the UN has brought together almost every nation on Earth for global climate summits called Conferences of the Parties (COPs). The $26^{th}$ annual summit – COP26 – took place in Glasgow last November.

As leaders from around the world made promises to tackle an existential threat to humanity, climate-change activists and experts railed against the hypocrisy that accompanied it. As outlined in a University of Southern California Annenberg Media report:

> ... a total of 400 private jets flew down to Glasgow from all over the world, carrying more than 100 leaders. This emitted 13,000 tonnes of carbon dioxide into the atmosphere. For comparison, the average person's carbon footprint globally is 7 tonnes per year and the carbon footprint of an average American is 21 tonnes per year. The leaders have been called out by critics as "eco-hypocrites" for emitting a huge amount of $CO_2$ while gathering for an event organized to curb greenhouse gas emissions.

Climate-change hypocrisy also extends to members of the British royal family. On numerous occasions over recent years, Prince Harry and Meghan Markle have been criticised for flying around the world in private jets while lecturing the world about climate change. A former UK government minister told *Newsweek*:

> It's completely hypocritical for Prince Harry or other members of the royal family to lecture people about climate change when they're emitting more carbon than almost everyone else on the planet. People using private jets are in the top one percent of carbon emitters in the world.

Many citizens understandably jump up and down about humanity's need to take climate change seriously. These same people typically look to governments and businesses to find eco-friendly solutions, when the real power for change is in our collective hands. We support governments with votes and businesses with dollars, which means that we can choose who governs and where we spend our money. We need to put our votes and our money where our mouths are!

"Hypocrisy is the natural state of the human mind", according to Robert Kurzban, author of *Why Everyone (Else) Is a Hypocrite.* Kurzban argues that our behavioural inconsistencies are caused by the mind's design, which consists of many specialised modules. These modules don't always work together seamlessly, resulting in contradictory beliefs and violations of our supposed moral principles.

Consequently, hypocrisy is everywhere and can manifest itself in countless ways. To pretend that we can live our lives without hypocrisy and contradiction is itself a form of deception. We must, therefore, exercise care before angrily lambasting others for their deeds, while doing the same ourselves. People who live in glass houses should not throw stones.

**We're all hypocrites; it's just a matter of scale.**

POSTING DATE | 22 MAY 2022

## How to change someone's mind

### FACTS ALONE ARE NOT ENOUGH

You are about to debate an important issue with a colleague with whom you have a differing perspective. You have developed a strong case to support your viewpoint, and it's backed up by hard, irrefutable data. Even though you're confident that your argument is watertight, you fail miserably to sway your opponent to your way of thinking.

You have just learned an invaluable lesson – you can't change a person's beliefs with facts and figures alone. How you present your case is just as important. Science has proven that evidence and logic don't win arguments. The ability to persuade others to change their minds requires a mix of communication skills, empathy, and respect.

Our opinions are often based on emotion. Humans have an innate tendency to hold on to pre-existing beliefs and convictions as our brains are wired to ensure the integrity of our worldview. Consequently, we seek out information that confirms what we already know (confirmation bias) and dismiss facts that are contrary to our core beliefs (the backfire effect).

So, berating another because they don't like our ideas, recommendations, or proposals is a recipe for disaster. If you want someone to see eye-to-eye with you, then – in the words of one writer – you need to remember that:

> When persuading someone to change their mind on a major topic, what's being said isn't always quite as important as how it's said. If a person feels attacked or disrespected or condescended to, they'll turn off their brain and block out the most rational, correct arguments on principle alone. Homo sapiens are odd, emotional creatures, more amenable to a convincing pitch than poorly presented rightness. It's why we vote for the guy we'd gladly have as a drinking buddy over the somewhat alienating candidates with a firmer grasp on the issues.

Productive exchanges between people are more likely to occur when there's mutual respect. Discussions, therefore, need to be held in an environment where no one is disparaged or shamed, and both sides are open to changing their minds. In short, there must be a goal shift from winning to understanding, and this requires empathy.

The late Stephen Covey wrote about the importance of empathy in his bestselling book, *The 7 Habits of Highly Effective People.* Habit 5 – seek first to understand, then to be understood – encourages us to alter the way we listen to others. To change someone's mind, you need to address their emotional attachment to what they believe, and this, Dr Covey argued, requires empathic listening.

According to Covey, people "listen with the intent to reply, not to understand". Most of us are so focussed on our own agenda that we don't hear the other person as we talk at or over them. In contrast, empathic listening helps us get inside another person's frame of reference, with the intent of truly understanding how they see the world. Covey writes:

> When another person speaks, we're usually "listening" at one of four levels. We may be *ignoring* another person, not really listening at all. We may practice *pretending.* "Yeah. Uh-huh. Right." We may practice *selective listening,* hearing only certain parts of the conversation. ... Or we may even practice *attentive listening,* paying attention and focusing energy on the words that are being said. But very few of us ever practice the fifth level, the highest form of listening, *empathic listening.*

We spend years learning to read, write, and speak but receive scant training in the art of listening. Just think of all the times that you have debated or argued with someone. Did preaching to them about right and wrong change their mind? Did acting like a "logic bully" cause them to see the light? Did accusing them of being closed-minded or unreasonable help your cause?

I'll bet that in each of these circumstances, you faced the same outcome – a stalemate. Why? Because we all want to be understood, valued, and affirmed, and this requires empathic listening. So, to change someone's mind, we must stop talking and start listening. Listening is the key pathway to changing someone's thinking, and until your conversation partner feels heard, it's almost impossible to change their mind.

Empathic listening is your secret weapon to influencing others and ensuring that you don't butt heads. A columnist for the online publishing platform, *Medium,* put it this way:

> When you come in guns blazing with all of your clear evidence, the other person will lock up. They'll feel bullied and incapable of hearing you out. The best arguers are proven to use a small number of key points. They don't rapid-fire or clap in the person's face while they talk. They ask questions. They know changing someone's mind is damn-near impossible. By asking questions, that person will change their own mind.
>
> Great arguers stay calm, kind, and empathetic – no matter how ignorant or stupid their target is. They often open by acknowledging the things they agree on. Quite often, they compliment their opponent in the first minute. Opening soft is disarming. It's unexpected. It highlights a desire for consensus rather than war and condescension.

Communications consultant and author Lauren Scheiffer urges us to "get to know the person you are trying to influence. What matters to them? What brings them joy? What makes them angry? Understanding even a little bit about them helps you walk in their shoes with empathy". You can then frame your message around the values of the other person, not your own.

In combination with empathic listening, another communication tool that you should consciously utilise is body language. Your non-verbal behaviours – facial expressions, gestures, posture, and tone of voice – send very clear messages which can be deciphered easily. If you roll your eyes or stamp your feet, for example, it's blindingly clear that you're not happy.

Your actions and mannerisms can speak louder than words, so remember that a genuine smile or tilt of the head will aid effective communication. Of course, it's impossible to read body language and gauge sentiment if you are not communicating face-to-face.

So, don't try to resolve important matters via emails or messaging apps.

In my recent post, *Has the world gone mad?*, I mentioned that science deniers – whether on vaccines, climate, or evolution – cherry-pick evidence and draw on flawed reasoning techniques. Still, we should not give up on them even though their detachment from verifiable reality is incomprehensible to science believers.

According to Lee McIntyre, a research fellow at Boston University, the only possible way to change the mind of science deniers is to talk to them calmly and respectfully. In his book, *How to Talk to a Science Denier*, McIntyre acknowledges that the truth is under assault, with feelings outweighing evidence.

Even so, he believes that for most science deniers, change is possible, and that if we don't try, things will only get worse. McIntyre states:

> Science denial is not just about doubt, it's about distrust. The way you overcome distrust is not through sharing accurate information, it's through conversation, face to face, in which you're calm and patient and show respect and listen. Having the right attitude is the only thing that gives hope of success.

The world is undeniably polarised, and our sense of shared reality is under attack. Denialism is dangerous and unfathomable, but one thing is clear:

**"The ability to hear is a gift. The willingness to listen is a choice."** – Mike Greene author of *60 Second Time Out*.

POSTING DATE | 19 JUNE 2022

## Should you always follow the orders of a superior?

### THE PERILS OF OBEDIENCE

It remains the most heinous crime in modern history. The Nazi genocide of six million European Jews during World War II was unsparingly barbaric and unfathomably evil. The state-sponsored mass murders were not carried out by Hitler himself, but by his trusted lieutenants. One of these henchmen was the notorious Adolf Eichmann.

Eichmann was an SS Lieutenant Colonel and a key figure in the "Final Solution" – the Nazi plan to systematically eradicate the Jews of Europe from the human race. Eichmann was in charge of identifying, assembling, and transporting Jews to extermination camps in German-occupied Poland, including Auschwitz. As the architect of the Holocaust, Eichmann was effectively the chief executioner.

At the Nuremberg war-crimes trials (following World War II), he was charged with managing the mass deportation of Jews to killing centres. Eichmann's defence – and that of other accused – was based on obedience. Eichmann claimed that he was just following orders from his Third Reich superiors. He portrayed himself as an unwilling accomplice, arguing that he was "forced to serve as a mere instrument" of the Nazi war machine.

In attempting to shift responsibility for the deaths of millions of Jews, Eichmann's "obedience defence" helped spark the interest of Stanley Milgram, a Yale University psychologist, in the topic of obedience. In July 1961, at the same time that Eichmann was on trial, Milgram began a series of experiments focussing on the conflict between obedience to authority and personal conscience.

The fundamental aim of Milgram's studies of obedience was to discover whether a person could be coerced into behaving heinously, like Eichmann. Specifically, Milgram tested whether "ordinary" folk would inflict harm on another person after following orders from an authority figure. Milgram dismayed the world when he revealed how easy it was to turn everyday people into torturers.

The volunteer participants recruited to the experiment were told that they were part of a study to investigate the effects of punishment on memory and learning ability. In reality, Milgram wanted to test how far his subjects (acting as "teachers") would go in punishing other subjects (acting as "learners") by administering potentially lethal electric shocks each time the learners made a mistake on a quiz.

The teachers were instructed by a man in a white lab coat (the "experimenter" authority figure) to deliver a shock of increasing intensity to the learners after each incorrect answer. Unbeknown to the teachers, the learners were in fact undercover actors. The actors initially took the shocks silently but then screamed after each jolt even though the shocks were not real – Milgram had built a fake shock machine. Regardless, the teachers believed the shocks to be real.

Milgram proved that ordinary people could be induced to abandon their moral instincts by a malevolent authority. A high proportion of the teachers delivered electric shocks – they felt disconnected from their actions when complying with orders. The shocking conclusion (pun intended!) from the Milgram experiment was that people obeying commands feel less responsible for their actions even though they are the ones committing the act.

Today, the Milgram experiment is criticised on both ethical and scientific grounds. Still, many psychologists argue that even with moral lapses and methodological holes, the basic finding of Milgram's work still holds up. Indeed, it has been used to explain atrocities from the Holocaust to the Vietnam War's My Lai massacre to the abuse of prisoners at Abu Ghraib.

In August 1971, social psychologist Philip Zimbardo expanded upon Milgram's research into the psychology of obedience. Zimbardo, a former classmate of Milgram, wanted to investigate further the impact of situational variables on human behaviour by using a two-week simulation of the rigid and uneven power structure in prison environments.

Zimbardo set up a mock prison in the basement of the Stanford University psychology department. He assigned his participants to play the roles of either "inmates" or "guards", with Zimbardo himself acting as the "prison warden". The behaviour of all involved was so extreme that the study had to be discontinued after a mere six days.

Soon after the experiment began, the guards began utilising authoritarian techniques to gain the obedience of inmates whom they humiliated and psychologically abused. The powerless prisoners, in turn, became submissive and accepted the abuse with little protest.

Like Milgram's obedience experiment, Zimbardo's Stanford Prison Experiment has become infamous and controversial for breaking ethical guidelines relating to the treatment of volunteers. Even so, the experiment demonstrated the power of roles, and the way ordinary people can turn cruel under the wrong circumstances.

Many, if not all, of the greatest human atrocities have been described as "crimes of obedience", according to scholars Herbert C. Kelman and V. Lee Hamilton in their 1990 book, *Crimes of Obedience*. The authors' initial impetus for researching and writing the book was provided by the trial of Lieutenant William Calley for crimes committed at the My Lai massacre, one of the most infamous atrocities of the Vietnam War.

During his court-martial, Calley used the Nuremberg defence – a "good soldier" simply "following orders" – to justify his premeditated murder of 22 villagers (infants, children, women, and old men) and the assault of a child of about two years of age. All the killings and the assault took place on 16 March, 1968. Calley's plea was that he dutifully followed his captain's order to kill everyone in My Lai.

Many Americans saw Calley as a scapegoat in the chain of command, and during his trial he received more than 10,000 letters of support. Following his conviction, the White House was inundated with mail objecting to the verdict. Calley was sentenced to life in prison, but after just three years of lax house arrest on military bases, he was released on parole in 1974 following the intervention of President Richard Nixon, who reduced his sentence.

Like the volunteers in the experiments conducted by Milgram and Zimbardo, Calley was a good and decent man. A *TIME* magazine reporter who got to know Calley said of him:

> There was nothing about Rusty Calley, as he was called, that would make you say that he was an explosion waiting to happen. He didn't have killer instincts. He didn't love guns. None of that was the case. He was a young guy from South Florida who loved being around people and going to parties. He was fun to be around.

It's clear that people can succumb to the demands of authority however immoral the consequences. Indeed, people have a propensity to obey the most abhorrent of orders – and not just on the battlefield. Obedience to authority is ingrained in all of us from an early age. Throughout our lives, we encounter authority figures to whom we are answerable, and this plays out in key relationships, such as between parent and child, teacher and student, boss and employee, priest and minor, and so on.

Humans have a strong predisposition to obey authority, and this is driven by a tendency to please authority figures. But when legitimate authority is abused, blind obedience to inappropriate orders can lead to destructive outcomes. Our challenge is to stand up against arbitrary or unjust authority and not allow another person to define for us what is right or wrong.

We all have a moral compass which guides our decision-making, and this can help us resist the urge to comply with commands that are at odds with our value system. As stated by the American Psychological Association:

> Acquiescence to the commands of an authority that are only mildly objectionable is often, as in Milgram's experiments, the beginning of a step-by-step, escalating process of entrapment. The farther one moves along the continuum of increasingly destructive acts, the harder it is to extract oneself from the commanding authority's grip, because to do so is to confront the fact that the earlier acts of compliance were wrong.

In the business world, employees can sometimes face unethical demands from employers. Some bosses fail to provide appropriate moral leadership by encouraging unethical practices in the workplace in the interests of, say, improving the bottom line. With regard to corporate scandals, some white-collar criminals trace their downfall to an excessive obedience to authority.

It's ironic that some of the greatest crimes in history have been committed by those who followed the rules, not by those who broke them. Blindly following orders can be a recipe for disaster, particularly when they conflict with common decency. While a civilised society needs rules, regulations, and policies, they should not be inviolable. In all walks of life, people must be allowed to use common sense and good judgment.

**We must think for ourselves and resist malevolent orders.**

POSTING DATE | 3 JULY 2022

## Why we need slow journalism in a fast world

NEWS DELIVERED DIFFERENTLY

There's always a lot going on in the world, which is why we are bombarded with news updates 24/7. As media readers, viewers, and listeners, we want to be informed about events and threats as soon as possible. Consequently, speed is a central part of contemporary journalism and has given rise to "fast journalism" and the thirst to be first with the latest news. But speed has morphed into a disease which has impacted the quality of journalism.

Accuracy is fundamental to good journalism, yet increasingly, it's being sacrificed for expediency. This particularly applies to early reports of breaking news with unfolding minute-by-minute developments. To help media networks maintain rolling coverage in times of crisis, talking heads masquerading as experts are wheeled out, and they invariably get essential facts wrong. One man's expert is another man's fool!

Flimsy or unsubstantiated reporting used as a basis for content runs counter to the long-held journalistic notions of truth-seeking and serving the public interest. News is meant to be a public good; however, as news cycles move ever faster in our digital age, the pressure to release stories quicker often results in reporters publishing only basic information with little in-depth analysis.

In all walks of life, slow and right beats fast and wrong, and the same holds true for journalism and news reporting. There is a growing slow news movement which operates outside the 24/7 news trap. Proponents of slow journalism take the time to get things right and turn out quality journalism, which is characterised by accuracy, depth, context, analysis, and expert opinion.

*Delayed Gratification* is the name of the world's first slow journalism magazine. It promotes itself as "a quarterly publication which revisits the events of the last three months to offer in-depth, independent journalism in an increasingly frantic world". The magazine swims against the tide in taking a stand against kneejerk reporting by providing slower but better news.

Commensurate with its tagline, "Last to breaking news", *Delayed Gratification* employs the benefit of hindsight to report on events *after* the dust has settled and the news agenda has moved on. This enables the magazine to get to the heart of a story by soberly reflecting on what's happened and then presenting a long-form story in its proper context.

Another slow news organisation is Tortoise Media. It was launched in 2019 by British journalist and former Director of BBC News, James Harding. He believes that "too many newsrooms chase the news but miss the story" and that we need to "slow down and wise up". The Tortoise website states:

> We don't do breaking news, but what's driving the news. We don't cover every story, but reveal a few. We take the time to see the fuller picture, to make sense of the forces shaping our future, to investigate what's unseen.

Someone else who believes that journalism needs reinvention is US journalism scholar Professor Jennifer Rauch. In her book, *Slow Media: Why "Slow" Is Satisfying, Sustainable, and Smart,* she makes the case for rethinking the way media is produced and consumed. Rauch is a fan of slow journalism as it requires reporters to spend weeks analysing the accuracy and perspectives of initial reports *before* publishing their own reports.

In an interview following the release of her book, Rauch stated that many journalists aren't getting to do the kind of in-depth, thoughtful, accurate reporting that drew them to the profession in the first place. She went on to opine that:

> Much news coverage is incomplete at best, inaccurate or misleading at worst. Too many news stories are dependent on press releases or official sources. You hear a lot about people getting news fatigue and avoiding the news because it makes them feel anxious.

Long before Rauch published her book in 2018, another academic, Professor Nassim Nicholas Taleb, called out the deficiencies with modern news reporting. In his 2007 global bestseller, *The Black Swan: The Impact of the Highly Improbable,* Taleb emboldened his readers "not to read newspapers, or follow the news in any way or form".

*The Black Swan* illuminated the severe limitations of our thinking and the fragility of our knowledge. Taleb was one of the first people to recognise news consumption as a serious problem. "The more information we absorb," he cautioned, "the more difficult it becomes to discern the relevant from the irrelevant". Taleb views journalism as "pure entertainment, not the search for the truth" and warned:

> Remember that we are swayed by the sensational. Listening to the news on the radio every hour is far worse for you than reading a weekly magazine, because the longer interval allows information to be filtered a bit.

It is alleged that Mark Twain once asserted: "If you don't read the newspaper, you are uninformed; if you do read the newspaper, you are misinformed". Sadly, Twain's quip is more relevant today than in his day, and many would agree with his claim.

It's my contention that to achieve one of journalism's prime purposes – the creation of an informed citizenry – we should adopt the classic strategy of *slow and steady wins the race* by embracing slow journalism.

Slow journalism is seen as the antidote to social media's need for speed. "If social media is a fast-food boxed meal", says *AdNews Australia,* "then slow journalism is a high-quality degustation. In a world of same-day delivery, instant noodles and push notifications ... it's hardly surprising that there are some people who just want things to move a little more slowly".

One media outlet which has embraced slow journalism is the Australian Broadcasting Commission (ABC). In 2018 the ABC launched a slow journalism initiative called the Remote Communities Project (RCP). The RCP created stories that provided audiences with an insight into life outside of metropolitan cities.

Reporters were able to work without the normal time constraints associated with fast journalism. They benefited greatly from spending up to a fortnight in the bush, learning first-hand about the issues and experiences of people living in isolated areas of Australia. Free from the tyranny of the 24-hour news cycle, reporters were able to uncover "the untold stories".

Since my retirement from full-time work in mid-2019, I have gravitated naturally toward longer-form, slow journalism and feel much better informed. The journals and magazines that I read are void of sensational and superficial storytelling but replete with investigative and factual journalism. The well-rounded and balanced articles which are delivered direct to my inbox are a joy to read.

While fast media feeds us small bites of trivial matter, slow media delivers big chunks of meaningful matter, with the latter content designed for those who take their news seriously and think deeply about the issues behind it.

*Elephant in the Room* is an example of slow media, as each post is written *after* a period of reflection and research. This blog is a place for reasoned argument supported by corroborating evidence. Its contentions aim to be intellectually compelling without being academic to give you a clear understanding of the forces shaping our world.

We know from Aesop's classic fable of "The Hare and the Tortoise" that being the fastest does not guarantee victory. When this lesson is applied to journalism, it's clear that filling the news abyss is not a sprint but a marathon. We need to recalibrate our relationship with the media and rethink how we consume information. The days of rocket-fast news ruling the media roost is being challenged by those who believe that we need to hasten slowly.

**In the race of life, the tortoise ultimately beats the hare.**

POSTING DATE | 31 JULY 2022

## Is the era of the specialist over?

### BECOME A DEEP GENERALIST

In 2018, the world held its collective breath as two Australian doctors spearheaded the rescue mission of 12 schoolboys and their soccer coach who were trapped underground in a flooded Thai cave. Both Aussie rescuers are proficient medicos and adept divers, and it was this atypical combination of skills that made the duo perfect for the daring operation.

Research has long shown that we can all gain from spending time outside of our specialism. With reference to the cave rescuers, they have formal training and acclaim in two unrelated domains – medicine and cave diving – and this qualifies each of them to be called a polymath. The word "polymath" is a 17th-century Greek term which describes a person with "many learnings".

Throughout history, many notable individuals have pursued multiple interests. Albert Einstein was an accomplished violinist as well as a physicist. Leonardo da Vinci was an artist, inventor, scientist, architect, and engineer. Thomas Edison was a prolific inventor, entrepreneur, poet, and writer. The world's most intriguing Renaissance men were all polymaths or deep generalists.

The label "polymath" is often applied to Elon Musk as he excels in multiple fields and has used his cross-discipline expertise as a physicist, engineer, economist, and entrepreneur to tackle some of society's most pressing challenges. He has built three multibillion-dollar companies in three disparate industries – aerospace (SpaceX), automotive (Tesla Inc.), and energy (SolarCity). But that's not all!

In 2016, Musk co-founded a mind-computer interface company (Neuralink Corp.) which is developing brain implants that can communicate with computers. In the same year, he started a tunnel construction business (the Boring Company) to create fast-to-dig transportation tunnels. Musk also came up with the idea for an ultra-high-speed futuristic transportation system (the Hyperloop).

Throughout his life, Musk has displayed a relentless pursuit of knowledge and an unrivalled talent for applying his learnings across a range of industries. He has been called the quintessential modern polymath. His world-changing intellect has become a symbol of the power of being an expert generalist with the ability to generate breakthrough insights and innovations.

Yet conventional wisdom still frowns on being a "jack-of-all-trades, master of none". From the time we enter school, we are constantly encouraged to specialise by choosing a clear path and then sticking with it. And once we enter the workforce, the pressure to specialise is ever present. Being a generalist has long been seen as the road to mediocrity.

Paradoxically, research shows that people with too many interests are more likely to succeed. This certainly holds true for the founders of five of the largest companies in the world – Bill Gates (Microsoft), Steve Jobs (Apple), Warren Buffett (Berkshire Hathaway), Larry Page (Google), and Jeff Bezos (Amazon). All are polymaths who follow the five-hour rule (minimum learning time each work week).

Polymaths see the world differently and make connections that are otherwise ignored. A case in point is Francis Crick, who discovered the structure of DNA. He began his scientific career in physics and later made the transition to biology. Crick claimed that this diverse background gave him the confidence to solve problems that other biologists couldn't.

Many of the world's other great inventions also arose as a result of multifaceted thinking. Nikola Tesla was a pioneer in many fields but is most remembered for inventing the radio. In doing so, he drew on his skills as an electrical engineer, theoretical physicist, mathematician, and futurist. Elon Musk's electric car company is named after Nikola Tesla.

Even though the world remains obsessed with specialisation, the evidence for deep generalists is growing. In his book, *Range: Why Generalists Triumph in a Specialized World*, David Epstein examines the world's most successful individuals across a range of human endeavours. He discovers that in most fields – especially those that are complex and unpredictable – generalists, not specialists, are the ones who excel.

Epstein reports that when researchers study great innovators, they typically find "systems thinkers" with an "ability to connect disparate pieces of information from many different sources" and who "read more than other technologists". Simply put, generalists invariably do better than specialists in putting two and two together across domains.

Charles Darwin is considered by Epstein to be the ultimate example of someone whose breadth of training enabled him to remain open-minded and innovative. Prior to sailing to the Galápagos Islands, Darwin studied natural history, medicine, theology, and geology. This cross-training enabled him to build the intellectual firepower that he would later need to overturn centuries of dogma.

The Digital Age has made it easier for us to become polymaths. Today, information is everywhere and, more often than not, it's free. Wannabe polymaths can become proficient in multiple fields by allocating at least one hour per day for deliberate learning and reading. The one habit that all high-performers share is reading books in various disciplines – and lots of them!

My desire to continually learn new things and improve my knowledge is one of the reasons I maintain a blog. Without exception, the research I undertake in writing each post helps broaden my horizons and aids my self-development. Moreover, learning keeps my brain active and stimulated, and this (hopefully!) helps maintain my cognitive health.

For readers of this blog, my posts are deliberately designed to make you think, as they tangle and weave through disparate but connected topics. By joining the dots, you will gain a helicopter view of where individual disciplines intersect and overlap. And by cross-pollinating ideas from a range of fields, you will be able to make new connections and see more creative solutions to contemporary problems.

Notwithstanding this, Western educational systems still lean towards deep specialisation, which is why UK researchers argue that we need a radical shake-up of school curriculums to ensure arts and sciences are no longer taught separately. Some educational experts believe that teaching children to think like Leonardo da Vinci would better prepare them for tackling complex issues.

When it comes to tertiary education, it has long been my contention that universities around the world will increasingly be challenged to turn out graduates with broader interdisciplinary degrees.

The answers to the big global issues we face – like climate change – cannot be found within traditional single disciplines, such as economics or science or politics, on their own.

For this reason, I believe that one subject that should be embedded in most university degrees is the study of biomimicry. Biomimicry is the art and science of emulating nature's best biological ideas and applying these solutions to product design, architecture, engineering, technology, business, and medicine. Biomimicry is relevant in every sector of society.

Velcro is probably the best-known example of innovation inspired by nature. The product's inventor, George de Mestral, stumbled upon the idea by examining how burrs stuck to the hair of his dog. By mimicking the strong attachment forces of the burrs' small hooks, he was able to develop Velcro straps and fasteners.

Similarly, Airbus observed how sea birds sense gust loads in the air with their beaks and adjust the shape of their wing feathers to suppress lift. As a result, Airbus installed probes on its A350 aircraft which detect gusts ahead of the wing and deploy moveable surfaces for more efficient flight. Airbus engineers continue to study the natural world for modern aircraft-design solutions.

Mother Nature is by far the smartest "person" I know. She is the ultimate polymath and genius, and we humans can learn much from her. She has been giving lessons in design and solving problems for billions of years, but only in recent times have we started "enrolling" in her classes. Using nature as a mentor, professionals from a range of fields are now studying biomimicry, but more of us need to look to nature for creative solutions.

It's never too late to pick up a new area to add to your repertoire of skills. If you can combine unique skills in creative ways, you may well be one of tomorrow's great problem-solvers and innovators. In an era of rapid-fire technological and social change, we all need to embrace our inner polymath because we are more than the sum of our parts.

**May polymaths inherit the Earth.**

POSTING DATE | 7 NOVEMBER 2021

## How the quiet many are drowned out by the outspoken few

### MODERATE VOICES MUFFLED

It's true – I'm a member of the "Silent Majority Party". My fellow members and I never demonstrate, wave placards, stage sit-ins, or stir up trouble. We are a quiet bunch with no media spokesperson. Although many of us are discontent with what is happening in society, we keep our opinions out of the public arena and quietly get on with our lives.

In my particular case, I express my views on contemporary issues via this blog, but that's where I draw the line. Like my fellow Silent Majority Party brethren, I leave the shouting, heckling, and disruption to the vocal minority. Their manipulative antics invariably capture the attention of the media, which provides prime-time coverage of their opinions – no matter how radical.

Non-peaceful protests, rallies, and marches tend to attract more media attention than peaceful demonstrations. "A little violence goes a long way," proclaims US political journalism company *POLITICO*, because "the press loves the sound of breaking glass, police-car sirens, and tear-gas grenades". Such activities certainly trump inaudible forms of protest like letter writing.

Political activists take to the streets over a diverse range of issues, grievances, and concerns. In addition to protest activities, organised interest groups lobby politicians, mobilise grassroots action, and orchestrate media campaigns to get their messages across. Swaying public opinion and influencing policy outcomes is the name of the game.

A US study claims that small groups which reach a critical mass of 25 per cent of the general population can overturn established norms. Decades of work in sociology, physics, and other disciplines have supported this idea. As noted in an article in *The Atlantic*:

> Small groups of people can indeed flip firmly established social conventions, as long as they reach a certain critical mass. When that happens, what was once acceptable can quickly become unacceptable, and vice versa. Two decades ago, most Americans opposed gay marriage, bans on public

smoking and the legalization of marijuana; now, these issues all enjoy majority support.

While I'm a passionate advocate for freedom of expression and would never stop anyone from exercising their democratic right to protest, the reality is that moderate voices are stifled by the clamour of minority interest groups and individuals. Since most citizens do not shout from the rooftops or force their beliefs and politics onto their fellow citizens, they are largely invisible.

According to the NSW Bar Association, freedom of speech is not an unfettered right to do and say what we want. "It is a personal right which, in any civilised society, carries with it, the corresponding duty to consider the rights of others. Freedom of speech is therefore a qualified right, not an absolute right, in accordance with international human rights law," wrote the association.

Research shows that being confident and loud is one way to win an argument – even if you are wrong. Shout louder than anyone else and people will assume you're right. In the world of politics, bolshie behaviour has been seen as the way to get ahead. US President Donald Trump shouted louder and more outrageously than any other politician, and this enabled him to dominate the news.

Nigel Farage – who led the former pro-Brexit UK Independence Party (UKIP) – is also a loud, rabble-rousing politician. His bombastic style convinced many Britons that breaking away from the European Union would be a good thing. He cleverly harnessed the power of voter discontent and exploited the populace's deepest fears about immigration.

Farage used xenophobic language to spruik a racist message, which had his misguided followers chanting "we want our country back". The UK is now suffering post-Brexit regret over its disastrous decision to leave the EU. In the words of former UK PM Gordon Brown, Farage "highjacked patriotism" by manufacturing distrust and disunity.

I've long observed that loud and aggressive people tend to get their way – they won't take "no" for an answer. They're the ones who will not accept that the doctor is booked until next week, but argue their way into the surgery that same day. They're the ones who become irked at airline cabin baggage restrictions and hog the overhead bin after airline staff relent in the interests of on-time departure.

These "entitled" individuals believe that the rules don't apply to them and that they deserve preferential treatment. Meanwhile, the rest of us graciously accept that the doctor can't see us today and that we need to stay within baggage allowance limits. So, should we all stomp our feet every time we are upset when things don't go our way? I think not.

We should not go through life being highjacked by our anger. To lose your temper and yell is not a constructive way to deal with a difficult situation – it's also damaging to relationships. Being calm and quiet, on the other hand, is not a bad thing. The world is full of quiet achievers. The best performing staff aren't necessarily the most vocal. Nor are the most valuable customers necessarily the loudest ones.

In the same way, quieter citizens are not necessarily apathetic. Rather, they dislike the politics of confrontation and prefer to cast an informed vote at each election. Politics based on "he who shouts loudest" often comes unstuck where it matters most – in the privacy of the polling booth.

Democracy gives each of us an equal say because of the principle of one-person, one-vote. Each person who casts a vote is equal to every other voter – no matter how much noise an individual may make. I care deeply about our nation and am an avid follower of the political system. This enables me to cast an informed vote for the party with the policies that I believe will serve our nation best.

In fairness, I must acknowledge that the electoral process is far from perfect. We like to believe that voters evaluate the evidence put in front of them over the course of a campaign and then make an informed decision at the ballot box. This, however, is fantasy, as research shows that the average voter is surprisingly unsophisticated. Most citizens don't make their voting decisions based on policy questions. Voters are poorly informed and make irrational decisions.

On the plus side, Australia's compulsory system saved us from Trumpism. As pointed out in an article in the Australian edition of *The Guardian*, Donald Trump was elected with only a quarter of eligible voters supporting him, and just 37 per cent of eligible Britons voted to leave the European Union. In 2015, (then) US President Barack Obama praised Australia's system, saying it would be "transformative" if everyone voted in the United States.

Notwithstanding my personal preference to voice my concerns in the privacy of a polling booth rather than publicly on the street, I accept wholeheartedly that political activism is part and parcel of a free and open society. Let those who wish to demonstrate without violence do so.

**But let's not criticise those who choose a less vocal way of expressing their views.**

POSTING DATE | 11 APRIL 2021

## Why global population is set to fall, and what it means

### SUSTAINED DECLINES IN FERTILITY

In every major city of the world, the story is the same – roads are clogged, trains are crowded, hospitals are overstretched, and suburbs are congested. Humanity's footprint is becoming denser, and we are feeling the crush of an increasingly populated world. Doom-mongers warn that the population explosion could ultimately lead to ecological and societal collapse. But is overpopulation panic justified?

Overpopulation is a hotly debated topic. Environmentalists warn that our planet's safe carrying capacity was not designed for 7.5 billion people and that this will create food scarcity and water shortages. Economists counter with their own cautionary tale about falling fertility rates leading to more senior citizens and less children, resulting in fewer workers supporting additional retirees, declining income-tax revenues, and reduced economic growth.

Overshadowing the dichotomy of environmental health versus economic health is a provocative prediction – the population of the world is headed for a steep decline. More than half of the world's population now live in countries where the fertility rate – the average number of babies born per woman – is below the replacement level of 2.1. This means that an increasing number of couples are not having enough children to replace themselves.

Due to falling global birth rates, a growing number of demographers estimate that the planet's population will peak at around nine billion sometime between 2040 and 2060, and then start to decline. If this is correct, alarmism and extreme measures to combat overpopulation are entirely unnecessary. This is the central assertion of *Empty Planet: The Shock of Global Population Decline* by Canadian authors Darrell Bricker and John Ibbitson.

The Canadian duo goes against the grain of conventional wisdom in arguing that world population will peak far lower and sooner than UN forecasts. Their contrarian view is that the world faces a birth dearth in lieu of a population explosion. Thus, the unfolding problem is one of depopulation, not overpopulation. The significance of a contracting global population is laid bare in the book's preface:

> The great defining event of the twenty-first century – one of the great defining events in human history – will occur in three decades, give or take, when the global population starts to decline. Once that decline begins, it will never end. We do not face the challenge of a population bomb but of a population bust – a relentless, generation-after-generation culling of the human herd. Nothing like this has ever happened before.

The authors add that by the end of this century, the planet's population could be back to where we are right now, and steadily growing fewer. The main driver of declining fertility is urbanisation. As explained by Bricker and Ibbitson: "On a farm, a child is an investment – an extra pair of hands to milk the cow, or shoulders to work the fields. But in a city a child is a liability, just another mouth to feed".

So, as rural folk escape poverty and nations grow richer, people opt for smaller families – a phenomenon called the fertility transition. Women in cities have more access to education, careers, and family planning, and these opportunities combine to lower rates of childbearing. As noted by the World Bank: "The higher the level of a woman's educational attainment, the fewer children she is likely to bear".

The authors note that one solution to a declining population is to import replacements. That's why German Chancellor Angela Merkel welcomed so many working-age refugees in to her country in 2015. Germany has an aging labour force and a declining birth rate and desperately needs an injection of young workers. But Merkel discovered that anti-immigration sentiment is alive and well in Germany – and the same holds true in other nations.

Few contemporary issues are more controversial than immigration. It emerged as a top issue in the 2016 US presidential election campaign. It was a driving force behind Brexit and the desire to restrict entry into the UK. And it has propelled right-wing parties in France and elsewhere that campaign on a "no more immigrants" platform. Around the world, hard nationalist and xenophobic politicians have galvanised support by whipping up fear over immigration.

"As the Brexit referendum revealed," note Bricker and Ibbitson, "many Brits want to turn the English Channel into a moat. To combat depopulation, nations must embrace both immigration *and* multiculturalism. The first is hard. The second, for some, may prove impossible".

Those who challenge the merits of immigration are often unaware that most advanced economies are heavily reliant on immigrants for labour growth. Japan has ignored this reality to its detriment. Japan allows very few people to immigrate and – as its fertility rate is less than 1.3 children per woman – it has a shrinking labour force. Japan is seen as the canary in the coal mine for assessing how population change affects economic growth.

Japan has been described as a slow-motion disaster, with a shrinking pool of taxable citizens and ballooning social-welfare costs for an increasing number of elderly. Japan has the highest national debt of any nation in the world (248% of GDP) as a result of its need to stimulate the economy through huge government spending programs. Economists argue that the world is now entering what Japan first experienced back in the 1990s when it suffered a "lost decade" of economic stagnation from which it has not recovered.

Beyond economics, Bricker and Ibbitson claim that population decline will influence the global contest for power.

> Population decline will shape the nature of war and peace in the decades ahead, as some nations grapple with the fallout of their shrinking, ageing societies. ... The defining geopolitical challenge in the coming decades could involve accommodating and containing an angry, frightened China as it confronts the consequences of its disastrous one-child policy.

Only time will tell if the authors are correct in predicting the looming demographic challenge of global population collapse. My sense is that they are on the money in forecasting that there will be significantly less of us. I have little doubt that my grandchildren will live in an emptier world populated by more grandparents than grandchildren.

**Another example of what goes up must come down.**

POSTING DATE | 8 MARCH 2020

## The world is doing much better than the media would have us believe

### IGNORE THE DOOM-MONGERS

There's no shortage of bad news – it dominates the headlines. The media concentrates on the negative aspects of life because bad news sells. As readers, viewers, and listeners, we thrive on human drama, so the news is replete with stories about terrorism, murders, epidemics, and crashes.

News broadcasts begin with the most traumatic story of the day, in line with the media's maxim "if it bleeds, it leads". This relentless death-and-destruction focus triggers our innate negativity bias and causes us to believe that the world is descending into disaster and chaos.

Following our exposure to a negative event, we tend to overestimate its significance due to a phenomenon called the availability bias. If you have just watched a news report of a plane crash in Sydney and are then asked about aviation safety, you might think (as it's top of mind) that plane crashes are a problem in Australia, whereas they rarely happen here.

In reality, the world is not full of doom and gloom – lots of positive things do happen. However, good news unfolds over time and receives fleeting coverage, whereas bad news – such as a rise in coronavirus cases – explodes daily and attracts rolling coverage. Steady progress – like a gradual fall in coronary disease – is not breaking news.

Most positive developments are not camera-friendly as they aren't built in a day. So, a single act of brutality will capture the headlines, while hundreds of acts of kindness over time are ignored. In the words of Harvard University Professor of Psychology Steven Pinker:

> News is about things that happen, not things that don't happen. We never see a journalist saying to the camera, "I'm reporting live from a country where war has not broken out" – or a city that has not been bombed, or a school that has not been shot up.

In a time when so many things seem dire, it's refreshing to learn how many important trends are improving. Providing a balanced view of humanity's progress is the motivation behind a book which helps us see how the world is really faring.

In *Ten Global Trends Every Smart Person Should Know,* Ronald Bailey and Marian Tupy debunk the belief that the world is getting worse. In fact, for the most part, it's getting better. The authors have assembled a superb collection of factual information which provides an uplifting report card on humanity's progress.

Despite its title, the book actually presents 78 trends. The first chapter, "Top 10 Trends", has a global focus. The remaining eight chapters identify other significant trends covering people, health, violence, work, natural resource, farm, technology, and US trends.

*Ten Global Trends* serves as a counter-argument to doomsayers and leaves the reader in no doubt that human progress over recent times has been nothing short of stunning. As the top ten trends reveal, the world is becoming richer, healthier, greener, safer, freer, and a more pleasant place to live.

**TREND 1 | THE GREAT ENRICHMENT**

The size of the world's economy has grown more than a hundredfold over the past two centuries. Economic growth leads to higher average incomes, enabling consumers to buy more goods and services and enjoy better standards of living. If global economic growth maintains its 2.8 per cent average rate since 2000, GDP will increase to a whopping $1.1 quadrillion by 2100.

**TREND 2 | THE END OF POVERTY**

Extreme poverty has plummeted from 84 per cent of the world's population in 1820 to under 10 per cent today. Over the course of the last generation, more than a billion people left the most destitute living conditions behind. Extreme poverty (living on less than $1.90 per day) is expected to retreat further by 2030, with less than 5 per cent of the world's population experiencing penury.

**TREND 3 | ARE WE RUNNING OUT OF RESOURCES?**

Despite claims to the contrary, humanity has not run out of a single supposedly non-renewable resource. Fossil fuels and most minerals are more abundant than in the past. Indeed, most resources are so plentiful they will last for centuries. There are compelling reasons to challenge the claims of resource depletion.

**TREND 4 | PEAK POPULATION**

World population will peak lower (at 8.9 billion) and sooner (by 2060) than the UN forecasts and will decline to 7.8 billion people by the end of the century. The significant decline in fertility rates in most nations means that global population will not continue forever on a runaway upward trajectory but will ultimately drop below its current level.

**TREND 5 | THE END OF FAMINE**

Famines have all but disappeared outside of war zones. Adequate nutrition is a basic requirement for human survival, yet throughout history, food has always been scarce. Today, the world's poorest region (Sub-Saharan Africa) enjoys access to food that is equivalent to that of Portugal in the early 1960s.

**TREND 6 | MORE LAND FOR NATURE**

The global tree canopy increased by 2.24 million square kilometres between 1982 and 2016. This equates to 7 per cent of the Earth's surface covered by new trees. Mother Nature is beating deforestation, resulting in expanding woodlands. There are just over three trillion trees on our planet – that's roughly 422 trees for every person on Earth.

**TREND 7 | PLANET CITY**

The world's urban population in 2018 was 4.2 billion people – more than the world's total population in 1975. Cities are the centres of innovation and the engines of growth. No country has grown to middle income without industrialising and urbanising, and none has grown to high income without vibrant cities. Urbanisation is also good for the environment – fewer humans habituating rural areas enables some land to revert to nature.

**TREND 8 | DEMOCRACY ON THE MARCH**

Since the collapse of the Berlin Wall in 1989, democracy has spread rapidly across the world, beating the communist and fascist regimes that had arisen since the 1920s. The supremacy of democracy is reflected in free elections, the rule of law, and constraints on executive power. Autocrats reject these democratic norms in favour of ruthless behaviour which limits rights and liberties.

## TREND 9 | THE LONG PEACE

Over the past half century, wars between countries have become rarer, and those which do occur kill fewer people. International trade offers a path to world peace as it encourages nations to live in harmony. Free trade raises the cost of war by making nations more economically interdependent. The more that people rely on trade with others, the greater the cost to all parties of a conflict.

## TREND 10 | A SAFER WORLD

The chances of a person dying in a natural catastrophe – earthquake, flood, drought, epidemic, etc. – has declined by nearly 99 per cent over the past century. Today, buildings are better constructed to survive earthquakes, weather satellites provide early storm warnings, and swift medical interventions limit the spread of diseases.

Clearly, the world is not going to the dogs, and these are not bleak times. Almost everywhere you turn, you can find evidence of some positive trend – if you are prepared to look. The remaining 68 trends outlined in *Ten Global Trends* show that on all key dimensions of human well-being, the world is in an extraordinarily better place today than just a few decades ago.

Most people are better educated, better fed, more literate, and have more life options than at any other time in human history. Incomes and life expectancy are rising, while child mortality and cancer death rates are falling. Stocks of nuclear warheads have plummeted, and digital technology has transformed how we live, work, and play.

The world isn't as horrific as we have been led to believe. Indeed, there's never been a better time to be alive. In bygone years, life was shorter, sicker, poorer, more dangerous, and less free. So, we need to stop bingeing on bad news and seek out the positives in the world, as good news lifts our spirits. We should also follow the advice of the Monty Python song "Always Look on the Bright Side of Life".

**And if you want to appreciate the simple things in daily life, just listen to the lyrics of Louis Armstrong's song "What a Wonderful World".**

POSTING DATE | 12 SEPTEMBER 2021

*Chapter Four*

# The Technological Landscape

Technology is rapidly changing and expanding in every field. In the gadget-filled 21st century, we are surrounded by robotics, artificial intelligence, iPhones, and laptops. As the pandemic unfolded, information technology played a crucial role in helping health experts track and understand the disease, while medical technology created vaccines which offered lifesaving protection against the virus. In this final chapter, we look at, *inter alia,* the development of COVID-19 vaccines, the reasons big tech companies were winners during the pandemic, the quest for healthy aging and longevity, and the cost of aerospace technology for Mars colonisation.

## COVID vaccines offer drug makers chance to salvage reputation

VILLAINS OR SAVIOURS?

The development of COVID-19 vaccines is a public-relations coup for the pharmaceutical industry. The arrival of vaccines has boosted public approval for drug companies. Thanks to the blanket press coverage of the global race to develop vaccines, "big pharma" brands like Pfizer, Moderna, and AstraZeneca have become household names.

The long-beleaguered drug manufacturing sector has become the hero of the hour. COVID-19 has provided the sector with a once-in-a-lifetime opportunity to reset its abysmal reputation. Less than two years ago, there was no business sector in the US as disliked as the pharmaceutical industry, according to a 2019 Gallup poll.

By providing the world with the ability to curb transmission of the virus, generations of ill will towards the industry seems to be melting away. Drug makers are currently basking in global plaudits – but will the adulation last? Will 2021 be a permanent reputational turning point, or will past disreputable behaviour (such as price gouging and the US opioid crisis) be repeated?

One health expert has argued that we should not be under any illusion that profit, not altruism motivated drug companies to develop COVID-19 vaccines. While no one knows precisely the extent to which these companies will profit from making vaccines, the shots are expected to collectively generate tens of billions of dollars in sales for the pharmaceutical industry.

Richer nations have gobbled up the majority of the global supply of vaccines, with poorer nations falling behind in the race for inoculations. This "me-first approach" is precisely the behaviour that the World Health Organization (WHO) feared and predicted. WHO Director-General Tedros Adhanom Ghebreyesus stated that "the world is on the brink of a catastrophic moral failure".

In January, Dr Ghebreyesus criticised inequalities in the global coronavirus-vaccine rollout, arguing that it was "not right" that younger adults in wealthy countries were getting vaccinated before older people or health-care workers in poorer countries. He also hit out at the profiteering of drug companies, accusing vaccine makers of targeting locations where "profits are highest".

Other experts have also expressed concern about vaccine nationalism and support Dr Ghebreyesus's call for countries and manufacturers to spread doses more fairly around the world. Suerie Moon, co-director of the Global Health Centre in Geneva, stated: "Richer countries will be able to vaccinate ... their whole populations before vulnerable groups in many developing countries get covered".

The WHO has urged countries and manufacturers to stop making bilateral deals. Such agreements have resulted in vaccine makers prioritising regulatory approvals in rich countries, where the profits are the highest, rather than submitting their data to the WHO for approval. "No country is exceptional and should cut the queue and vaccinate all their population while some remain with no supply of the vaccine," said Dr Ghebreyesus.

According to an opinion piece in *The New York Times,* drug companies will "make a killing" from the coronavirus. While other sectors of the business world have struggled to survive the mayhem from the pandemic, the pharmaceutical industry is set to profit handsomely. Sales of treatments and vaccines will pad bottom lines, and this is expected to create a windfall for the industry.

But drug companies are not the only profiteers. A December 2020 article in the *Los Angeles Times* reported that executives at some pharmaceutical companies received huge paydays by selling shares around the time their companies announced positive news about coronavirus vaccines. This practice is common in the health-care industry, with executives using prearranged stock sale plans to unload shares on days when their companies release good news.

Pre-planned stock trades are not illegal and can be very lucrative. According to the *Los Angeles Times* article:

> Pfizer Chief Executive Albert Bourla shed 60% of his holdings in the company Nov. 9, the same day his firm announced the results of trials that showed its vaccine

> was highly effective in preventing the disease caused by the coronavirus. The news caused the company's stock to jump 15%. Bourla is one of seven Pfizer executives who collectively have earned $14 million from stock sales this year. ... That amount is dwarfed by sales made by executives at Moderna, a Cambridge, Mass.-based firm that has never brought a product to market but has produced a vaccine reported to be nearly as effective as Pfizer's. Executives there collectively made $287 million from stock sales this year. ... Moderna's CEO, Stéphane Bancel, has accounted for $81 million of the sales ...

The public has largely bankrolled the hunt for COVID-19 vaccines. Yet, even though taxpayers have footed the bill for much of the research and development, we have no say in how vaccines are priced and distributed. This is at the sole discretion of pharmaceutical companies, which will use government-granted legal monopolies – in the form of patents – to charge whatever price they wish.

Allowing drug makers to get rich from a global health emergency does not sit well with the average citizen. As we Aussies like to say, this arrangement fails the pub test. Patents should not come before patients. Picking up on this theme, Owen Jones, a columnist for *The Guardian* (UK), published an opinion piece, "The Covid vaccine will benefit humanity – we should all own the patent", wherein he stated:

> Pfizer and its German biotech partner, BioNTech, stand to make an astonishing £9.8bn [in 2021] from a coronavirus vaccine. Suggestions that pharmaceutical companies should not profit from the world's most severe crisis since the second world war were dismissed in July [2020] as "radical" by Pfizer's CEO. ... But Pfizer's claim to "have never taken any money from the US government or from anyone" does not stand up to scrutiny. ... Essentially, pharmaceutical companies are global monopolies, which are given the right to charge whatever the market is willing to tolerate for the new medicines they produce.

Many believe that the current drug-development model is broken as it does not deliver affordable drugs to the masses. This is exactly what happened when a treatment for HIV infection was developed over two decades ago. The drug was expensive at a whopping US$15,000 – per person per year – making it completely unaffordable to people in Africa. While AIDS sufferers in the West were able to afford the breakthrough treatment, millions needlessly died in Africa from the AIDS epidemic. The drug company blocked access to a low-cost generic AIDS medication to protect its investment.

Another fundamental flaw of the medicine-patent scheme is that it motivates innovation only if potential patent-holders believe that they can make a substantive return on their investment. From a shareholder perspective, this is fair and understandable, but not always in the best interests of society. An example is the 2018 decision by pharmaceutical giant Pfizer to cease research on a treatment for dementia as it did not stack up financially.

This dashed the hopes of millions suffering from Alzheimer's and Parkinson's and those at risk of developing one of these devastating diseases. The need to generate value for shareholders saw Pfizer re-allocate R&D funding to other areas. Still, this was cold comfort for patients and their families affected by neurological diseases.

Unsurprisingly, there have been calls for future coronavirus vaccines to be treated as global public goods, with equal access for all, without profit. We have a golden opportunity to reshape the biomedical research and development system in a way that prioritizes people over profits. The belief that monopolies and high prices are a "necessary evil" in financing the development of new medicines needs to be challenged.

The current medicine-patent system is flawed, and governments must do more of the heavy lifting regarding financing research into new drugs. This might be a bitter pill for drug companies to swallow, but a welcome tonic for the masses. With research costs paid upfront by governments, most drugs would be available for the same price as a bottle of generic aspirin.

I'll leave the final word on this contentious topic to *The Guardian*'s Owen Jones: "Rather than being a PR triumph for big pharma, coronavirus should serve as a reminder of the disastrous consequences of leaving a life-saving industry in the hands of a profiteering monopoly."

**Perhaps it was unrealistic to expect a leopard to change its spots.**

POSTING DATE | 14 FEBRUARY 2021

## Big technology companies thrive during coronavirus

### WINNERS IN A PANDEMIC ECONOMY

COVID-19 has wrought economic disruption on a monumental scale. Around the world, businesses of all shapes and sizes have fought a life-and-death battle. Business owners have grappled with forced closures, plummeting revenues, and surging losses. Despite drastic measures – including slashing jobs – many businesses have been unable to stay afloat.

The decision by policymakers to induce massive economic suffering to save lives was a brutal trade-off – but not for the technology industry. While other industries were decimated by store, restaurant, and office closures, the technology sector powered ahead. Government stay-at-home orders were a godsend for technology companies – demand for their just-a-click-away services skyrocketed.

Specifically, the COVID crisis turbo-charged the profits and share prices of the technology industry's titans – Alphabet (Google's parent company), Amazon, Apple, Facebook, and Microsoft. The quintet benefited enormously from a greater reliance on their services during the pandemic, as the world moved almost entirely online for work, school, and entertainment.

Each of these leading digital powers was able to capitalise on being viewed as an essential service for a public in lockdown, with their shares enjoying a jaw-dropping bull run. As noted in a report in *The Wall Street Journal*, their combined revenue during 2020 surged by a fifth to a mammoth $1.1 trillion, while their aggregate market capitalisation soared by half to a staggering $8 trillion.

Thanks to the pandemic, the technology conglomerates now make up five of the six largest companies in the world. During 2020, their stocks soared to dizzying heights, and all are now valued at over $1 trillion. According to an analysis conducted in March this year by MacKeeper, these companies are worth more than most countries. MacKeeper noted that:

- Apple's gargantuan $2.2-trillion valuation makes it richer than 96 per cent of the world. Only seven countries have annual GDP figures that outrank Apple's market capitalisation.

- Microsoft's colossal $1.8-trillion market cap puts its value on par with the GDP of Canada and makes it richer than many developed economies, including Australia. Only nine countries are worth more than the developer of Windows.
- Amazon's $1.6-trillion valuation would make it the 14th richest "country". Its revenue per employee is $351,531 annually, which exceeds the highest GDP per capita in the world.
- Alphabet, Google's parent company, is valued at $1.4-trillion, putting it ahead of all but 12 nations.
- Facebook, while falling short of the trillion-dollar mark, is valued at a respectable $763-billion. (NB: Facebook's cap passed $1-trillion on 28 June 2021.)

The economic effects of COVID have catapulted the tech titans to heights that few would have imagined possible prior to the pandemic. They now account for nearly a quarter of the total value of companies in the S&P 500 Index – the barometer of corporate America – and that is almost double the percentage of just five years ago. Never before has this level of market influence been seen from one sector.

These behemoths have phenomenal corporate power and have been dubbed the "Frightening Five", which is why some believe that their wings need to be clipped. Together, they control much of the critical digital infrastructure which underpins global commerce. Over recent years, their digital services have played a greater role in our daily lives.

The imposition of social distancing and travel restrictions during the pandemic dramatically increased our dependence on digital platforms to service our basic needs, including staying connected with family, friends, and colleagues. This reliance was tangibly demonstrated in the exponential rise in spending on computers, online retailing, cloud-computing services, and digital advertising.

The pandemic has made a clutch of tech firms an even more integral part of work and personal life. Indeed, the coronavirus has created huge tailwinds for these juggernauts by driving behavioural shifts that will long outlive the health crisis. "Digital adoption curves aren't slowing down – they're accelerating", said Microsoft Chief Executive Satya Nadella.

Big tech is on a roll, and its deep pockets will enable it to withstand almost any challenge to its market dominance. Investors have been astonished at its earnings growth and resilience in marching unscathed through the health chaos. In the words of one analyst, "the digital revolution is here to stay, and these businesses are embedded in our lives".

People who have tried to live without the tech heavyweights claim that it is impossible. Journalist Kashmir Hill found that she could reduce but not eliminate the Frightening Five from her life. Despite her goal of wanting to "excise these companies from my life as completely as possible," she discovered that "these tech giants dominate the Internet in so many invisible ways," it's not possible to avoid them.

According to an article in *The New York Times*, the Big Five's platforms "are inescapable; you may opt out of one or two of them, but together, they form a gilded mesh blanketing the entire economy". Many of these digital platforms generate what economists call "network effects" – they keep getting more indispensable as more people use them.

Millions of people find it hard to imagine going through a single day without using an Apple iPhone, conducting a Google search, reading a Facebook News Feed, receiving a package from Amazon, or launching Microsoft Office. Even so, these same people find it unsettling that a handful of unelected tech executives wield so much power.

Governments around the world also worry about the misuse of monopoly powers and the gobbling up of competitors. Government probes have been conducted into the business practices of the tech giants, and these have uncovered privacy concerns and data security breaches. Governments from Australia to the US are starting to crack down on big tech companies to rein in their power.

Over recent times, US tech companies have faced increased scrutiny in Washington over their size and power. Republican and

Democratic lawmakers have banded together to introduce a package of bills which will change antitrust laws regulating the conduct of business corporations. The legislation should level the playing field by ensuring that tech companies are held to the same rules as everyone else. As outlined in one report:

> The new laws would make it easier for the government to break up dominant companies. It could also prevent these companies from snuffing out competition through pre-emptive acquisitions. And it could curtail the tech giants from entering different businesses where they'd be able to use their market power to crush smaller competitors.

In any market, regulators like to see competition, as this gives consumers choice. Having one dominant player lessens competition, which typically leads to higher prices. But in the case of Google and Facebook, their services are free thereby making concerns over pricing irrelevant. The companies themselves say they are successful because of the quality of their offerings, so why punish success? To quote *Bloomberg Technology*:

> Consumers appear to agree it's hard to beat Google's suite of free products or Amazon's convenience. Their dominance may not be about predatory practices so much as the nature of competition in the digital marketplace, where tech platforms benefit from network effects: As more people use them, the more useful – and dominant – the platforms become.

So, the focus must be on whether there are other harmful political, economic, or social effects. Some believe that the tech giants have become more like governments than companies, given the staggering amount of money at their disposal and the enormous influence they have over democracy in society. Case in point, Facebook has become a global political force as the largest and most influential entity in the news business.

The digital economy knows no national borders, and this is a threat to the jurisdiction of governments around the world. Given this, we will likely see increasing friction between the Big Five companies that rule the tech industry and the governments that rule the lands these companies are invading. The nation-state is fighting not to lose its grip.

Love them or hate them, there's no escaping the tech superstars. They have become part of the fabric of our lives and will continue to cast a long shadow over the political, economic, and social landscapes. They have created an Internet oligopoly which has changed the face of modern capitalism and made them indomitable.

## The Big Five have only one question: What pandemic?

POSTING DATE | 4 JULY 2021

## The quest for healthy aging and longevity

### NEVER SAY DIE

The human species has a natural shelf life due to aging – a debilitating condition that no one can escape. Our biological functions decay over time and the Grim Reaper eventually catches up with all of us. Despite the amazing advances in medicine and the resultant rise in life expectancy, you can't keep Father Time at bay forever. Still, there are those who believe that humans can significantly extend their expiry date.

It is generally accepted that the apparent limit to the human lifespan is about 120 years. The life-extending treatments necessary to ward off the ailments that accompany old age and stop people living well beyond 120 years do not currently exist. So, at this stage, we are all doomed to age and die – assuming that some other fatal event does not take us out first.

That said, the good news for those who want to stay young and live longer is that scientists are working to recalibrate the human body clock. It's already evident that people over 50 aren't aging as fast or poorly as their parents, and anti-aging research is set to improve this trend. Over time, medical treatments to head off the slow march towards death will become increasingly common.

We know that the duration of human life is influenced by genetics, the environment, and lifestyle. Yet the causes of aging are extremely complex and unclear. With the rise in longevity clinical trials, more answers – and questions – are emerging. Scientists are now asking whether our natural genetic makeup is limited to a maximum span of 120 years, or whether this boundary can be breached.

The study of longevity is a developing science. Our genes harbour many secrets to a long and healthy life, and researchers are trying to find the key within our genome to edit out bad stuff. Genes are akin to little packets of information found in each cell in our body. These packets contain critical instructions which tell our body how to grow and develop.

An online article by *Nature Education* explains that:

> The action of a single gene can have huge effects on how long a creature lives. This may seem hard to believe because so many things go into determining lifespan, including a host of lifestyle factors and a long list of diseases. Nonetheless, remarkable effects on lifespan are seen when particular genes are deleted from an animal's genetic sequence. Furthermore, research – particularly that involving microscopic roundworms – continues to provide scientists with tantalizing clues about the molecular pathways involved in aging.

Researchers at the University of Rochester have discovered that one of the keys to longevity resides in a gene called Sirtuin 6 or SIRT6. The Sirtuin family of genes and their proteins play a role in controlling aging by repairing damaged DNA, thereby preserving health and youthfulness. SIRT6 has also been identified as a critical regulator of telomere integrity.

Telomeres are an essential part of human cells that affect how our cells age. Telomeres are caps at the end of each strand of DNA which protect our chromosomes, just like the plastic coating (tips) on the ends of shoelaces. Without tips, shoelaces would become frayed and no longer able to do their job. In the same way, without telomeres, DNA strands become damaged, resulting in the inability of cells to fully replicate.

The cells in your body are continually dividing and renewing. With each round of cell division, telomeres become shorter. Eventually, our telomeres become so short that the genes they protect could be damaged, so the cells stop dividing and self-destruct. This programmed cell death (called apoptosis) contributes to aging.

Apoptosis is "cell suicide", and scientists believe that reducing the rate of telomere shortening could slow the body's cellular clock. Research shows that longer telomeres are associated with a longer lifespan, while shorter telomeres are connected with the ailments of aging: heart disease, cancer, and osteoporosis. If scientists can preserve or elongate telomeres, humanity will be one step closer to a genetic Fountain of Youth.

While most scientists are purely trying to extend life, some researchers are brazenly focussed on helping people dodge death altogether, by turning science fiction into science fact. To many, the quest for immortality seems nonsensical. Even so, Ray Kurzweil, Google's Director of Engineering, preaches that "immortality is within our grasp".

Google co-founder, Larry Page, has invested \$1.5 billion of Google's money into a R&D project called Calico, which aims to "cure death". Calico is short for the California Life Company, and the mission of this Google-backed biotech firm is to "harness advanced technologies to increase our understanding of the biology that controls lifespan". For the masters of the universe at Google, death is the ultimate engineering problem to be solved. The company believes that it will eventually be successful at hacking the code of life.

Aging and death are existential certainties, which is why many consider Google's anti-death project to be unbridled hubris. While the search for immortality is an epic goal, few believe that Google will solve "the problem" of death. A more likely outcome is that Calico will find ways to dramatically extend human life. That, in itself, raises a series of socio-economic questions regarding overpopulation, class divisions, and the affordability of anti-aging technologies.

What seems forgotten by Calico's backers in their conquest of death is that mortality has value, which is why immortality is not an easy sell. Research reveals that most people don't like the idea of living forever. As outlined in a 2017 *Smithsonian Magazine* article:

> ... a large percentage of today's population also subscribes to religious beliefs in which the afterlife is something to be welcomed. When the Pew Research Center asked Americans in 2013 whether they would use technologies that allowed them to live to 120 or beyond, 56 percent said no. Two-thirds of respondents believed that radically longer lifespans would strain natural resources, and that these treatments would only ever be available to the wealthy.

Google has resourced its science start-up with some serious intellectual firepower, and these scientists and researchers are working behind the scenes to challenge the inevitability of death. The proponents of a "transhumanist" movement called the Church of Perpetual Life support Google's initiative. They believe that technology could one day see our consciousness digitised into computers, turning us from biological humans into robots – the so-called singularity. (Some fear that this will see artificial intelligence morph into a modern-day Frankenstein's monster!)

For Silicon Valley's death-cheating initiative to be successful, it must find a way to defy the laws of thermodynamics so that an individual can live forever. The key to immortality is tied to the second law of thermodynamics which states that everything must decay. The cells in our bodies follow that rule and eventually deteriorate. That leads to entropy – the inescapable and irreversible process of disorder and eventual death.

Turnover is a basic characteristic of life. Ergo, the search for the elixir of everlasting life runs against the natural order of things, as all living organisms ultimately die. Humans are not biologically immortal, and no amount of R&D money can alter that fact. We will all eventually kick the bucket as immortality – the Holy Grail of biological sciences – is a fairy tale. Even if it were possible, I think that a never-ending life would be a fate worse than death.

**The death of death has been grossly exaggerated.**

POSTING DATE | 23 MAY 2021

## Why the future may not need us

### RISE OF SENTIENT ROBOTS

Attempting to predict the future is always a roll of the dice. No one can see around corners, but that has not stopped think-tanks and other forecasters from trying to gaze a few years down the road. Every other week, another report or book is released telling us how tomorrow is going to unfold.

Yet the future has too many variables for anyone to say with certainty what will happen. Long-promised gizmos like flying cars, robot maids, and personal jetpacks have failed to materialise for the masses. Similarly, bringing cryogenically frozen corpses back to life remains firmly in the realm of science fiction.

History shows that some innovations turn the world upside down while others flop spectacularly. Determining which discoveries will disrupt the status quo is fraught with danger. This is particularly the case with digital technologies which are taking us into uncharted waters.

I'm not a seer when it comes to the future, nor is Yuval Noah Harari. Professor Harari does not claim to know for certain what's in store for humanity. Nonetheless, his book – *Homo Deus: A Brief History of Tomorrow* – provides a provocative and fascinating insight into what might lie ahead.

Harari is a professor of history at the Hebrew University of Jerusalem. His preceding book, the global bestseller *Sapiens: A Brief History of Humankind* laid out the last 70,000 years of human history. It examined how humanity managed to rein in famine, plague, and war.

While *Sapiens* showed us where we have been, *Homo Deus* points to where we are going. Harari openly admits that predicting the future isn't as easy as deconstructing the past. Even so, his future-orientated sequel provides a glimpse of the forces that will shape the $21^{st}$ century.

Harari's central claim is that Homo sapiens (Latin for "wise man") will become Homo deus (Latin for "God man"). We are on the cusp of an evolutionary transition in history that may witness the creation of a new species of superhumans – the man-gods of Harari's title.

Harari is an atheist, so when he uses the word "God", he is not referring to a supreme deity who is all-powerful (omnipotent), all-knowing (omniscient), and all-present (omnipresent). Rather, he means humans with life spans greatly extended by science, and intelligence vastly enhanced by technology.

Harari believes that humans will increasingly focus on God-like pursuits such as chasing enduring happiness (well-being) and everlasting life (wellness). "In seeking bliss and immortality," he writes, "humans are in fact trying to upgrade themselves into gods".

Achieving this upgrade will take "divine powers" and will happen through new "techno-humanism" technologies, such as genetic modification, artificial intelligence, and cyborg engineering. We are approaching a crossroads in evolution where machines will become more human-like and humans will allegedly become more machine-like.

Biology and computing are coming together and could theoretically result in a human brain being directly connected to a computer. That "distant possibility", says Harari, will be reserved for a tiny number of elites – a superclass of humans – given the significant cost of biotechnology.

There will also be a massive "useless class" who will be pushed to one side by intelligent machines which will do jobs better than people can. The list of occupations where people will be "unemployable" include bus drivers, bartenders, construction labourers, veterinary assistants, and telemarketers.

One of the divides between the superclass and useless class will be biological, with the former having superior physical and cognitive capacity and living much longer. A second dividing line between the classes will be artificial intelligence, which will give unprecedented power to the few who control the algorithms which run our lives.

To illustrate, at some stage in the future, all vehicles are predicted to be self-driving, and one corporation may well control the algorithm that runs the entire transport market. In that scenario, all the economic power previously shared by thousands will be in the hands of a single corporation.

A second example can be found in the operation of the military. Armies – which once consisted of millions of men – are increasingly being dominated by small groups of super-warriors who control technologies like drones which can fight cyber wars. The best armies today require a small number of highly professional soldiers using very high-tech equipment.

Across the board, human authority is shifting to algorithms and external data processing systems which, according to Harari, may "know us better than we know ourselves". Harari envisages that "Dataism" – a universal faith in the power of algorithms – will become sacrosanct.

Our lives will be dominated by non-conscious but highly intelligent algorithms as we are sucked deeper into the online world and turned into faceless data. In this brave new digital world, Dataism will purportedly become our 21$^{st}$ century religion, replacing a homo-centric world with a data-centric world.

Billions of people around the world are regular users of social media and share intimate details of their lives on platforms such as Facebook, YouTube, WhatsApp, and Twitter. But all that free browsing and connecting comes at a price – your entire life (which is why I'm not a user, albeit I do utilise Google).

Harari warns that when you get something for free, you are the product. He points out that "in the twenty-first century our personal data is probably the most valuable resource most humans still have to offer, and we are giving it to the tech giants in exchange for email services and funny cat videos".

The dehumanisation of decision-making is being facilitated by everyday citizens. The algorithms that nowadays make automated decisions – which were formerly the exclusive remit of humans – are being fed a diet of data supplied by us. As noted in an online article by two mathematicians:

> An algorithm is a digital recipe: a list of rules for achieving an outcome, using a set of ingredients. Usually, for tech companies, that outcome is to make money by convincing us to buy something or keeping us scrolling in order to show us more advertisements. The ingredients used are the data we provide through our actions online – knowingly or otherwise.

Harari believes that "humankind is poised to replace natural selection with intelligent design, and to extend life from the organic realm into the inorganic". Still, he is not asserting that the future has to unfold this way – his book maps the different possibilities that humankind is facing. He states that our species:

> … is likely to upgrade itself step by step, merging with robots and computers in the process, until our descendants will look back and realise that they are no longer the kind of animal that wrote the Bible, built the Great Wall of China and laughed at Charlie Chaplin's antics.

Frankly, I find Harari's predictions chilling and hope that they do not come to pass. I don't want my great-grandchildren to be bio-engineered. I don't want humans to be turned into flesh-and-silicon cyborgs. And I don't want the techno super-rich to live forever by implanting their brains into robots.

My attitude to immortality was outlined in a recent post, *The quest for healthy aging and longevity*. Assuming I'm right and immortality is never achieved, the unequal availability of life-extending procedures will nonetheless take a toll on society. For Harari this means that:

> … we might see the emergence of the most unequal societies that ever existed … economic inequality will be translated into biological inequality.

**I hope that the world is not spinning too fast to avoid this grim future.**

POSTING DATE | 20 JUNE 2021

## Is exploring and colonising Mars worth the investment?

### JUSTIFYING THE COST OF INTERSTELLAR TRAVEL

The need to explore is at the heart of human existence. People have always explored the world around them as part of a primordial journey of discovery. Great explorers – like Marco Polo, Christopher Columbus, and James Cook – led the spread of civilisation and helped humanity discover the unknown.

From the Stone Age to the Space Age, humans have pushed new frontiers to overcome what was once thought impossible. Human ventures have resulted in us navigating the seas, discovering new lands, conquering the skies, and exploring the cosmos.

For eons, Earthlings have looked at the heavens and wondered about the celestial bodies in our solar system. Mars, the big red dot in the night sky, has long fascinated us. Indeed, no other planet has fired the human imagination as much as our neighbouring planet.

Throughout history, Mars has been embraced in myths (home of little green men), religions (named after the Roman god of war), literature (sci-fi tomes such as *The War of the Worlds* about extraterrestrial invaders), and cinema (Hollywood has released dozens of movies about Mars and Martians).

The lure of the Red Planet has also proved irresistible to NASA. America's space agency wants to land a human crew on Mars in the 2030s – potentially as early as 2035. Between now and then, hundreds of billions of dollars will be spent in the countdown to put boots on the red Martian surface. But is it worth the stratospheric cost?

Astronauts are not budget travellers, which is why spaceflights are so expensive. A manned mission to Mars is an extremely complex and long-timescale project which will burn through stacks of money – perhaps as much as half a trillion dollars.

No one in their right mind would consider this amount of money to be small change. Even so, it is – in the opinion of Mars exploration advocates – a sound and sensible investment. Opponents, of course, have a different view and see deep space exploration as an extravagance that we can ill afford.

The tension between those dreaming of a second home on a Red Planet and those prioritising the home we currently have on our Blue Planet is the most polarising issue in the Mars debate. The opportunity for Homo sapiens to shrug off their terrestrial bonds has divided us.

Many believe that the long-term benefits of space exploration are overshadowed by short-term earthly concerns. Those focussed on the "here and now" invoke the old catch-cry that the money could be better spent elsewhere on more pressing issues, such as the fight against world hunger.

Critics of interplanetary exploration also believe that the claimed scientific and social benefits of such pursuits are pie-in-the-sky. They would prefer to see their tax dollars deployed to yield immediate improvements in tangible areas, such as national infrastructure and health care.

Personally, I am a proponent of humankind's next giant leap to colonise another world. I accept that establishing a permanent human settlement on Mars is an eyebrow-raising idea. Yet it's a dream that has captured the collective imagination of humankind more than any other.

Whether it's private companies like SpaceX or government organisations such as NASA, the race to Mars is well and truly on. The shared space vision of many countries seems to be "Conquer Mars". Only four entities – the US, Russia, India, and the European Space Agency – have successfully entered the Martian orbit. However, membership in this elite club is set to expand.

Last July, America, China, and the United Arab Emirates all launched unmanned spacecraft to Mars. The closeness of the three launches was no coincidence. Each was timed to take advantage of a one-month window in which Mars and Earth were in the nearest alignment on the same side of the Sun. This allowed for the shortest possible trip – a mere 55 million kilometres!

The space route to the Red Planet is becoming increasingly busy. A growing number of nations are blasting off to Mars, with each looking to find their specific niche. While they have different objectives, Mars is shaping up as the next symbol of humanity's enduring quest for exploration.

Many prominent scientists believe that establishing a colony on Mars is a worthwhile endeavour which will produce myriad long-term benefits for society. The three most often cited payoffs are as follows.

**1. Ensure the future of humankind**

Prior to his death, Professor Stephen Hawking made the bleak prediction that humanity must colonise another planet within 100 years or face possible extinction. "With climate change, overdue asteroid strikes, epidemics, and population growth, our own planet is increasingly precarious," warned Hawking.

Like Elon Musk, Hawking believed that we have no choice as a species but to become multi-planetary – starting with the colonisation of Mars. Musk views Mars as a "backup planet" should something apocalyptic destroy the Earth. Dinosaurs roamed the Earth for 165 million years until a colossal asteroid wiped them out – and the fear is that it could happen again.

If humans ever need to beat a retreat from Earth due to some doomsday event, we will need somewhere to go. Musk thinks that we may be ready to start shuttling people between Earth and Mars in the next decade or so. If all goes well, then perhaps 40 or 100 years later, Mars could be a self-sustaining colony of a million people.

**2. Search for signs of life on Mars**

Understanding whether extraterrestrial life exists and/or existed elsewhere in the universe is a fundamental question of humankind. While Mars today is dry and barren, it wasn't always a desolate wasteland. Water, which is critical to life, was stable on the surface of Mars for about a billion years. In the same way that life evolved on Earth, it is likely to have followed a similar path on Mars.

As noted in an article authored by political scientist Darrell West, and published by *The Brookings Institution*, the question of the origins of life is central to science, religion, and philosophy. Humans have long assumed that life was unique to Earth and not present elsewhere in the solar system, let alone the universe. We have constructed elaborate religious and philosophical narratives around this assumption and built our identity along the notion that life exists exclusively on Earth.

If future space missions cast doubt on that assumption or outright disprove it by finding remnants of microbial life on other planets, it will be both invigorating and illusion-shattering. We humans will be forced to confront our own myths and consider alternative narratives about the universe and the place of Earth in the overall scheme of things.

**3. Develop new technologies**

Many everyday conveniences we use in our daily lives stem from innovations in space technology. For example, the memory foam you lie on for a good night's rest was initially developed to improve the comfort of astronauts on long space flights. Also, every photo you snap on your smartphone is possible due to small imaging sensors originally developed by NASA. Further, the water-purification systems developed for the International Space Station are now used to help remote communities address water shortages.

Pushing the boundaries of human exploration invariably leads to discoveries in science and technology which deliver unintended benefits to humanity. The world already benefits greatly from space technology, especially with regard to satellites and global positioning systems which have revolutionised banking, navigation, and everyday communications.

Space technology orbits our daily lives without us even noticing, and the Mars missions will undoubtedly deliver further benefits. Successfully landing on and colonising Mars will require NASA and other space agencies to pioneer further innovations, and the technology developed will ultimately find its way into our lives. To illustrate, laser-based technology being developed for Mars landings will likely be used on Earth to make self-driving cars safer.

As a young boy, I watched in awe as Neil Armstrong walked on the Moon, and I hope that in my lifetime I will also get to see humans walk on the Red Planet. Mars is a modern-day New World, and a human colony on this planet is the next great adventure. Let the countdown begin.

**Three, two, one ... we have lift off!**

POSTING DATE | 28 FEBRUARY 2021

## Why gigantic numbers baffle the mind

### A SMALL PROBLEM WITH BIG NUMBERS

Our ancient ancestors had no need to understand excessively large numbers as their everyday dealings were with single digits, such as two fish or three spears. Unlike us, they did not live in a world comprised of millions of streets, billions of people, and trillions in debt. And they certainly never encountered a Rubik's cube with 43 quintillion possible configurations (that's 18 zeros)!

In contrast, today's news broadcasts often report absurdly huge numbers as businesses, scientists, and governments increasingly think in terms of millions (of dollars), billions (of stars), and trillions (in bailouts). These mathematical names are tossed around with casual disregard, thereby sealing their place in common parlance. Still, many of us do not have a visceral grasp of their size.

Understanding giant numbers is far from second nature – they perplex the human mind, which is yet to latch on to the modern world's explosion of massive numbers. As noted by one leading anthropologist, as a species we have evolved capacities that "... are naturally good at discriminating small quantities and naturally poor at discriminating large quantities".

While getting a solid handle on incredibly big numbers isn't easy, it's not a problem for Google founders Larry Page and Sergey Brin, who both grew up fascinated with mathematics. So, when they registered the name of their new Internet search company in 1997, they chose the mathematical term "googol". Googol is the label for 10 raised to the hundredth power ($10^{100}$) or 1 followed by 100 zeros.

Our young tech entrepreneurs thought that googol was an appropriate name for their search engine as it was going to index an unfathomable number of Internet web pages. However, due to a typographical error, the name was incorrectly typed as "Google"; the name stuck and Google Inc. was born.

Big numbers befuddle us – and not because we misspell them. Numbers as large as a googol are hard to comprehend, and referring to them by name doesn't help. There is not a googol of anything in the universe, as the number is so mind-bogglingly mammoth it has no practical application.

Of course, smaller numbers used to quantify commonplace things – such as 2 dogs, 25 people, and 1,000 cars – are easy to comprehend. But when we encounter larger numbers, like a quadrillion, it becomes increasingly difficult to conceptualise them. Such numbers are so abstract, our eyes glaze over.

Consider a trillion – it effortlessly rolls off the tongue. Yet, when we express it in exponential format ($10^{12}$) or its full format (1,000,000,000,000), we start to get a sense of how gargantuan it is. One trillion is a thousand billion, or comparably a million million. Whichever way you look at it, there are too many noughts to make sense of, so let's put this number into perspective.

If you had spent $1 million a day since the birth of Jesus Christ, you still wouldn't have chalked up $1 trillion in purchases. If you travelled back in time by a trillion seconds, you would end up circa 30,000 BC. And if you were to spend $1 million an hour, non-stop for 24 hours a day, it would take you 114 years to burn through $1 trillion.

In August 2018, Apple became the first company in the world to cross over into the four-comma club when its market capitalisation surpassed $1 trillion. Two years later, Apple's market value doubled, making it the first publicly traded US company to pass the $2 trillion threshold.

World Bank data reveals that only seven countries have annual GDP figures greater than Apple's $2 trillion value. With this amount to spend, you could buy Australia and New Zealand and still have a pocket full of change. You could also end world hunger many times over according to the United Nations.

Investopedia calculated that to equal Apple's $2 trillion market cap, you would have to combine the net worth of the world's top 24 billionaires. This provides a nice segue to our next humongous number – a billion. Using scientific notation, this number is expressed as $10^9$ – the superscript tells you how many zeros there are after the one.

After discussing a trillion, a billion might sound small – but it's not. Each billion is equivalent to a thousand million. Could you live on a billion dollars for the rest of your life? Well, spare a thought for the world's richest individuals, who each face the challenge of surviving on personal fortunes of over $100 billion.

In March each year, the American business magazine, *Forbes*, publishes a list of the wealthiest billionaires in the world. The 2021 *Forbes* list shows that Amazon founder Jeff Bezos is the world's richest person, with a net worth of $177 billion.

Entrepreneur Elon Musk rocketed into the number two spot with a $151 billion fortune. French luxury-goods tycoon Bernard Arnault took third place with $150 billion under his Louis Vuitton belt. And rounding out the top four in the centibillionaire club is Microsoft co-founder Bill Gates, whose riches swelled to $124 billion.

The number of billionaires on *Forbes* 35$^{th}$ annual list exploded to an unprecedented 2,755 people, who are collectively worth $13.1 trillion, up from $8 trillion on the 2020 list. Just to provide some perspective to this staggering wealth, Oxfam International reported that, prior to the pandemic, the (then) 2,153 billionaires in the world had more wealth than the 4.6 billion people who made up 60 per cent of the planet's population.

If we drop down one notch on our scale of large numbers, we arrive at a more digestible number – a million – which has a power-of-10 notation of $10^6$, where 10 is the base and the $^6$ is the exponent. A million is a thousand thousand, and while it's the smallest of the big boys, a million remains the classic benchmark for other massive numbers.

As a million sits at the bottom of the "illions" ladder, it's easy to view this as a paltry amount, but is that really the case? When was the last time you encountered a million in your daily life? Do you own a million of anything? Have you ever driven a million miles? Do you work in an office with a million employees?

When I was a boy, a millionaire was a very wealthy person, whereas today in Australia that is considered to be a modest level of wealth. Nevertheless, a million is still a large number, and anyone reading this post would be thrilled to strike it rich with a seven-figure windfall. Also, die-hard social-media influencers work overtime trying to rack up a million-plus followers.

Humans are visual creatures, so a common strategy for comprehending big numbers is to devise visual representations which provide a sense of scale. You can put a million into perspective by saying that one million acres is the size of 16 million tennis courts. Or that planting one million trees would cover an area of more than 15,000 football fields.

The trick to thinking about large numbers is to relate them to something that is meaningful – even something as simple as seconds. A million seconds takes almost 12 days to elapse; a billion seconds is about 32 years; and a trillion seconds equates to around 32,000 years. In a similar vein, you could say that counting to a million would take days, counting to a billion would take years, and counting to a trillion would be impossible in one lifetime.

Telling a child that you could line up 109 Earths across the face of the Sun is far more comprehendible than clinically blurting out that the Sun's diameter is 1.392 million kms. Equally, reporting that a destructive bushfire has rapidly burned an area equivalent to the size of a football field every second is easier to visualize than saying that millions of acres were destroyed.

Mathematics is the universal language of humanity, and it connects all of us. Around the world and across civilisations, anyone with an elementary education can understand tens, hundreds, and thousands, but many of us struggle to quantify millions, billions, and trillions. So, instead of hurling brain-bending numbers at each other, we should break them down so that they make sense for our own experience.

**What's next – getting our minds around a quadrillion ($10^{15}$)?**

POSTING DATE | 13 FEBRUARY 2022

# Resource List

This resource list acknowledges my debt to the many and varied sources of data and ideas I drew upon in researching and writing the 50 blog posts contained in this book. The list is arranged under the medium of publication, and each citation includes sufficient information – including a URL where appropriate – to allow that source to be located and retrieved.

## PUBLISHED BOOKS

Achen, Christopher H. and Bartels, Larry M. 2016. *Democracy for Realists: Why Elections Do Not Produce Responsive Government.* New Jersey: Princeton University Press.

Andersen, Kurt. 2017. *Fantasyland: How America Went Haywire: A 500-Year History*. London: Ebury Publishing.

Bailey, Ronald and Tupy, Marian L. 2020. *Ten Global Trends Every Smart Person Should Know: And Many Others You Will Find Interesting*. Washington DC: Cato Institute.

Bessen, James. 2015. *Learning by Doing: The Real Connection between Innovation, Wages, and Wealth.* New Haven: Yale University Press.

Bricker, Darrell and Ibbitson, John. 2019. *Empty Planet: The Shock of Global Population Decline*. Toronto: Signal.

Chang, Ha-Joon. 2010. *23 Things They Don't Tell You about Capitalism*. London:Penguin Books.

Covey, Stephen R. 2020. *The 7 Habits of Highly Effective People*. 30th anniversary edn. New York: Simon & Schuster.

Epstein, David. 2019. *Range: Why Generalists Triumph in a Specialized World*. New York: Riverhead Books.

Harari, Yuval Noah. 2015. *Sapiens: A Brief History of Humankind*. London: Vintage.

____________2017. *Homo Deus: A Brief History of Tomorrow*. London: Vintage.

Kelman, Herbert and Hamilton, V. Lee. 1990. *Crimes of Obedience: Toward a Social Psychology of Authority and Responsibility*. New Haven: Yale University Press.

Kurzban, Robert. 2010. *Why Everyone (Else) Is a Hypocrite: Evolution and the Modular Mind*. New Jersey: Princeton University Press.

Lee, Bandy X. 2020. *Profile of a Nation: Trump's Mind, America's Soul*. New York: World Mental Health Coalition, Inc.

McIntyre, Lee. 2021. *How to Talk to a Science Denier: Conversations with Flat Earthers, Climate Deniers, and Others Who Defy Reason*. Cambridge: The MIT Press.

Mudde, Cas and Kaltwasser, Cristóbal Rovira. 2017. *Populism: A Very Short Introduction*. New York: Oxford University Press.

Norberg, Johan. 2003. *In Defense of Global Capitalism*. Washington DC: Cato Institute.

Rauch, Jennifer. 2018. *Slow Media: Why "Slow" is Satisfying, Sustainable, and Smart*. New York: Oxford University Press.

Schweizer, Peter. 2006. *Do As I Say (Not As I Do): Profiles in Liberal Hypocrisy*. New York: Doubleday.

Sowell, Thomas. 2011. *Economic Facts and Fallacies*. New York: Basic Books.

Taleb, Nassim Nicholas. 2007. *The Black Swan: The Impact of the Highly Improbable*. London: Penguin Books.

Tanner, Lindsay. 2011. *Sideshow: Dumbing down democracy*. Melbourne: Scribe Publications Pty Ltd.

Wood, Geoffrey E. 2014. *Fifty Economic Fallacies Exposed*. London: The Institute of Economic Affairs.

## NEWSPAPER ARTICLES

Alcorn, Gay. 2019. 'How Australia's compulsory voting saved it from Trumpism'. *The Guardian* Australian Edn. (online). 8 March. Available: https://www.theguardian.com/australia-news/2019/mar/08/how-australias-compulsory-voting-saved-it-from-trumpism

Andersen, Kurt. 2017. 'How America lost its mind'. *The Atlantic* (online). 28 December. Available: https://www.theatlantic.com/magazine/archive/2017/09/how-america-lost-its-mind/534231/

Best, Isabel. 2016. 'Should we even go there? Historians on comparing fascism to Trumpism'. *The Guardian* (online). 2 December. Available: https://www.theguardian.com/us-news/2016/dec/01/comparing-fascism-donald-trump-historians-trumpism

Bramesco, Charles. 2021. 'Look away: why star-studded comet satire Don't Look Up is a disaster'. *The Guardian* (online). 27 December. Available: https://www.theguardian.com/film/2021/dec/27/look-away-why-star-studded-comet-satire-dont-look-up-is-a-disaster

Brooks, Arthur C. 2019. 'Conspiracy theories are a dangerous threat to our democracy'. *The Washington Post* (online). 3 September. Available: https://www.washingtonpost.com/opinions/2019/09/03/conspiracy-theories-are-dangerous-threat-our-democracy/

Brown, Gordon. 2019. 'There's a new battle for Britain: resistance to Nigel Farage'. *The Guardian* (online). 30 May. Available: https://www.theguardian.com/commentisfree/2019/may/30/new-battle-britain-resistance-nigel-farage

Bruni, Frank. 2019. 'The Real Horror of the Anti-Vaxxers'. *The New York Times* (online). 9 March. Available: https://www.nytimes.com/2019/03/09/opinion/sunday/the-real-horror-of-the-anti-vaxxers.html

Buranyi, Stephen. 2020. 'Big Pharma Is Fooling US'. *The New York Times* (online). 17 December. Available: https://www.nytimes.

com/2020/12/17/opinion/covid-vaccine-big-pharma.html?auth=login-email&login=email

Butler, Sarah. 2018. 'Is fast fashion giving way to the sustainable wardrobe?'. *The Guardian* (online). 30 December. Available: https://www.theguardian.com/business/2018/dec/29/fast-fashion-giving-way-sustainable-wardrobe

Cave, Damien. 2021. 'Australia's States Are Feuding Like Siblings. What Else to Do but Laugh?'. *The New York Times* (online). 14 January. Available: https://www.nytimes.com/2021/01/14/world/australia/state-border-restrictions-coronavirus.html

Cohen, Nick. 2017. 'Trump's lies are not the problem. It's the millions who swallow them who really matter'. *The Guardian* (online). 5 February. Available: https://www.theguardian.com/commentisfree/2017/feb/05/donald-trump-lies-belief-totalitarianism

Daragahi, Borzou. 2020. 'Coronavirus could be used by authoritarian leaders as excuse to undermine democracy, experts warn'. *The Independent* (online). 17 March. Available: https://www.independent.co.uk/news/health/coronavirus-us-cases-government-pandemic-democracy-covid-19-a9407011.html

De Stropper, Bart. 2018. 'Dementia is too big a problem to walk away from – for Pfizer or any of us'. 11 January. *The Guardian* (online). Available: https://www.theguardian.com/commentisfree/2018/jan/11/dementia-pfizer-alzheimers-research-big-pharma

Dooley, Ben. 2019. 'Modern Monetary Theory's Reluctant Poster Child: Japan'. *The New York Times* (online). 5 June. Available: https://www.nytimes.com/2019/06/05/business/modern-monetary-theorys-reluctant-poster-child-japan.html?auth=login-email&login=email

Eyers, James. 2021. 'Digital finance CRC wins $181m from government, partners'. *Australian Financial Review* (online). 30 June. Available: https://www.afr.com/companies/financial-services/digital-finance-crc-wins-181m-from-government-partners-20210629-p585ad

Gray, Dylan. 2013. Big pharma's excuses for the monopolies on medicine won't wash'. *The Guardian* (online). 23 February. Available: https://www.theguardian.com/commentisfree/2013/feb/22/hiv-aids-deaths-pharmaceutical-industry

Groch, Sherryn. 2020. 'Why are so many nations blasting off to Mars?'. *The Sydney Morning Herald* (online). 31 July. Available: https://www.smh.com.au/national/why-are-so-many-nations-blasting-off-to-mars-20200730-p55gyr.html

Harari, Yuval Noah. 2020. 'Yuval Noah Harari: the world after coronavirus'. *Financial Times* (online). 20 March. Available: https://www.ft.com/content/19d90308-6858-11ea-a3c9-1fe6fedcca75

Helm, Toby., Graham-Harrison, Emma and McKie, Robin. 2020. 'How did Britain get its coronavirus response so wrong?'. *The Guardian* (online). 19 April. Available: https://www.theguardian.com/world/2020/apr/18/how-did-britain-get-its-response-to-coronavirus-so-wrong

Henley, Jon and Roy, Eleanor Ainge. 2020. 'Are female leaders more successful at managing the coronavirus crisis?'. *The Guardian* (online). 25 April. Available: https://www.theguardian.com/world/2020/apr/25/why-do-female-leaders-seem-to-be-more-successful-at-managing-the-coronavirus-crisis

Herrman, John. 2021. 'What, Exactly, Is Amazon Web Services?'. *The New York Times* (online). 9 February. Available: https://www.nytimes.com/2021/02/09/style/amazon-web-services.html

Hewson, John. 2017. 'Career politicians aren't qualified to run the country'. *The Sydney Morning Herald* (online). 23 February. Available: https://www.smh.com.au/opinion/career-politicians-arent-qualified-to-run-the-country-20170223-guj8gw.html

Horowitz, Jason., Bubola, Emma and Povoledo, Elisabetta. 2020. 'Italy, Pandemic's New Epicenter, Has Lessons for the World'. *The New York Times* (online). 21 March. Available: https://www.nytimes.com/2020/03/21/world/europe/italy-coronavirus-center-lessons.html

'How Big Tech Got Even Bigger'. *The Wall Street Journal* (online). 6 February, 2021. Available: https://www.wsj.com/articles/how-big-tech-got-even-bigger-11612587632

Ingle, Sean. 2022. 'China opens Winter Olympics with peace doves and a mighty provocation'. *The Guardian* (online). 5 February. Available: https://www.theguardian.com/sport/2022/feb/04/china-opens-winter-olympics-with-peace-doves-and-a-mighty-provocation

Irvine, Jessica. 2020. 'Don't add government debt to your list of things to worry about'. *The Sydney Morning Herald* (online). 8 April. Available: https://www.smh.com.au/business/the-economy/don-t-add-government-debt-to-your-list-of-things-to-worry-about-20200408-p54ibp.html

Jabour, Bridie. 2021. 'It is astonishing to witness the Australian "border wars" given our COVID response so far'. *The Guardian* (online). 7 January. Available: https://www.theguardian.com/commentisfree/2021/jan/07/it-is-astonishing-to-witness-the-australian-border-wars-given-our-covid-response-so-far

Jericho, Greg. 2020. 'With borrowing effectively free, why be scared of government debt?'. *The Guardian* (online). 8 March. Available: https://www.theguardian.com/business/commentisfree/2020/mar/08/with-borrowing-effectively-free-why-be-scared-of-government-debt

Jones, Owen. 2020. 'The Covid vaccine will benefit humanity – we should all own the patent'. *The Guardian* (online). 13 November. Available: https://www.theguardian.com/commentisfree/2020/nov/12/covid-vaccine-patent-pharmaceutical-industry-profits-public-sector

Krugman, Paul. 2003. 'Lumps of Labor'. *The New York Times* (online). 7 October. Available: https://www.nytimes.com/2003/10/07/opinion/lumps-of-labor.html

Lau, Maya. 2020. 'Good vaccine news and a flurry of stock sales by executives. There's a pattern, study finds'. *Los Angeles Times* (online). 7 December. Available: https://www.latimes.com/business/story/2020-12-07/good-vaccine-news-executive-stock-trades

Lowrey, Annie. 2020. 'Don't Blame Econ 101 for the Plight of Essential Workers'. *The Atlantic* (online). 13 May. Available: https://www.theatlantic.com/ideas/archive/2020/05/why-are-americas-most-essential-workers-so-poorly-treated/611575/

Manjoo, Farhad. 2016. 'Tech's "Frightful 5" Will Dominate Digital Life for Foreseeable Future'. *The New York Times* (online). 20 January. Available: https://www.nytimes.com/2016/01/21/technology/techs-frightful-5-will-dominate-digital-life-for-foreseeable-future.html

____________ 2016. 'Why the World Is Drawing Battle Lines Against American Tech Giants'. *The New York Times* (online). 1 June. Available: https://www.nytimes.com/2016/06/02/technology/why-the-world-is-drawing-battle-lines-against-american-tech-giants.html

Mazzucato, Mariana and Momenghalibaf, Azzi. 2020. 'Drug Companies Will Make a Killing From Coronavirus'. *The New York Times* (online). 18 March. Available: https://www.nytimes.com/2020/03/18/opinion/coronavirus-vaccine-cost.html?auth=login-email&login=email

Minevich, Mark. 2020. 'Can China use coronavirus to pave the way to a new world order?'. *The Hill* (online). 2 April. Available: https://thehill.com/opinion/international/490816-can-china-use-coronavirus-to-pave-the-way-to-a-new-world-order/

Parker, Kristy and Mounk, Yascha. 2020. 'Authoritarian Populists Have Six Classic Moves. Trump's Response to COVID-19 Uses Five of Them'. *The Atlantic* (online). 2 April. Available: https://www.theatlantic.com/ideas/archive/2020/04/trumps-authoritarian-covid/609304/

Partington, Richard. 2019. 'Is it time to end our fixation with GDP and growth?'. *The Guardian* (online). 17 June. Available: https://www.theguardian.com/news/2019/jun/17/is-time-to-end-our-fixation-with-gdp-and-growth

Pinker, Steven. 2018. 'The media exaggerates negative news. This distortion has consequences'. *The Guardian* (online). 17 February. Available: https://www.theguardian.com/

commentisfree/2018/feb/17/steven-pinker-media-negative-news

Rajagopal, Divya. 2021. 'Covid: WHO criticises countries, vaccine companies over bilateral deals'. *The Economic Times* (online). 19 January. Available: https://economictimes.indiatimes.com/news/international/world-news/who-criticises-countries-vaccine-cos-over-bilateral-deals/articleshow/80335236.cms?from=mdr

Reyburn. Scott. 2021. 'JPG File Sells for $69 Million, as "NFT Mania" Gathers Pace'. *The New York Times* (online). 11 March. Available: https://www.nytimes.com/2021/03/11/arts/design/nft-auction-christies-beeple.html

Romm, Cari. 2015. 'Rethinking One of Psychology's Most Infamous Experiments'. *The Atlantic* (online). 29 January. Available: https://www.theatlantic.com/health/archive/2015/01/rethinking-one-of-psychologys-most-infamous-experiments/384913/

Rooduijn, Matthijs. 2018. 'Why is populism suddenly all the rage?'. *The Guardian* (online). 21 November. Available: https://www.theguardian.com/world/political-science/2018/nov/20/why-is-populism-suddenly-so-sexy-the-reasons-are-many

Rosen, Julia. 2021. 'The Science of Climate Change Explained: Facts, Evidence and Proof'. *The New York Times* (online). 6 November. Available: https://www.nytimes.com/article/climate-change-global-warming-faq.html

Rowland, Christopher., Johnson, Carolyn Y. and Wan, William. 2020. 'Even finding a COVID-19 vaccine won't be enough to end the pandemic'. *The Washington Post* (online). 11 May. Available: https://www.washingtonpost.com/business/2020/05/11/coronavirus-vaccine-global-supply/

Rubin, Jennifer. 2015. 'Why the voters are to blame'. *The Washington Post* (online). 31 July. Available: https://www.washingtonpost.com/blogs/right-turn/wp/2015/07/31/the-voters-are-to-blame/

Rubin, Trudy. 2020. 'Trump joins "Ostrich Alliance" of loser leaders who put politics above coronavirus science'. *The Philadelphia Inquirer* (online). 22 April. Available: https://www.inquirer.com/opinion/coronavirus-covid-trump-liberate-science-michigan-20200421.html

Sample, Ian. 2019. 'Scientists attempt to recreate 'Overview effect' from Earth'. *The Guardian* (online). 26 December. Available: https://www.theguardian.com/science/2019/dec/26/scientists-attempt-to-recreate-overview-effect-from-earth

Sanger, David E. et al. 2020. 'Search for Coronavirus Vaccine Becomes a Global Competition'. *The New York Times* (online). 19 March. Available: https://www.nytimes.com/2020/03/19/us/politics/coronavirus-vaccine-competition.html

Serhan, Yasmeen. 2020. 'The EU Watches as Hungary Kills Democracy'. *The Atlantic* (online). 3 April. Available: https://www.theatlantic.com/international/archive/2020/04/europe-hungary-viktor-orban-coronavirus-covid19-democracy/609313/

Sperling, Gene B. 2020. 'Martin Luther King Jr Predicted This Moment'. *The New York Times* (online). 24 April. Available: https://www.nytimes.com/2020/04/24/opinion/sunday/essential-workers-wages-covid.html

Tharoor, Ishaan. 2020. 'Trump and Bolsonaro see coronavirus more as a political hassle than a public threat'. *The Washington Post* (online). 25 March. Available: https://webcache.googleusercontent.com/search?q=cache:c8f71Lh1uhIJ:https://www.washingtonpost.com/world/2020/03/25/trump-bolsonaro-see-coronavirus-more-political-hassle-than-public-threat/+&cd=1&hl=en&ct=clnk&gl=au

Tisdall, Simon. 2020. 'From Trump to Erdoğan, men who behave badly make the worst leaders in a pandemic'. *The Guardian* (online). 26 April. Available: https://www.theguardian.com/commentisfree/2020/apr/26/trump-to-erdogan-men-who-behave-badly-make-worst-leaders-pandemic-covid-19

van Leeuwen, Hans and Smith, Michael. 2020. 'Search for COVID-19 vaccine morphs into geopolitical battle'. *Australian*

*Financial Review* (online). 19 July. Available: https://www.afr.com/companies/healthcare-and-fitness/search-for-covid-19-vaccine-morphs-into-geopolitical-battle-20200717-p55cvc

'What is the best way to share out a future Covid-19 vaccine?'. *Bangkok Post* (online). 4 September 2020. Available: https://www.bangkokpost.com/world/1979943/what-is-the-best-way-to-share-out-a-future-covid-19-vaccine-

Yong, Ed. 2018. 'The Tipping Point When Minority Views Take Over'. *The Atlantic* (online). 8 June. Available: https://www.theatlantic.com/science/archive/2018/06/the-tipping-point-when-minority-views-take-over/562307/

## MAGAZINES & PERIODICALS

Anderson, Cami. 2020. 'Why Do Women Make Such Good Leaders During COVID-19?'. *Forbes* (online). 19 April. Available: https://www.forbes.com/sites/camianderson1/2020/04/19/why-do-women-make-such-good-leaders-during-covid-19/?sh=5707e5ba42fc

Atkin, Emily. 2019. 'Climate Change Is the Symptom. Consumer Culture Is the Disease'. *The New Republic* (online). 12 June. Available: https://newrepublic.com/article/154147/climate-change-symptom-consumer-culture-disease

Barajas, Joshua. 2016. 'How Nazi's Defense of "Just Following Orders" Plays Out in the Mind'. *Scientific American* (online). 19 February. Available: https://www.scientificamerican.com/article/how-nazi-s-defense-of-just-following-orders-plays-out-in-the-mind/

Bartlett, Jamie. 2017. 'Return of the city-state'. *Aeon* (online). 5 September. Available: https://aeon.co/essays/the-end-of-a-world-of-nation-states-may-be-upon-us

Berkley, Seth. 2020. 'In the COVID-19 vaccine race, nobody wins unless everyone wins'. *Fortune.* (online). 8 July. Available: https://fortune.com/2020/07/08/covid-19-vaccine-alliance-update-cooperation-coronavirus-vaccines/

Bollyky, Thomas J. and Bown, Chad P. 2020. 'The Tragedy of Vaccine Nationalism'. *Foreign Affairs* (online). September/

October. Available: https://www.foreignaffairs.com/articles/united-states/2020-07-27/vaccine-nationalism-pandemic

Buchanan, Leigh and O'Connell, Andrew. 2006. 'A Brief History of Decision Making'. *Harvard Business Review* (online). January Magazine. Available: https://hbr.org/2006/01/a-brief-history-of-decision-making

Chamorro-Premuzic, Tomas. 2020. 'Are Women Better at Managing the Covid19 Pandemic?'. *Forbes* (online). 10 April. Available: https://webcache.googleusercontent.com/search?q=cache:H22K2TpShCkJ:https://www.forbes.com/sites/tomaspremuzic/2020/04/10/are-female-leaders-better-at-managing-the-covid19-pandemic/+&cd=1&hl=en&ct=clnk&gl=au

Conca, James. 2015. 'The Fukushima Disaster Wasn't Disastrous Because Of The Radiation'. *Forbes* (online). 16 March. Available: https://www.forbes.com/sites/jamesconca/2015/03/16/the-fukushima-disaster-wasnt-very-disastrous/?sh=7e2530196b2d

Davidson, Adam. 2015. 'Debunking the Myth of the Job-Stealing Immigrant'. *The New York Times Magazine* (online). 24 March. Available: https://www.nytimes.com/2015/03/29/magazine/debunking-the-myth-of-the-job-stealing-immigrant.html?_r=0

Deel, Gary. 2020. 'COVID-19 and Respecting Expertise When It's Most Crucial'. *EDGE* Australian Military University (online). 30 March. Available: https://amuedge.com/covid-19-and-respecting-expertise-when-its-most-crucial/

Dolan, Kerry A. 2021. 'Billionaires List: Facts and Figures 2021'. *Forbes* (online). 6 April. Available: https://www.forbes.com/sites/kerryadolan/2021/04/06/forbes-35th-annual-worlds-billionaires-list-facts-and-figures-2021/?sh=7949b8c25e58

Doraisamy, Jerome. 2019. 'Expansion of free speech laws may infringe upon other human rights'. *LawyersWeekly* (online). 8 January. Available: https://www.lawyersweekly.com.au/politics/24778-expansion-of-free-speech-laws-may-infringe-upon-other-human-rights

Dunning, David. 2016. 'The Psychological Quirk That Explains Why You Love Donald Trump'. *POLITICO Magazine* (online).

25 May. Available: https://www.politico.com/magazine/story/2016/05/donald-trump-supporters-dunning-kruger-effect-213904/

Gallagher, Felix. 2020. 'Is GDP an outdated metric of economic success?'. *Oxford Business Review* (online). 15 December. Available: https://oxfordbusinessreview.org/is-gdp-an-outdated-metric-of-economic-success/

Haass, Richard. 2020. 'The Pandemic Will Accelerate History Rather Than Reshape It'. *Foreign Affairs* (online). 7 April. Available: https://www.foreignaffairs.com/articles/united-states/2020-04-07/pandemic-will-accelerate-history-rather-reshape-it

Harari, Yuval Noah. 2020. 'In the Battle Against Coronavirus, Humanity Lacks Leadership'. *TIME* (online). 15 March. Available: https://time.com/5803225/yuval-noah-harari-coronavirus-humanity-leadership/

Ikenberry, G. John. 2011. 'The Future of the Liberal World Order'. *Foreign Affairs* (online). May/June. Available: https://www.foreignaffairs.com/articles/2011-05-01/future-liberal-world-order?check_logged_in=1

'Jennifer Rauch on why Slow Media is satisfying, sustainable and smart'. *Delayed Gratification* (online). 23 April 2019. Available: https://www.slow-journalism.com/delayed-gratification-magazine/jennifer-rauch-on-why-slow-media-is-satisfying-sustainable-and-smart

Karlson, Nils., Stern, Charlotta and Klein, Daniel B. 2020. 'Sweden's Coronavirus Strategy Will Soon Be the World's'. *Foreign Affairs* (online). 12 May. Available: https://www.foreignaffairs.com/articles/sweden/2020-05-12/swedens-coronavirus-strategy-will-soon-be-worlds

Katwala, Amit. 2020. 'Coronavirus could kill handshakes'. *WIRED* (online). 6 March. Available: https://www.wired.co.uk/article/coronavirus-handshakes

Keep, Elmo. 2017. 'Can Human Mortality Really Be Hacked?'. *Smithsonian Magazine* (online). June. Available: https://www.

smithsonianmag.com/innovation/human-mortality-hacked-life-extension-180963241/

Knight, Will. 2020. 'China Goes Back to Work as the Coronavirus Rages on Elsewhere'. *WIRED* (online). 27 March. Available: https://www.wired.com/story/china-goes-work-coronavirus-rages-elsewhere/

Lauer, Alex. 2020. 'Elon Musk is the Ultimate Armchair Epidemiologist'. *InsideHook* (online). 1 May. Available: https://www.insidehook.com/article/science/elon-musk-armchair-epidemiologist-coronavirus

Lewis, Hyrum. 2017. "It's Time to Retire the Political Spectrum'. *Quillette* (online). 3 May. Available: https://quillette.com/2017/05/03/time-retire-political-spectrum/

Lewis, Tanya. 2021. 'The "Shared Psychosis" of Donald Trump and His Loyalists'. *Scientific American* (online). 11 January. Available: https://www.scientificamerican.com/article/the-shared-psychosis-of-donald-trump-and-his-loyalists/

McIntyre, Lee. 2021. 'Talking to science deniers and sceptics is not hopeless'. *Nature* (online). 5 August. Available: https://www.nature.com/articles/d41586-021-02152-y

Mack, Eric. Undated. 'Elon Musk Succeeds by Doing the Exact Opposite of What We're all Told to Do'. *Inc.com* (online). Available: https://www.inc.com/eric-mack/elon-musk-succeeds-again-and-again-by-ignoring-this-piece-of-advice-we-all-hear.html

Mayell, Hillary. 2004. 'About 1.7 billion people belong to the global consumer class'. *National Geographic* (online). 12 January. Available: https://www.nationalgeographic.com/environment/article/consumerism-earth-suffers

Newman, Steph. 2019. '"Slow media" the antidote to social media's need for speed?'. *AdNews* (online). 1 March. Available: https://www.adnews.com.au/opinion/slow-media-the-antidote-to-social-media-s-need-for-speed

Nossel, Suzanne. 2021. 'The World Still Needs the UN'. *Foreign Affairs* (online). 18 March. Available: https://www.

foreignaffairs.com/articles/world/2021-03-18/world-still-needs-un

Pazzanese, Christina. 2020. 'Battling the "pandemic of misinformation"'. *The Harvard Gazette* (online). 8 May. Available: https://news.harvard.edu/gazette/story/2020/05/social-media-used-to-spread-create-covid-19-falsehoods/

Ralph, Elizabeth. 2020. 'The Dangerous Race for the Covid Vaccine'. *POLITICO* (online). 7 July. Available: https://www.politico.com/news/magazine/2020/07/07/vaccine-race-covid-national-pride-348072

Range, Peter Ross. 2018. 'Only One Man Was Found Guilty for His Role in the My Lai Massacre. This Is What It Was Like to Cover His Trial'. *TIME* (online). 16 March. Available: https://time.com/5202268/calley-trial-my-lai-massacre/

Rothman, Joshua. 2018. 'Are Things Getting Better or Worse?'. *The New Yorker* (online). 16 July. Available: https://www.newyorker.com/magazine/2018/07/23/are-things-getting-better-or-worse

Royston, Jack. 2021. 'Prince Harry and Meghan Markle Called Hypocritical for Flying 21 Private Jets in Two Years'. *Newsweek* (online). 28 September. Available: https://www.newsweek.com/prince-harry-meghan-markle-hypocritical-21-private-jets-since-2019-climate-change-environment-1633426

Salzman, Avi. 2021. 'Why Visa Bought an NFT for $150,000'. *Barron's* (online). 26 August. Available: https://www.barrons.com/articles/why-visa-bought-an-nft-for-150-000-51630006729

Seneca, Christopher. 2020. 'How to Break Out of Your Social Media Echo Chamber'. *WIRED* (online). 17 September. Available: https://www.wired.com/story/facebook-twitter-echo-chamber-confirmation-bias/

Shafer, Jack. 2018. 'Why the Press Didn't Cover Your Demonstration'. *POLITICO Magazine* (online). 22 January. Available: https://www.politico.com/magazine/story/2018/01/22/why-the-press-didnt-cover-your-demonstration-216499/

Taylor, Paul. 2020. 'Coronavirus brings out best (and worst) in world leaders'. *POLITICO* (online). 25 March. Available: https://www.politico.eu/article/coronavirus-brings-out-best-and-worst-in-world-leaders/

Wittenberg-Cox, Avivah. 2020. 'What Do Countries with The Best Coronavirus Responses Have In Common? Women Leaders'. *Forbes Magazine* (online). 13 April. Available: https://www.forbes.com/sites/avivahwittenbergcox/2020/04/13/what-do-countries-with-the-best-coronavirus-reponses-have-in-common-women-leaders/?sh=72bf09a73dec

## MEDIA OUTLETS

'Backstory: How "slow journalism" is uncovering untold stories in remote communities'. *ABC News* (online). 6 September 2018. Available: https://www.abc.net.au/news/redirects/backstory/regional/2018-09-06/backstory-remote-communities-project/10178276

Bayram, Burcu A. 2017. 'Rise in globalism doesn't mean the end for nationalists'. *The Conversation* (online). 11 August. Available: https://theconversation.com/rise-in-globalism-doesnt-mean-the-end-for-nationalists-81463

Berglöf, Erik. 2020. 'A Pandemic Strategy as Global as COVID-19'. *Project Syndicate* (online). 19 March. Available: https://www.project-syndicate.org/commentary/covid19-pandemic-g20-cooperation-by-erik-berglof-2020-03?barrier=accesspaylog

Blackburn, Christine Crudo. 2020. 'Commentary: COVID-19 exposes US reliance on China for pharmaceuticals and medical devices'. *Channel News Asia* (online). 19 February. Available: https://www.channelnewsasia.com/commentary/covid-19-wuhancoronavirus-china-us-medical-medicine-supply-chain-778041

Boscovic, Dragan. 2021. 'How nonfungible tokens work and where they get their value – a cryptocurrency expert explains NFTs'. *The Conversation* (online). 31 March. Available: https://theconversation.com/how-nonfungible-tokens-work-and-where-they-get-their-value-a-cryptocurrency-expert-explains-nfts-157489

Calland, Richard. 2020. 'All world leaders face mega COVID-19 crises: how Ramaphosa is stacking up'. *The Conversation* (online). 26 March. Available: https://theconversation.com/all-world-leaders-face-mega-covid-19-crises-how-ramaphosa-is-stacking-up-134682

Campbell, Eric and McGregor, Lisa. 2020. 'These five strategies have helped Singapore fight off the coronavirus outbreak. Can they keep it at bay?'. *ABC News* (online). 31 March. Available: https://www.abc.net.au/news/2020-03-31/coronavirus-singapore-how-it-fought-the-virus/12100072

Carmody, James. 2020. 'Row over coronavirus border closures escalates as WA Premier hits back at NSW with Ruby Princess jibe'. *ABC News* (online). 20 May. Available: https://www.abc.net.au/news/2020-05-20/wa-escalates-coronavirus-state-border-closure-row-with-nsw/12266628

Chang, Charis and Maiden, Samantha. 2020. 'Australia joins "first movers" group of nations that have kept coronavirus under control'. *News.com.au* (online). 7 May. Available: https://www.news.com.au/national/politics/australia-joins-first-movers-group-of-nations-that-have-kept-coronavirus-under-control/news-story/997f1cc7f0eba65f3739f85b66fafe12

Eng, James. 2015. '3 Trillion: Study Finds Many, Many More Trees Than Previously Estimated'. *NBC News* (online). Available: ttps://www.nbcnews.com/science/environment/3-trillion-study-finds-many-many-more-trees-previously-estimated-n420456

Forthomme, Claude. 2019. 'Populism's Promises: Are Populist Leaders Delivering on Them?'. *Impakter* (online). 6 January. Available: https://impakter.com/populisms-promises-are-populist-leaders-delivering-on-them/

Goldman, Dana., Conti, David and Kahn, Matthew E. 2020. 'Why COVID-19 vaccines need to prioritize "superspreaders"'. *The Conversation* (online). 4 September. Available: https://theconversation.com/why-covid-19-vaccines-need-to-prioritize-superspreaders-145232

Greifeld, Robert. 2020. 'Op-ed: Pandemic moves Modern Monetary Theory from the fringes to actual US policy'. *CNBC* (online). 29

April. Available: https://www.cnbc.com/2020/04/29/op-ed-pandemic-moves-modern-monetary-theory-from-the-fringes-to-actual-us-policy.html

Hutchens, Gareth. 2020. 'Australia's net debt likely to jump to more than $500 billion as massive coronavirus stimulus unleashed'. *ABC NEWS* (online). 31 March. Available: https://www.abc.net.au/news/2020-03-31/how-will-130-billion-dollar-coronavirus-stimulus-be-paid-for/12105774?section=analysis

Knight, Ben. 2020. 'Coronavirus pandemic shakes up Australian workplaces, as businesses prepare for the other side'. *ABC News* (online). 4 May. Available: https://www.abc.net.au/news/2020-05-04/coronavirus-working-from-home-jobs-divide-women-men/12207694

Lassa, Jonatan A and Booth, Miranda. 2020. 'Are populist leaders a liability during COVID-19?'. *The Conversation* (online). 8 April. Available: https://theconversation.com/are-populist-leaders-a-liability-during-covid-19-135431

Lee, Jong-Wha. 2020. 'A Coordinated Response to COVID-19'. *Project Syndicate* (online). 25 March. Available: https://www.project-syndicate.org/commentary/covid19-pandemic-g20-cooperation-by-lee-jong-wha-2020-03?barrier=accesspaylog

Lexchin, Joel. 2020. 'Can a pharma company change? Profit, not altruism, motivates COVID-19 vaccine development'. *The Conversation* (online). 15 December. Available: https://theconversation.com/can-a-pharma-company-change-profit-not-altruism-motivates-covid-19-vaccine-development-151739

Lufkin, Bryan. 2020. 'Coronavirus: The psychology of panic buying'. *BBC* (online). 5 March. Available: https://www.bbc.com/worklife/article/20200304-coronavirus-covid-19-update-why-people-are-stockpiling

Mitchell, Lewis and Bagrow, James. 2020. 'Do social media algorithms erode our ability to make decisions freely? The jury is out'. *The Conversation* (online). 12 October. Available: https://theconversation.com/do-social-media-algorithms-erode-our-ability-to-make-decisions-freely-the-jury-is-out-140729

Reid, Julie. 2020. 'The media often conflates malicious criticism with genuine critique: why it shouldn't'. *The Conversation* (online). 2 July. Available: https://theconversation.com/the-media-often-conflates-malicious-criticism-with-genuine-critique-why-it-shouldnt-141486

Robertson, David. 2020. 'Coronavirus has some of you calling for Tasmania's border to close. Here's what the experts say'. *ABC News* (online). 17 March. Available: https://www.abc.net.au/news/2020-03-17/coronavirus-tasmania-border-close-what-do-experts-say/12060600

Smith, David. 2020. 'Donald Trump blames everyone but himself for the coronavirus crisis. Will voters agree?'. *The Conversation* (online). 16 April. Available: https://theconversation.com/donald-trump-blames-everyone-but-himself-for-the-coronavirus-crisis-will-voters-agree-135205

Sutton, Malcolm. 2020. 'Sensationalist coronavirus reporting a 'bigger contagion' than the virus itself'. *ABC News* (online). 6 March. Available: https://www.abc.net.au/news/2020-03-06/sensationalist-coronavirus-media-coverage-a-bigger-contagion/12029416

Taylor, Catherine. 2021. 'Australia has a COVID opening plan, but the states are now more divided. Here's where it stands'. *ABC News* (online). 4 September. Available: https://www.abc.net.au/news/2021-09-04/covid-opening-strategy-federal-state-differences-on-plan/100432944

Thoma, Mark. 2016. 'Why GDP fails as a measure of well-being'. *CBS News* (online). 27 January. Available: https://www.cbsnews.com/news/why-gdp-fails-as-a-measure-of-well-being/

'Viewpoint: Is inequality about to get unimaginably worse?'. *BBC* (online). 28 April 2017. Available: https://www.bbc.com/news/world-39706765

Wang, Yanan. 2020. 'Mask-clad Chinese workers cautiously return to the office'. (American) *ABC News* (online). 10 March. Available: https://abcnews.go.com/Health/wireStory/mask-clad-chinese-workers-cautiously-return-office-69479163

Wong, Luke. 2019. 'Space exploration brings both everyday innovations and massive economic benefits to Earth'. *ABC News* (online). 17 July. Available: https://www.abc.net.au/news/2019-07-17/how-space-exploration-innovations-benefit-earth/11314176

## DIGITAL NEWS SITES

Illing, Sean. 2017. 'Two eminent political scientists: The problem with democracy is voters'. *Vox* (online). 24 June. Available: https://www.vox.com/policy-and-politics/2017/6/1/15515820/donald-trump-democracy-brexit-2016-election-europe

Leetaru, Kalev. 2020. 'Media Coverage and Coronavirus Panic: What the Numbers Show'. *RealClear Politics* (online). 2 March. Available: https://www.realclearpolitics.com/articles/2020/03/02/media_coverage_and_coronavirus_panic_what_the_numbers_show_142539.html

Matthews, Dylan. 2019. "Modern Monetary Theory, explained'. *Vox* (online). 16 April. Available: https://www.vox.com/future-perfect/2019/4/16/18251646/modern-monetary-theory-new-moment-explained

Nash, Ethan. 2019. 'Google's $1.5 billion research center to "solve death"'. *TOTT News* (online). 14 March. Available: https://tottnews.com/2019/03/14/google-calico-solving-death/

Orwig, Jessica. 2015. '5 undeniable reasons humans need to colonize Mars – even though it's going to cost billions'. *BusinessInsider* (online). 21 April. Available: https://www.businessinsider.com/5-undeniable-reasons-why-humans-should-go-to-mars-2015-4

Prager, Dennis. 2020. 'Coronavirus Becomes Latest Excuse for Mass Hysteria'. *The Daily Signal* (online). 3 March. Available: https://www.dailysignal.com/2020/03/03/coronavirus-becomes-latest-excuse-for-mass-hysteria/

Reardon, Marguerite. 2021. 'Here's how new antitrust legislation could affect Big Tech... and you'. *CNET* (online). 15 June. Available: https://www.cnet.com/news/politics/heres-how-new-antitrust-legislation-could-affect-big-tech-and-you/

Verhofstadt, Guy. 2020. 'Is COVID 19 Killing democracy?'. *Balkan Insight* (online). 18 May. Available: https://balkaninsight.com/2020/05/18/is-covid-19-killing-democracy/

Walker, Iain and Leviston, Zoe. 2022. 'There are three types of climate change denier – and most of us are at least one'. *Quartz* (online). 21 July. Available: https://qz.com/1726232/the-three-types-of-climate-change-denial/

Yusuf, Huma. 2020. 'World leaders are using Covid-19 to undermine democracy – and history won't judge them well for it'. *Scroll-in* (online). 25 March. Available: https://scroll.in/article/957114/world-leaders-are-using-covid-19-to-undermine-democracy-and-history-wont-judge-them-well-for-it

## ASSORTED WEBSITES

Adams, Jill U. 2008. Genetic Control of Aging and Life Span. *Nature Education* 1 (1):130 (online). Available: https://www.nature.com/scitable/topicpage/genetic-control-of-aging-and-life-span-847/

Barlow, Rich. 2021. 'How to Talk to a Science Denier'. *Boston University Today* (online). 13 October. Available: https://www.bu.edu/articles/2021/lee-mcintyre-how-to-talk-to-a-science-denier/

Benyamin, Chaya. 2020. 'How Similar are the Far-Left and the Far-Right?'. *The Perspective* (online). Available: https://www.theperspective.com/debates/politics/similar-far-left-far-right/

Bidshahri, Raya. 2017. 'Why We Should Send All Our Politicians to Space'. *SingularityHub* (online). 21 August. Available: https://singularityhub.com/2017/08/21/why-we-should-send-all-our-politicians-to-space/

Bonfiglioli, Catriona. 2020. 'Responsible journalism in a time of coronavirus'. *Journalism Education & Research Association of Australia* (online). 23 April. Available: https://jeraa.org.au/responsible-journalism-in-a-time-of-coronavirus/

Bronner, Stephen J. 2020. 'Leadership Experts Share 10 Simple Methods to Change Someone's Mind'. *Inverse* (online). 14

August. Available: https://www.inverse.com/mind-body/10-simple-methods-to-changing-someones-mind

Brumfiel, Geoff. 2020. 'Countries Slammed Their Borders Shut to Stop Coronavirus. But Is It Doing Any Good?'. *Goats and Soda* (online). 15 May. Available: https://www.npr.org/sections/goatsandsoda/2020/05/15/855669867/countries-slammed-their-borders-shut-to-stop-coronavirus-but-is-it-doing-any-goo

Cherry, Kendra. 2021. 'List of Common Cognitive Biases'. *VeryWellMind* (online). 20 January. Available: https://www.verywellmind.com/cognitive-biases-distort-thinking-2794763

Diamandis, Peter H. 2020. 'A Renaissance of Genomics and Drugs Is Extending Human Longevity'. *SingularityHub* (online). 26 June. Available: https://singularityhub.com/2020/06/26/a-renaissance-of-genomics-and-drugs-is-extending-human-longevity/

Donovan, John. 2020. 'Why Is Populism So Popular Again'. *HowStuffWorks.* (online). 7 October. Available: https://people.howstuffworks.com/oligarchy.htm

Dorić, Marko. 'Slow Journalism… the importance of explaining the news, not just breaking it'. *What's new in publishing* (online). Available: https://whatsnewinpublishing.com/slow-journalism-the-importance-of-explaining-the-news-not-just-breaking-it/

Farmer, Catherine. 2021. '"They were just following orders". *UCL* (online). 27 January. Available: https://www.ucl.ac.uk/ioe/research-projects/2022/jan/they-were-just-following-orders

'Forget the "Fountain of Youth", Longevity Lies in a Gene'. *Technology Networks, Genomics Research* (online). 23 April 2019. Available: https://www.technologynetworks.com/genomics/news/forget-the-fountain-of-youth-longevity-lies-in-a-gene-318524

'Google Strategy Teardown: Google Is Turning Itself into an AI Company As It Seeks to Win New Markets Like Cloud and Transportation'. *CB Insights* (online). 16 August 2018. Available: https://www.cbinsights.com/research/report/google-strategy-teardown/

Hail, Steven. 2020. 'Modern monetary theory, COVID-19 and the economy'. *Independent Australia* (online). 29 March. Available: https://independentaustralia.net/politics/politics-display/modern-monetary-theory-covid-19-and-the-economy,13726

Hill, Kashmir. 2019. 'Life Without the Tech Giants'. *Gizmodo* (online). 22 January. Available: https://gizmodo.com/life-without-the-tech-giants-1830258056

Lishchuk, Ruslana. 2021. 'How large would tech companies be if they were countries?'. *MacKeeper* (online). 13 August. Available: https://mackeeper.com/blog/tech-giants-as-countries/

Mabe, John. 2016. 'Amazon, FedEx and Adjacent Innovation'. *Tech Gistics* (online). September 19. Available: https://www.techgistics.net/blog/2016/9/17/amazon-fedex-and-adjacent-innovation

'McDonald's Business Model Case Study'. *What is the business model of* (online). 10 October 2021. Available: https://whatisthebusinessmodelof.com/business-models/mcdonalds-real-estate-company/

'McDonald's Real Estate: How They Really Make Their Money'. *Wall Street Survivor* (online). 6 January 2022. Available: https://www.wallstreetsurvivor.com/mcdonalds-beyond-the-burger/

Michel, Matt. 2015. 'Ten Reasons Why Capitalism Is Morally Superior'. *Contracting Business* (online). 25 September. Available: https://www.contractingbusiness.com/residential-hvac/article/20868486/ten-reasons-why-capitalism-is-morally-superior

Mistry, Lajja. 2021. 'Climate justice or climate hypocrisy?' *Annenberg Media,* University of Southern California (online). 2 November. Available: https://www.uscannenbergmedia.com/2021/11/02/climate-justice-or-climate-hypocrisy/

'Obeying and Resisting Malevolent Orders'. *American Psychological Association* (online). 25 May 2004. Available: https://www.apa.org/topics/forensics-law-public-safety/order

QJ, Steve. 2020. 'The True Danger of Trump's Bottomless Coup'. *Medium* (online). 13 December. Available: https://medium.

com/illumination-curated/the-true-danger-of-trumps-bottomless-coup-2ccf8b499967

Taylor, Jim. 2012. 'Six Reasons Why Politicians Believe They Can Lie'. *Psychology Today* (online). Available: https://www.psychologytoday.com/au/blog/the-power-prime/201209/six-reasons-why-politicians-believe-they-can-lie

Trimarchi, Maria. 2013. '10 of the Worst Decisions Ever Made.' *HowStuffWorks* (online). 22 May. Available: https://history.howstuffworks.com/historical-events/10-worst-decisions.htm

Van Lerven, Frank and Jackson, Andrew. (Undated). 'A government is not a household'. *Positive Money* (online). Available: https://positivemoney.org/2018/10/a-government-is-not-a-household/

Wenham, Clare. 2020. 'Is reporting of the coronavirus producing viral panic?'. *BMJ* (online). 3 January. https://blogs.bmj.com/bmj/2020/01/31/is-reporting-of-the-coronavirus-producing-viral-panic/

'What is a telomere'. *T.A. Sciences* (online). Available: https://www.tasciences.com/what-is-a-telomere.html

## INTERNATIONAL ORGANISATIONS

Armstrong, Drew. 2020. 'The World's Most Loathed Industry Gave Us a Vaccine in Record Time'. *Bloomberg Business Week* (online). 23 December. Available: https://www.bloomberg.com/news/features/2020-12-23/covid-vaccine-how-big-pharma-saved-the-world-in-2020

Boadle, Anthony. 2020. 'COVID-19 crisis shakes Brazil, but Bolsonaro keeps impeachment at bay'. *Reuters* (online). 5 June. Available: https://www.reuters.com/article/us-brazil-politics-analysis/covid-19-crisis-shakes-brazil-but-bolsonaro-keeps-impeachment-at-bay-idUSKBN23C1FM

'Campaigners warn that 9 out of 10 people in poor countries are set to miss out on COVID-19 vaccine next year'. *Oxfam International* (online). 9 December 2020. Available: https://www.oxfam.org/en/press-releases/campaigners-warn-9-out-10-people-poor-countries-are-set-miss-out-covid-19-vaccine

Marchant, Natalie. 2021. 'Thinking like Leonardo da Vinci will help children tackle climate change'. *World Economic Forum* (online). 11 May. Available: https://www.weforum.org/agenda/2021/05/da-vinci-interdisciplinary-learning-climate-change-education/

McLaughlin, David. 2017. 'Are Facebook and Google the New Monopolies?: Quick Take Q&A'. *Bloomberg* (online). 13 July. Available: https://www.bloomberg.com/news/articles/2017-07-13/antitrust-built-for-rockefeller-baffled-by-bezos-quicktake-q-a#xj4y7vzkg

Woods, Ngaire and Batniji, Rajaie. 2020. 'There's only one option for a global coronavirus exit strategy'. *World Economic Forum* (online). 11 April. Available: https://www.weforum.org/agenda/2020/04/there-s-only-one-option-for-a-global-coronavirus-exit-strategy/

'World's billionaires have more wealth than 4.6 billion people'. *Oxfam International* (online). 20 January 2020. Available: https://www.oxfam.org/en/press-releases/worlds-billionaires-have-more-wealth-46-billion-people

## BLOGS

'Confirmation Bias and the Power of Disconfirming Evidence'. *fs.blog* (online). Available: https://fs.blog/confirmation-bias/

Hughes, Melissa. 2019. 'Confident or cocky?'. *Melissa Hughes Rocks* (online). 15 November. Available: https://www.melissahughes.rocks/post/confident-or-cocky

Kernan, Sean. 2020. 'How to Win Arguments with Stupid, Stubborn People'. *Medium* (online). 17 February. Available: https://medium.com/mind-cafe/how-to-win-arguments-with-stupid-stubborn-people-db2a47968f37

MillenniYo. 2018. 'We are all not equal'. *Medium* (online). 15 October. Available: https://millenniyo.medium.com/we-are-not-all-equal-98ba24b20d5c

Smith, Richard. 2016. 'How humans might divide into a superclass and a useless class'. *The bmjopinion* (online). 7 September. Available: https://blogs.bmj.com/bmj/2016/09/07/richard-smith-how-humans-might-divide-into-a-superclass-and-a-useless-class/

## THINK-TANKS

Friedman, Jeffrey. 1999. 'Public Ignorance and Democracy'. *Cato Institute* (online). July/August. Available: https://www.cato.org/policy-report/july/august-1999/public-ignorance-democracy

West, Darrell, M. 2020. 'Five reasons to explore Mars'. *The Brookings Institution* (online). 18 August. Available: https://www.brookings.edu/blog/techtank/2020/08/18/five-reasons-to-explore-mars/

## SCHOLARLY PUBLICATIONS

Daly, Tom Gerald. 2020. 'How COVID-19 is hitting some democracies harder than others'. *Pursuit* (online). University of Melbourne. 3 June. Available: https://pursuit.unimelb.edu.au/articles/how-covid-19-is-hitting-some-democracies-harder-than-others

'Effect of Globalization on Sovereignty of States'. 2011. *Department of International Law and Jurisprudence, Faculty of Law, Nnamdi Azikiwe University, Awka* (online). Nigeria. Vol 2 (2011). Available: https://www.ajol.info/index.php/naujilj/article/view/82410

Gates, Bill. 2020. 'Responding to Covid-19 – A Once-in-a-Century Pandemic?'. 2020. *The New England Journal of Medicine* (online). 30 April. Available: https://www.nejm.org/doi/full/10.1056/NEJMp2003762

Held, David, et al. 'Global Transformations'. *ReVision*, vol. 22, no. 2, fall 1999, p. 7. *Gale Academic OneFile*. Accessed 20 July 2022. Available: https://go.gale.com/ps/anonymous?id=GALE%7CA59085553&sid=googleScholar&v=2.1&it=r&linkaccess=abs&issn=02756935&p=AONE&sw=w

Kildis, Hüseyin Pusat. 2020. 'Horseshoe Theory and Covid-19'. *E-International Relations* (online). 23 July. Available: https://www.e-ir.info/2020/07/23/horseshoe-theory-and-covid-19/

McClosky, Herbert and Chong, Dennis. 2009. 'Similarities and Differences Between Left-Wing and Right-Wing Radicals'. *British Journal of Political Science,* Volume 15, Issue 3, July 1985, pp. 329 – 363. Published online 27 January 2009. Available: https://www.cambridge.org/core/journals/british-journal-of-political-science/article/abs/similarities-and-differences-between-leftwing-and-rightwing-radicals/C46411F0228745583D2EB8E91A19D881

University of Pennsylvania School of Medicine. 2020. 'Who Should Get the COVID-19 Vaccine First? Penn-Led Team Lays Groundwork for Fair Distribution'. *Penn Medicine News* (online). 3 September. Available: https://www.pennmedicine.org/news/news-releases/2020/september/who-should-get-the-covid-19-vaccine-first

University of Pennsylvania School of Medicine. 2020. 'Who should get the COVID-19 vaccine first? Team of global experts offer a model that would prioritize reducing premature deaths' *ScienceDaily*. (online). 3 September. Available: www.sciencedaily.com/releases/2020/09/200903145011.htm

## BUSINESS PUBLICATIONS

Richardson, Chris. 2020. 'Who's afraid of the big bad debt?'. *Deloitte Access Economics* (online). 3 April. Available: https://www2.deloitte.com/au/en/pages/media-releases/articles/whos-afraid-big-bad-debt-030420.html

# About the Author

Paul Thomas worked in the financial services industry for over 40 years. His journey from bank teller to bank CEO began in 1976. He followed an old-fashioned career path that saw him rise through the ranks. Along the way, he gained broad experience in retail banking across a range of financial institutions.

Versed in all aspects of management, Paul developed a reputation as a high-calibre executive with particular expertise in strategy development and execution. Post-retirement, his deep knowledge of contemporary issues and his passion for communication find expression in his fortnightly blog, *Elephant in the Room*. He writes respectfully and insightfully – but without fear or favour – for the public at large.

Paul has developed a reputation as a thought leader and commentator on the contemporary political, economic, social, and technological issues facing business and society. He offers informed insights and opinions in an authoritative voice that is authentic and engaging.

An accomplished public speaker and writer, Paul holds an MBA and a Diploma in Financial Services. He is also a graduate of the Australian Institute of Company Directors.

Made in the USA
Monee, IL
04 November 2026

67387550R00154